VISUAL DIGITAL CULTURE

Digital entertainment, from video games to simulation rides, is now a central feature of popular culture. Computer-based or digital technologies are supplanting the traditional production methods of television, film and video, provoking intense speculation about their impact on the character of art. Examining the digital imaging techniques across a wide range of media, including film, music video, computer games, theme parks and simulation rides, *Visual Digital Culture* explores the relationship between evolving digital technologies and existing media, and considers the effect of these new image forms on the experience of visual culture.

Andrew Darley first traces the development of digital computing from the 1960s and its use in the production of visual digital entertainment. Through case studies of films such as *Toy Story*, key pop videos such as Michael Jackson's *Black or White*, and computer games like *Quake* and *Blade Runner*, Andrew Darley asks whether digital visual forms mark a break with traditional emphases on story, representation, meaning and reading towards a focus on style, image performance and sensation. He questions the implications of digital culture for theories of spectatorship, suggesting that these new visual forms create new forms of spectatorship within mass culture.

Andrew Darley is Senior Lecturer in Critical and Theoretical Studies at The Surrey Institute of Art and Design.

SUSSEX STUDIES IN CULTURE AND COMMUNICATION

Series Editors: Roger Silverstone, London School of Economics; Craig Clunas, University of Sussex; Jane Cowan, University of Sussex

Books in this series express Sussex's unique commitment to interdisciplinary work at the cutting edge of cultural and communication studies. Transcending the interface between the social and the human sciences, the series explores some of the key themes that define the particular character of life, and the representation of life, at the end of one millennium and the beginning of the next.

Our relationships to each other, to our bodies and to our technologies are changing. New concepts are required, new evidence is needed, to advance our understanding of these changes. The boundaries between disciplines need to be challenged. Through monographs and edited collections the series will explore new ways of thinking about communication, performance, identities and the continual refashioning of meanings, messages and images in space and time.

VIRTUAL GEOGRAPHIES
Bodies, space and relations
Edited by Mike Crang, Phil Crang and Jon May

THE HOUSE OF DIFFERENCE
Cultural politics and national identity in Canada
Eva Mackey

CULTURAL ENCOUNTERS
Edited by Elizabeth Hallam and Brian Street

Forthcoming:

A NATIONAL JOKE
Andy Medhurst

VISUAL DIGITAL CULTURE

Surface play and spectacle in new media genres

Andrew Darley

London and New York

First published 2000
by Routledge
11 New Fetter Lane, London EC4P 4EE

Simultaneously published in the USA and Canada
by Routledge
29 West 35th Street, New York, NY 10001

Reprinted 2002

Routledge is an imprint of the Taylor & Francis Group

Typeset in Galliard by Taylor & Francis Books Ltd
Printed and bound in Great Britain by Biddles Ltd, Guildford and King's Lynn

British Library Cataloguing in Publication Data
A catalogue record for this book is available from the British Library,

Library of Congress Cataloging in Publication Data
A catalog record for this book has been applied for

ISBN 0–415–16554–7 (hb)
ISBN 0–415–16555–5 (pb)

FOR MIKE

CONTENTS

CONTENTS

ILLUSTRATIONS

The intention was to include more illustrations than those that eventually made it into the following pages. That I was unable to incorporate a more representative sample of the range of examples discussed is due to difficulties in obtaining copyright permissions.

FIGURES

ACKNOWLEDGEMENTS

This book arises from research into the digital image as mass culture undertaken from the end of the 1980s. During the 1990s, at both practical and critical levels, colleagues and students alike have negotiated the incursion of digital technology into the established domains of animation, photography, film and video. Being part of this particular encounter with the new technology and party to the stimulating work and discussion it has generated has had considerable bearing on the development of my own perspective and interests. I owe much to the various kinds of encouragement, support and direct commentary that has come from colleagues and students in the past few years. Among those who – whether they are aware of it or not – have helped me in the current endeavour I should like to mention Peter Hall, Martin Conboy, Sylvie Bringas, Helen Davies, Jill McGreal, John Henshaw, Matthew Rampley, Liz Wilkinson, Claire Mussell, Jaid Mindang, Claire Underwood, Dominic Sidoli, Gwynneth Wilkey and Roy Greener.

For their constant encouragement and close support I should particularly like to thank David Bate and Roger Noake. The Surrey Institute of Art and Design gave concrete help for my research and writing in the form of a generous research secondment that reduced my teaching duties between May 1996 and December 1998. Of course, without such assistance the writing of this book would have been all the more difficult.

I owe an especial debt to Roger Silverstone, general editor of the series in which this book appears. Over the past decade he has been a superb teacher: generous with his time, patient, always stimulating when offering critical commentary and a constant source of inspiration and encouragement. Indeed, if not for his urging I am uncertain that I would have produced a book proposal at all. Finally, I must thank Elisabetta Tenenti not just for her helpful suggestions with prose and the 'horrors' of editing, but also for the unfailing reassurance she extended throughout the process of writing. As is customary, I should stress that the arguments and ideas set out in the ensuing pages are my own responsibility.

INTRODUCTION

Video games, digital films, simulation rides, these have become commonplace cultural experiences as we move into the twenty-first century. They form part of the central subject of this book, which concerns itself with a group of cultural genres or forms that I am relating under the overarching term *visual* ~~Form~~ *digital culture*. The forms in question are spectacle cinema, computer anima- ~~includes~~ tion and certain modes of music video and advertising; special venue attractions and simulation rides; and arcade and computer games.[1] Looked at as cultural phenomena these forms appear to be extremely new-fashioned, having only emerged as modes of mass culture within the past twenty years or thereabouts.

As these latest genres of visual culture are what this book is about, it is useful at the outset to have a description of them and some idea of how they have emerged and come to be the way they are. For this reason, Part I is historical.

Histories do now exist covering facets and certain individual instances of the digital image-based forms explored in these pages (see, for example, Haddon 1988; Darley 1990; Coyle 1993). However, as far as I am aware, there has been no attempt to produce the kind of inclusive explication – relating them together – which appears in subsequent chapters. This is hardly surprising; previous accounts have of necessity been exploratory and tentative in character. They have been attempts to make sense of a cultural space which was still in its forma- tive stages; a cultural space which, despite the still rapid changes which mark its development, has only recently begun to settle into more stable institutional modes and genres. It is impossible to tell just how enduring these will prove to be, still, they do now exist thereby making this most recent constellation of forms, related by the same technology and cultural location, susceptible to the kind of comparative aesthetic treatment undertaken in this book.

The first chapter covers a relatively short period of time stretching from the 1960s to the present day. The aim is to trace the main ways in which the digital computer has been developed and used in the production practices of the incip- ient visual forms at issue. I sketch their emergence describing how each has taken shape and say something about the enabling role which digital techniques have played in this gestation process.

1

Chapters 2 and 3 introduce further historical considerations as a way of beginning to throw more light on the aesthetic make up of the visual digital genres at issue. Forgoing the expository mode adopted in the first chapter, they strive instead to understand and explain the place of visual digital culture *within*, and in relation to, a larger history – or, better perhaps, histories – of modern culture itself. In the first place, I reflect on the forms at issue in the context of a broader cultural history – one involving technologically based popular entertainments and stretching back into the last century (and beyond). After which, I consider them in relation to contemporary culture and the historical idea of what is variously termed 'late' or 'post'-modernism. One of the things I hope to demonstrate is that in order to begin to understand the formal/aesthetic dimension of visual digital culture we are required to move beyond an explanation centred solely around a chronology of technological development – instructive though this may be. Yet, perhaps the major area of concern revolves around considerations of the importance and significance of the *continuities* and *discontinuities*, the *similarities* and *differences* that exist between corresponding technologically based visual forms: those both of the past and the present and those that exist in the digital present itself. I explore these lines of continuity as well as their disjunctive correlates in terms of both the genres themselves and their cultural-aesthetic contexts, attempting to describe and explain the ways in which they are significant.

Part II involves a more extended enquiry into the character of the visual digital aesthetic itself. In chapters 4 and 5 I undertake a close exploration of several of the genres at issue. By examining specific expressions of digital animation, advertising, cinema and music video I intend to demonstrate in more detail how each in their *various* ways continues the tradition of popular spectacle introduced in the previous section. At the same time I begin to show how the aesthetic dimension of each is a manifestation of a very different historical moment: one that is enabled and encouraged by new technological developments and subject to the prevailing forces of a mass culture dominated by 'electronic intertexuality'.[2]

In addition to producing more concrete aesthetic examinations of digital image forms than is usually attempted (chapters 4, 5 and 7) I move, in chapter 6, to related wider considerations. I understand the genres in question to be particular instances of a more general tendency within much of late twentieth-century culture towards an increasing preoccupation with visual form and surface (introduced in chapter 3). I explore the implications of this by looking at a cluster of underlying and mutating concepts that – with respect to the aesthetic make-up of visual digital genres (and thereby, at least, much of mass visual culture in general) – appear either to be in the ascendant or on the wane. Thus, I suggest that whilst certain developments stemming from practices involving notions such as repetition and montage have a strong part to play both in the constitution and the understanding of current neo-spectacle impulses, conversely, once-central notions such as authorship and genre do not.

The final section, Part III, shifts the focus more directly on to spectator experience and spaces of aesthetic consumption. Chapter 7 performs a kind of bridging function between the more obvious or direct 'poetic' considerations of the previous section and the more concerted look at spectator issues in the last chapter. Thus, whilst discussing the aesthetic character of computer games and special venue attractions I have attempted to close in much more on issues of spectator activity and response. The immediate reason for this being the rather novel ways in which this aspect figures in these genres: that is, with reference to what are commonly known as their 'interactive' and 'immersive' capabilities. I suggest that what the 'players' and 'riders' of games and simulation attractions are doing can be construed as in many respects broadly typical of the spectator experience involved in the other genres of visual digital culture.

Chapter 8 pursues this question of spectators and visual digital genres analysing what it is that they share in common. I locate and begin to describe a shift away from prior modes of spectator experience based on symbolic concerns (and 'interpretative models') towards recipients who are seeking intensities of direct sensual stimulation. As a possible avenue for further understanding what is occurring within this new aesthetic space of neo-spectacle, concepts of play are introduced and discussed. Considerations of how such a mode of spectatorship might be appraised are introduced and, in an attempt to indicate how we might begin to gain more insight into spectator or viewing experiences, I return to the history of spectacle entertainments and the changing character of exhibition sites and consumption contexts. Once again, I consider continuities, similarities and differences, understanding one crucial difference – a key factor affecting contemporary spectator activity and experience – to rest with the rise of *private* modes and contexts of exhibition and reception. Finally, pondering the more general context in which the spectators of visual digital forms exist, I turn to some current attempts within the cultural sphere to conceptualise so-called 'postmodern' experience. Though there is a certain congruence here with the spectator activity I have begun to elucidate with respect to digital forms and neo-spectacle, I urge caution against being too quick to generalise. I argue instead for the presentiment that contemporary culture is far more nuanced or differentiated at the aesthetic level than first it may appear: we need more clarity as to the ways in which this is so. Even the aesthetic that I begin to elucidate in the chapters that follow remains surprisingly rich and diverse despite the extraordinary regularities operating across its different forms.

The complexities of contemporary spectacle

This book's treatment of its subject stands in marked contrast to most approaches to understanding the digital image to date. For the most part, those who, like myself, have been concerned with the aesthetic aspect have preferred to concentrate on the more marginal practices of computer art. Those, on the other hand, sharing my concern with mass cultural developments either fail to acknowledge aesthetics at all, or else tend to view the concept in ways that are quite different to that with which I operate here.

It is tempting to suggest that my use of history and what may be described as a rudimentary 'poetics' to understand the aesthetic dimension of visual digital culture have everything to do with my subject. For how does one begin to make aesthetic sense of a spectacle tradition and a spectacle culture if not through attending to appearances and the sensual aspect? And yet, things are not quite so simple. For, clearly, the questions that lie at the heart of the approach adopted in these pages – questions that revolve around beginning to understanding form, style and the dynamics of spectating – also have an application that stretches beyond my own object of study.

It is fair to say, however, that the majority of contemporary approaches to understanding the genres and expressions of contemporary visual culture consider such concerns to be secondary to more pressing problems. Dominant critical approaches treat such cultural phenomena as texts the meaning of which needs to be variously explained or uncovered both at the particular and the general level. Such endeavours are, of course, vital. Yet, in what follows I adopt the more unfashionable approach. Taking my cue from the likes of Susan Sontag (1967), Kristin Thompson (1981) and, most recently, David Bordwell (1991), I endorse the view that the somewhat neglected aesthetic dimension is equally important to understanding cultural practices such as those explored in these pages.

The understanding I propound below of how spectators engage with recent expressions of digital visual culture such as spectacle cinema, music video or computer games, is one which, broadly speaking, involves the idea of 'passivity'. At least this is so as long as passivity is understood or conceived in terms of intellection and processes of meaning-making, 'reading' or interpretation. For the aesthetic character of visual digital forms, though by no means homogeneous, leans heavily towards foregrounding the *sensuous*. It is to terms such as form, style, decoration, simulation, illusion and, in particular, spectacle that I turn most often when discussing examples. Indeed, I suggest that it is possible to discern a distinct diminution in concern with meaning-construction at the level of textual production itself in the expressions and genres that I analyse. Spectators are solicited and engaged in that case at more immediate and surface levels. And I dare to suggest that such engagement entails something of a shift in sensibility towards far more involvement with surface appearances, composition and artifice – towards too, increased connections with more directly sense-based aesthetic experiences.

What of the *cultural* evaluation of the aesthetic I propose and describe in these pages? It may seem strange to be revisiting the so-called 'high' and 'low' culture debates here, particularly – as is so often claimed – contemporary culture ('postmodernism') is thought to be making such distinctions increasingly obsolete (see, for example, Fiske 1994: 254). However, certain echoes of this distinction still reverberate within critical attitudes to contemporary culture and particularly with the genres and expressions at issue. Of course, the fact that the then contemporary custodians and critics of aesthetic and ethical values regarded the popular visual entertainments of the nineteenth century with suspicion and general disdain comes as no surprise to us. It was after all precisely within the nineteenth century that the idea of the 'artist as genius', and with it the distinction between 'high' and 'low' forms of art, was consolidated. Within this evaluative framework the newer technologically informed and commercialised modes of culture – photography, the cinema, the amusement park – came to be regarded as manufactured diversions, mere ephemera. From this perspective, forms of pure spectacle – image for image's sake – along with their adjuncts in mechanised modes of physical stimulation and vertigo, are deemed the least worthy of serious consideration. They are looked upon as trivial and aesthetically sterile.

Of course, I do not say that things have not changed in the intervening years. Cultural history and criticism (in its broadest sense) has done much to dispel regressive and romantic notions of art. Popular and mass forms of culture have been admitted to the fold and in the process a healthy caution has been injected by the wider acknowledgement that art, like everything else, is a social phenomenon – one, moreover, that cannot properly be grasped outside of historical development and the specificity of social context (see Wolff 1981). Still, it would be wrong to assume that the deep-seated prejudices of an earlier era have thereby been eliminated. Neither should it be assumed that these newer forms of criticism do not themselves – explicitly or otherwise – take sides with respect to aesthetic judgement. I am unsure about the extent or the precise nature of the affinity that much current cultural criticism seems to share with a prior high cultural critical sensibility that was primarily literary in orientation (see Sontag 1967; Huyssen 1984: 5–52). It does seem, however, that regardless of how, ultimately, we are to understand and appraise the genres and expressions at issue here, we must take account of the fact that prejudices and dispositions – both explicit and contingent – continue to influence the way in which they are perceived *as culture*.[3]

David Bordwell (1991) has raised the concern that within the field of film studies the dominant preoccupation with interpretation-centred approaches has retarded the development of alternative ways of critically understanding film. The hegemony of the 'hermeneutic presumption' that Bordwell locates in film studies is more extensive however: it pervades and is dominant in almost every branch of the broad field of cultural studies. Undoubtedly, its paradigm discipline – at least in the current phase of dominance – has been literary criticism. Indeed, one of the reasons for the lack of alternative approaches may well be that methods designed for understanding literary texts in particular have been imported wholesale into making sense of visual ones. In making these observations it is not my intention to deride interpretative approaches to understanding cultural products. Neither do I want to deny that interpretation (the search for hidden meanings) is *central* to critical endeavour in any field of the human

[handwritten marginal note: too much emphasis on meaning-making]

sciences. I want rather to suggest that it is vital to recognise – and in this respect I am very much on Bordwell's side – that other elements are always going to be present in any kind of cultural expression. Moreover, the importance or significance of extra-semantic elements should never be taken for granted. For, if there is a problem with meaning-centred approaches it rests precisely in this: their very dominance – their success and certitude – which makes not only themselves blind to other dimensions of 'texts', works, genres or forms, but which also discourages the pursuit of such avenues by others. More significantly, the hegemony of meaning-centred approaches within the field of academic critical study may contribute to both the continued aesthetic misapprehension of expressions such as those at the centre of this discussion and also, thereby, or so I am suggesting, to their continued cultural relegation.

The visual digital genres and expressions explored in these pages appear to fit most comfortably within that tradition of the arts known as the 'decorative' (which is to say the 'lesser' forms of art or culture). They tend greatly to play up form, style, surface, artifice, spectacle and sensation, and they dilute meaning and encourage intellectual quiescence. They tend towards pure diversion, consisting of forms that are immediate and ephemeral in their effect. Certainly, from some perspectives they are related to superfluity, to prodigality. Insofar as they tend *not* to concern themselves with representation or meaning in anything other than a formal sense, then they are viewed as wasteful – decadent even.

And yet is this really so – is it not possible to mount a positive case for such an aesthetic? Is ornamentation, style, spectacle, giddiness really aesthetically inferior or, rather, just different (other) to established notions of literary, classical, modernist art? Is an aesthetic without depth necessarily an impoverished aesthetic, or is it rather, another kind of aesthetic – misunderstood and undervalued as such? For what – on the face of it – is wrong with the delight, pleasure, excitation, thrill, wonder, amazement, sensation and so forth experienced by recipients of such forms? Even before we begin to entertain notions as to whether or not such contemporary spectators are resisting or escaping the system by consuming such texts, there is a relatively new and distinctive (and still opaque) aesthetic to recognise and understand.[4]

It is important to acknowledge that a shift has occurred – at least within an important swathe of contemporary visual culture – towards an aesthetic that foregrounds the dimension of appearance, form and sensation. And we must take this shift seriously at the aesthetic level. Naturally, this entails discarding the prejudices and dismissals of earlier approaches, which claim such work is far too shallow and obvious to be susceptible to serious study. It also means accepting that *in the first instance* rather than problems of 'implicit or repressed meanings' it is more likely to be questions of a sensuous and perceptual character that will produce most by way of aesthetic understanding. A rush into interpretation before the aesthetic itself has been more clearly apprehended may follow an all too easy dismissal of such a spectacle aesthetic on grounds that it is facile, already transparent or really about something else. It almost certainly *is* about

[handwritten marginalia: characteristic of texts.]

[handwritten marginalia: end of empire decadent games]

[handwritten marginalia: how to value aesthetic of spectacle]

[handwritten marginalia at bottom: I would link this aesthetic's hegemonic dominant to politics of empire, though the link is not inherent & the aesthetic appears elsewhere as in AIDS quilt, etc]

something else, but it is also and equally about (relatively) poorly understood but clearly powerful modes of aesthetic practice. Disentangling, detailing and describing these practices of form and spectacle in this more tangible and partial sense is a vital *part* of understanding our society's more general preoccupation with surfaces.[5]

We might acknowledge here in the recent expressions of visual digital culture an instance of the historical durability of certain ways of addressing the eyes and the senses. This is manifest in ways that are rather distinctive from the past. Yet there are also lines of continuity as well as shifts and breaks in the persistence of this aesthetic space. There are certainly two important and related dimensions to understanding what this involves. From the perspective of spectatorship there is the question of understanding what is involved in the processes of engagement with and appreciation of the forms themselves. There is also the issue – frequently overlooked or dismissed – of the artifice and skills involved in their construction. Indeed, as I shall suggest, it is – in part at least – precisely these latter, i.e. legerdemain, pyrotechnics, stage-effects and so forth that are being admired by spectators and players not just the *effects* so produced. Indeed, it may well be that appreciation of composition is precisely more entrenched as an element of spectator engagement here than in other forms of mass visual culture. I may be guilty myself of implying (or presuming) at times that the technics of production in the contemporary forms at issue here are largely formulaic and instrumentalist. There may well be good reasons for such an attitude. Yet might we not also concede that what may also be occurring here are certain kinds of preoccupation with skill (in the production of various visual effects) that are not particularly well understood, precisely because they have always been viewed as both immediately transparent and inferior. Far from being obvious I would suggest that they be related to an aesthetic tradition that remains relatively opaque – a tradition that this book is concerned to open up for further scrutiny.

I do not claim that attempting to produce a clearer understanding of the aesthetic workings of the latest expressions of the spectacle tradition is all that we should be doing. Nor that this provides a somehow indispensable platform for broader considerations. I am concerned, however, that we do not cast the same critical light of past approaches on the latest developments. We should certainly recognise the validity and complexity of such practices and the expressions and forms they generate. Further, we must acknowledge that understanding their operation and character calls for methods that revolve around rather different elements and processes to those we expect to find in immediately prior modes of mass visual culture. In short, increased clarity and understanding with regard to the (broadly) aesthetic character of the cultural space in question can only aid critical/interpretative forays into understanding its place or function in the broader scheme of things.

[margin handwritten notes: appreciation of function of apparatus]

[margin handwritten notes: reason such a study necessary]

Part I

HISTORY

1

A BACK STORY: REALISM, SIMULATION, INTERACTION

From a purely technological perspective the 1960s, a formative stage in the history of the modern computer, can be said to constitute the prehistorical era of the cultural forms and genres that I am concerned to explore here.[1] As functional performance improved and computation technologies became much more practicable (smaller, faster, more powerful *and* less expensive) it became possible to discern within the field a multiplication of possible lines of development, a focusing-in on areas for further research. This was coupled with a greatly increased alertness as to the nascent and future commercial opportunities that were opening up as work in the field progressed. The work undertaken in the research laboratories of the 1960s in areas such as information processing, modelling, remote control and manipulation, and graphic displays seems a far cry from today's computer animated cinema, arcade games and special venue attractions. Yet this is precisely where the technological link with these contemporary cultural forms resides.

Beginnings

One important example of the kind of focusing that commenced at this time is computer graphics. Highly sophisticated techniques of computer imaging are absolutely vital to the digital visual genres under investigation in these pages. At the beginning of their technological evolution, in the late 1950s, however, they consisted of little more than lines and dots on a cathode ray display screen. Efforts to improve and develop both the display screen itself and its graphics capabilities began at this time: both with respect to the visualisation of calculations under way in the computer, and in terms of its advantages as a user input mode. Similarly, the computer's ability – given the correct program and enough computing power – to model processes, events, states and so forth was another significant motive for pursuing visualisation technologies.

Engineers and artists

Most of the early work put into developing such potential came from engineers and computer scientists working in corporate or academic research environments. A key example of such research was that into real-time interactive computer graphics. This came to practical fruition in 1963 in a system called *Sketchpad*, which allowed a user to draw directly on to a cathode display screen with a 'light-pen' and then to modify or 'tidy-up' the geometrical image possibilities so obtained with a keyboard. Though extremely primitive by today's standards, *Sketchpad* is viewed as a crucial breakthrough from which have sprung most of the later technical developments in the areas of so-called 'paint' and interactive graphics systems. By the mid-1960s, a similar system involving computer image modification was being used in the design of car bodies – a precursor of current CAD/CAM (Computer Aided Design/Computer Aided Manufacture) systems. And by 1963, computer generated wire-frame animation films – visual simulations of scientific and technical ideas – were being produced using the early vector display technique.

Many of the digital technologies and techniques underpinning current forms of visual digital culture were first developed in relation to research goals and technical problems that were construed in ways which had little to do with aesthetic applications. For the most part, the concern of those early computer scientists involved with computer graphics research was with perfecting and developing further what they saw as the computer's latent and extensive functional potential. Such work was undertaken in relation to ongoing research on commercial and military applications such as flight simulators and computer aided design. It would be incorrect, however, to claim that there was no aesthetic impulse operating in connection to these early centres of computer research. Some of the scientists and technicians involved in this nascent field of computer imaging began to look at their graphics in aesthetic as well as functional terms (see, for example, Franke 1971; Davis 1973: 97–105). In addition to concerted efforts aimed at various computer design processes and applications on the part of scientists, artists of the time began to see in the computer a new and potentially exciting means of aesthetic experimentation.

Those artists who began to explore this new means of image production did so as a way of augmenting their current aesthetic practices. For the most part the individuals concerned were mainstream modernists in aesthetic outlook and approach. Committed to modes of formalist image-making involving a sort of continual reworking of the self-same aesthetic axiom through experimentation with technique, they saw the computer as an instrument with great potential for the production of innovation in aesthetic form (see, for example, Vanderbeek 1970; Le Grice 1974).

Perhaps the best known of these early computer-artist experimenters is the late John Whitney.[2] Whitney's computer film work was guided by his attempts to draw a working analogy between abstract visual experimentation and music with its power to 'evoke the most explicit emotions directly by its simple patterned configurations of tones in time' (Whitney 1971: 26). His involvement in computer imaging began in the 1950s. Utilising outdated computing equipment junked by the military after the war Whitney began to construct computerised drawing machines. This led to the development of a fully automated system involving high precision integrated coordination and control of the entire production process (including drawing, motions, lighting and exposures) – a mechanical analogue computer, specifically designed to produce complex abstract film animations.

Like Whitney the majority of artists involved with computer image production in the 1960s worked in close collaboration with computer scientists and program researchers.[3] And many of the engineers and scientists who came into working contact with artists came to consider themselves – if they did not already do so – as producers of 'computer art' in their own right (see, for example, Noll 1967). To understand more fully the character of such collaborations and the shifting viewpoints they seem to represent, it is important to mention the broader context in which they were occurring.

Cybernetic serendipity

The 1960s is not only an era of intense practical development of new electronically and digitally based technologies, but also one of increased conjecture as to the nature of such technology and the promise it held for the future of society. Speculation was rife within the academic, political, cultural and business communities. The area was thought about in terms of the new cultural forms that would spring from it, the new aesthetics it would inaugurate, the new disciplines it would spawn, and the profound effects it would have on industry, work and leisure. The dominant tone of this thinking was of intense optimism: technology, particularly the new computer-based technology, was invoked as a panacea for the ills of the present.

Many within the artistic community shared this perspective towards the burgeoning new electronic technology and the cybernetic discourse surrounding it. Indeed, it is clear that the artist/technician collaboration already mentioned within the ambit of computer imaging, was an important aspect of a much broader 'investment' in new technology then being pursued by artists. Two exhibitions that now stand as emblematic of this tendency are the *9 Evenings: Theater and Engineering* performance events held in New York in 1966 and the 1968 London based exhibition *Cybernetic Serendipity* (see Whitman and Kluver 1967; Reichardt 1968).

The former involved works that issued from a collaboration between a group of American artists (associated with diverse fields that ranged from painting, theatre and choreography, to music) and a group of engineers. The latter was less parochial, drawing on work from the United States, Japan and Europe, it differed significantly from the former insofar as its focus was exclusively the computer and computer-related (or cybernetic) systems (see Reichardt 1968, 1971). It was an exhibition that attempted to demonstrate that the new computer technologies were soldering the unification of art and technology; producing a hybridisation of engineering and more properly artistic concerns. At the time, perhaps the most important theoretical advocate of this new technological optimism – at least as far as artists were concerned – was the media and cultural theorist Marshall McLuhan (see McLuhan 1968).

Another event, however, displays the more mundane and pragmatic dimensions of a maturing field. At the international symposium, Computer Graphics 70, there was a session on computer art – though a glance at the proceedings (Parslow and Green 1970) reveals it to be almost wholly overshadowed by the more utilitarian and commercial considerations that characterised the event. Here, clearly, we are already in a different world: back in the space of applied research and development where computer graphics were being viewed either as 'practical industrial tools' or 'research instruments'.

The proto-realists

It is within this functional/technical space of early computer imaging that we can locate the emergence of a problem that has preoccupied many of those working in the area to this day. It started out as a concern with the production of representational imagery by computer and, as the potential was realised, subsequently turned into a fixation with the perfection of simulated photo-realism. This preoccupation has considerable bearing on the development of the forms at the heart of this study. By and large, figurative representation was not a problem that troubled the first artists to become involved with computer graphics, it was, rather, the serendipitous possibilities for formal experimentation offered up by computer programming that they seized upon. On the other hand, representational concerns were present almost from the first in many of the uses to which computer scientists wanted to put computer images.

The desire on the part of scientists to model or simulate physical processes and events in space (and time) was a central impulse in the production of the earliest computer graphics and films. Whilst concurrent with the initiation of applied forms, work was under way on computer produced figurative imagery as a research activity in its own right. Even the work conducted in collaboration with artists had a decided leaning towards more figurative kinds of imagery.[4] At the end of the 1960s experimentation began into the production of algorithms for the production and manipulation of still, line-based figurative images.

Thus, a picture begins to emerge of computer imaging in the 1960s, which involves a complex and somewhat tangled set of interests and pursuits. There was the growing applied research and development into the area on the part of scientists, engineers and corporate researchers. But there was also an early and significant aesthetic interest on the part of experimental artists. There are clearly moments when the aims and explorations of artists and engineers appear to coincide. Indeed, it would seem that these mainly corporate-funded collaborations were highly productive, even when what the artist was getting out of them diverged from what the technician was learning. The artistic impulse certainly contributed to establishing and advancing the field in the first instance and undoubtedly the commitment of most of these early computer artist pioneers to a non-functional exploration of a pure visual aesthetic continues to this day as a certain marginal tendency within computer imaging.

Simulation and interaction

In the early 1970s the enthusiasm of certain of the 'hard' computer engineers for the possibilities that had been awakened in the previous decade begins to coincide with those of art critics and some of the artists themselves. At least this is so with respect to what were viewed as being the most likely aspects of future development in the field. Thus, computer scientist Ivan Sutherland, having extended his initial research on real-time interactive computer graphics into the realm of the simulated experience of three-dimensional space, claimed that through his computer displays he had, 'landed an airplane on the deck of a moving carrier, observed a nuclear particle hit a potential wall and flown a rocket at the speed of light' (cited in Davis 1973: 103). One can already discern in this statement a fascination with two key concerns: *simulation* and *interaction*. In this respect it is illuminating to compare Sutherland with McLuhanite art and technology critic Gene Youngblood. Writing at the same time about trends in computer imaging – or as he calls it, 'cybernetic cinema' – Youngblood argues:

> If the visual subsystems exist today, it's folly to assume that the computing hardware won't exist tomorrow. The notion of 'reality' will be utterly and finally obscured when we reach that point ... [of generating] totally convincing reality within the information processing system ... We're entering a Mythic age of electronic realities that exist only on a metaphysical plane.
>
> (1970: 206)

Meanwhile, video artist Nam June Paik began, in the late 1960s, to talk of future art forms in which he anticipated completely new levels of interaction and interfacing between the artist and/or participant and the work itself, calling such work 'Direct-Contact Art' (see Davis 1973: 106).

Those engineers, artists and critics of the 1960s who, somewhat prophetically, saw a cultural future for the new computer-based technology in terms of interaction and simulation were quite right. More than anything else this formative or primitive era of computer graphics established a set of interests and research pursuits which form the basis for later developments in such areas as image manipulation, real-time interactive usage, three-dimensional image simulation, animation and realistic image synthesis. In their different ways these have become central to recent cultural forms such as computer games, special effects cinema and simulation experiences. Simulation, understood as the representational copying or modelling of phenomenal reality both on a two-dimensional screen and in terms of three-dimensional *virtual* space, has increasingly engaged the attention of computer image research since the turn of the 1980s.

However, the domains within which it has developed, the applications to which it has been put and the different cultural forms that have grown out of it, have diverged markedly from those anticipated by 1960s art. If anything, it is the enthusiastic remarks of the technician Sutherland which best capture what has subsequently taken place in the cultural domain: in terms both of content *and* form. As we shall see, it is in the mass cultural domain that the potential of interaction and simulation has been most extensively employed.

Digital cinema

The rise of mainstream digital cinema, computer animation and certain significant and related sub-genres of both music video and advertising are intimately tied to the development of computer imaging which I began to unfold above. Yet, how did we arrive at the current situation typified by the ultra-realistic animation and spectacular effects of films such as *Jurassic Park* (1993), *The Mask* (1994), *Toy Story* (1995), *Mission: Impossible* (1996) and *Armageddon* (1998)?

We left the story at the beginning of the 1970s having noted a growing interest in representational image production on the part of certain computer graphics researchers as the 1960s wore on. This interest was to turn into a fixation by the end of the 1970s. By then, however, certain technical developments, which had encouraged the attentions of the commercial cultural establishment, had conspired to shift this preoccupation with figurative imagery to another level.

Realism

The upshot of this became the dogged pursuit of a somewhat revised goal: the development of digital techniques for the production of so-called 'realism'. The notion of 'realism' has dominated computer image research and practice from the late 1970s and by and large it still prevails today. Until the 1970s image production had come to rely on the vector display technique for image generation: a process that limited the kinds and complexity of images produced. Eventually a different process of image manufacture and display emerged. Turning upon the calculation and display of 'pixel' values – so-called 'raster displays' and 'frame-store' techniques – these were much more conducive to the production of 'realistic' imagery. There are, of course, a host of differing and often contradictory conceptions of what constitutes representational realism. The one that came to discursive prominence within computer image research and practice is perhaps the one with which we are all most familiar. Quite simply it turns upon the notion of the proximate or accurate image: the 'realisticness' or resemblance of an image to the phenomenal everyday world that we perceive and experience (partially) through sight. For the majority of those involved with digital imaging at the time, the yardstick of such verisimilitude was photographic and cinematographic imagery.

Beyond the ultimate goal of producing 'photographic' imagery by other means, the motives for such a fixation with realism are diverse and appear to depend upon imperatives that are active within the particular domain in which they develop.[5] If the factors shaping the representational and 'realist' thrust in practical and scientific domains tended to have a functional basis, in the sphere of mass visual culture – the domain of entertainment cinema – the support for realism was part of a more general ideal, indeed, it comprised the predominant aesthetic regime. Clearly, computer imaging only really becomes interesting to the producers and distributors of Hollywood cinema when it can operate effectively within the parameters of its own established commercial aesthetic. By the middle of the 1980s the popular or journalistic criticism attached to Hollywood had, on the whole, embraced computer imaging and was enthusiastic in support of its potential. The pundits clearly believed they could see in this new imaging technology, intimations of novel extensions of the Hollywood aesthetic. They envisage the computer introducing a new degree of expressive 'freedom' to the established media of photography and cinema: one that would maintain the look of photography whilst cutting it loose from its referential ties (see, for example, Sutherland 1976; Sørenson 1984a and 1984b). Eventually, what began to fulfil such expectations was the computer's phenomenal rejuvenation of special visual effects, so intimately tied to the perfection of photo-realism. But we are jumping ahead of ourselves.

A considerable time was to elapse before digital imaging techniques became firmly established within mainstream cinema and related domains such as television, advertising and music video. Work in both software (or program) and hardware (machinery) development was angled towards techniques of animation, image manipulation and processing, image compositing, motion control and three-dimensional (still and moving) image generation. At various moments in the early years of this process such research fed into the production of particular films. Thus *Westworld* (1973), *Futureworld* (1976), *Tron* (1982), *Star Trek: The Wrath of Khan* (1982) and *The Last Starfighter* (1985) are now viewed as milestones in the history of digital cinema. The latter was hailed at the time of its release as a milestone of 'realist' computer graphics – the beginning of the gradual, yet eventual, takeover of Hollywood by computers (see Robley 1984; Sørenson 1984a).

By the mid-1980s many computer graphics companies had begun to make significant inroads in introducing digital imaging to television advertising, music video and animation (see, for example, Onosko 1984; Baker 1993). The work of developing systems and software for digital moving image production which had been undertaken in preceding years was now reaching fruition. Among the most celebrated work to appear in the commercial material shown at the annual ACM-SIGGRAPH (Association for Computer Machinery, Special Interest Group in Computer Graphics and Interactive Technology) Convention of 1986, was the music video for Mick Jagger's *Hard Woman*, the 'gold series' TV advertisements for Benson and Hedges, and the short entertainment animation *Luxo Junior*. Collectively these texts displayed the huge strides that had been taken with respect to the goal of 'realistic' digitally generated imagery and in terms of digitally assisted image compositing.

Significantly, by this time much of the research and development for commercial cultural applications had begun to leave the laboratories and was taking place within the computer graphics companies themselves. By 1985 some of these companies were also beginning to market their own proprietary hardware and software graphics systems to other producers.

Manipulation and synthesis

It is from the mid-1980s onwards that various modes of digital imaging finally establish a significant presence within the moving image forms of mass culture. Two somewhat distinctive strands of research and development underpin this advance and yet they are often closely related in terms of their deployment in the production of moving image texts. They are commonly referred to as 'image manipulation' and 'image synthesis'.

In *digital image manipulation* the computer is frequently employed to effect changes in images which it has not itself been involved in producing. There are basically two dimensions to this kind of work, though increasingly in productions associated with the moving image domain, these are combined or employed together. The first is connected to techniques of what is known as 'image processing', the second to techniques of image compositing. Image processing involves already existing imagery, for example, photographs, photographic reproductions, films and videos being digitally stored in the computer to be subsequently worked on or altered in a multitude of possible ways. These range from the addition and/or removal of blur, the undetectable removal of a particular part of the digitised image, the enhancement or changing of colour, to the 'crispening', 'warping' and merging of parts of the image. The compositing dimension, on the other hand, refers to the aspect of image combination. Here the already existing images may include 'found images', images deliberately produced for combination, or a mixture of both. If it is the former, then digital compositing may be employed along with some of the techniques of image processing to superimpose imagery from one source on to imagery of another. When this involves moving images, then techniques of digital motion control may be utilised together with techniques of image processing to ensure the seamless combination of the disparate source images within the frame or shot.

Such techniques are now widely used within television, advertising, publishing, video and cinema production. Indeed, these new and still evolving means have led to a new emphasis on the so-called 'post-production' aspect of moving image-making, and a host of new companies based on this increasingly important aspect of moving image production have sprung up since the mid-1980s.

Digital image synthesis is perhaps the area in which the 'realist' aesthetic goal has been most tenacious and influential. The key defining feature of image synthesis or image generation is that the images so produced are created *within* the computer. This involves the input of mathematical data to the computer's memory that effectively describes or models and then stores whatever is to be imaged. Once this is done the model can be manipulated, altered or refined in some way. Next, the model is converted into a picture: a particular view of the model is chosen and various techniques are then employed to complete or render the final image. A variety of techniques have been developed both for the initial introduction of the abstract model into the computer's memory and for the completion process – the viewing and rendering – of the final image. Especially after the adoption of the raster display system, researchers were much preoccupied with developing ways to produce 'convincing' lighting effects and surface textures to the objects and scenes imaged. Most of the concentration in recent years has been centred upon the generation of three-dimensional imagery, so-called because of the initial model described and stored in the computer. An underlying model which is three-dimensional, even though it will eventually be seen as a flat image, perhaps printed on paper or displayed on a video monitor or film screen, produces solid looking and hence more 'realistic' imagery. These basic procedures are more or less the same in both moving and still image generation, though the animation of scenes is obviously far more complex, requiring additional kinds of computation to produce and capture both the movement of figures and the virtual camera within the virtual three-dimensional set that contains the action.[6]

Pixar and 'ILM': flagships of manipulation and simulation

As early as the 1970s the general trajectory of developments in digital cinema to date had *already* been anticipated. In a popular review of the feature film *Futureworld* (1976), among the first Hollywood films to include computer generated images, areas of work are located and certain technical potentialities fixed upon that have been embraced and sustained as goals for research and development right up to the present (Sutherland 1976). Thus the aim of eventually being able to produce films without the present technical apparatus of sets, props, cameras, lights and the like is introduced. So also is the notion that soon there will exist synthetic actors playing scenes in such synthetic settings.

19

The necessity is underlined, particularly in the entertainment sphere, of the urgent drive for near-photographic realism in digitally synthesised imagery, the suggestion being that the computer film will only really be a success when this is achieved. The reviewer's final speculation is that in the future there may well be forms which involve experiential interaction within a computer simulated world: what we now call 'virtual reality'.

In 1995 the first feature-length computer synthesised film *Toy Story* was released. This film realises, in part at least, the expectations raised in the 1970s of producing a film without the traditional apparatus. The film is a highly sophisticated and accomplished example of three-dimensional computer animation. It certainly adds a new quality or dimension of 'realistic-ness' to traditional Disney-style cartoon animation – one might even say a certain photo-realism is achieved relative to the rest of the genre. Ultimately though, one still has to say that the characters *are* clearly cartoon characters and that they all operate within generically familiar cartoon scenarios: the computer generated film that replaces live action has yet to appear. The technical possibilities mooted over twenty years ago have partly been met, certainly they are still being striven for, but, as usual, what is more interesting is what has been happening in the meantime (see, for example, Dixon 1995–6).

Two companies stand as emblematic of the two main trends of development within digital imaging since the 1980s: Pixar and Industrial Light and Magic (ILM). Pixar is primarily associated with computer image synthesis. It represents the important *animation* dimension of current digital cinema. Perhaps more purist in its approach to computer image production than companies operating within the live action sphere, it strives to produce *all* of its moving imagery with the computer itself. This imagery is, within its cartoon-influenced terms of reference, highly realistic. It involves refined techniques (programs), many of which were first developed by the company's own research team, for the various phases and procedures involved in three-dimensional modelling, animation and rendering. Work on perfecting software that further polishes the movement of figures, facial expression, lip-synch and so forth, as well as the refining of programs for rendering the scene all contribute to the underlying 'project' of seeking to produce synthetic photo-realistic imagery by other means. Although the content of the films produced over the years by Pixar is rather unexceptional, particularly to those who are familiar with Disney cartoons, the images themselves are not. *The Adventures of André and Wally Bee* (1985), *Luxo Junior* (1986), *Red's Dream* (1987), *Tin Toy* (1988), *Knick Knack* (1989), *Toy Story* (1995) and *A Bug's Life* (1998) are, above all else, films which have introduced striking novelty and effects at the level of the image to the domain of moving images.

The main business of the company ILM lies with techniques of special effects in all their different aspects, and from the very beginning computer imaging was crucial to this work. Over the years the development and use of digital techniques has come to play an increasingly central role in ILM's work for the numerous live action-based film productions that the company has been involved in. The studio first used digital techniques for the special effects on *Star Wars*. The choreography of spectacular space battles and spaceship footage in this film was realised with a convincing verisimilitude that wholly overshadowed previous work of a similar kind. This impression was achieved in large part by the digital pre-programming of camera movement: a technique offering both an extraordinary degree of precision and the possibility of infinite repeatability. Now, not only could many layers of moving imagery be superimposed and married together seamlessly, but also the camera itself could appear to move freely (i.e. pan, tilt, zoom, track and so forth) within the space that was being represented.

What is important about the above from the point of view of this account is the recognition that digital techniques are associated from the beginning with *assisting* in the production of visual effects within already established forms such as live action feature film. Indeed, so-called 'special effects' have, since the production of *Star Wars*, been enjoying a remarkable renaissance. ILM (along with the numerous similar enterprises that have emerged subsequently) have played a significant part in the progress of this renaissance. The emergence of visual digital cultural genres themselves coincides with this regeneration of special effects. Broadly, it might be argued that much of the time these companies have developed and used digital techniques as a means both of improving the integration of established visual effects techniques and of enabling their further refinement.

Thus, it must be stressed that the computer has only *partially* replaced live action cinematography as an originator of images and scenes of apparent digital photo-realism. For, despite the increasing use of computer generated imagery in the 1990s, such scenes are still far more likely to have been contrived through a combination of computer assisted and manipulated traditional effects than through pure computer generated image production. Fuelling such development are recent improvements in techniques for converting original 35 mm film footage into a high-resolution format susceptible to digital manipulation and then back to film again with negligible loss of image quality.

Over the years ILM have worked on numerous films containing such effects.[7] Many of these are included in a distinctive corpus to have emerged within new Hollywood cinema as a predominant genre or type in the late 1980s and 1990s (see chapter 5). Cutting across traditional genres such as adventure, science fiction, fantasy and the like, these films should perhaps be more properly defined not by what kind of fiction they exemplify so much as by their sheer technological density, a characteristic that is evident in their display of outlandish and spectacular illusionism.[8]

21

Television and video

Just as certain mainstream feature films now rely on the renovation brought to special effects by the computer, so too do advertising, music video and, latterly, television production draw heavily on the potential of the computer in this regard. Since the 1970s TV advertising and the music video have both acted as key sites for the development and exposure of techniques of digital image generation and animation, and of digital image manipulation. Like the cinema, both advertising and music video have since the late 1980s each produced a significant corpus or sub-genre that has formed around displaying the distinctive imaging capabilities of digital techniques (for examples, see chapters 4 and 5 below). In certain respects – though, crucially, not all – advertising and music video, have used the new technology in ways that deviate somewhat from the aesthetic predominating in the cinema. This, I believe, is attributable to their particular and distinctive overall aesthetic goals; or, more technically perhaps, to their differing institutional modes of representation (see, chapter 5).

The rapid advances in programming technologies coupled to the process of circuit miniaturisation that first began to take effect in the 1960s has meant that within a period of barely twenty years, digital imaging techniques have not only integrated with established means of production but in certain respects are now starting to replace them. In the domain of mass visual culture the technological shift from analogue to digital now appears to be irrevocable. With the emergence of the computer, entirely new ways of making images, together with distinctive ways of assisting and augmenting traditional methods and techniques of moving image production have become commonplace within contemporary forms of visual cultural production. Nowadays it is safe to assume – even when the work of the computer does not figure in a displayed manner in a music video or TV advertisement – that it has been involved nevertheless. So pervasive have digitally based techniques become in post-production processes, that even the music tape or advertisement that is being produced in a 'traditional' manner will have had some digital input, even if that input has had no tangible effect on the final outcome of the piece. Digital techniques have developed to the stage where they now appear to be on the brink of effectively replacing previous mechanical (analogue) technologies as the predominant means of producing moving images. A whole industry – increasingly multinational in character – of hardware and software producers together with a multitude of companies specialising in computer generated animation, digital special effects, digitally based post-production work and so forth, has grown up in relation to this development. Of course, new Hollywood and its immediate moving image family (advertising, music video and television) are not the only domains of contemporary visual culture to be affected by digital technologies. I must now introduce and sketch the rise of two further members of this extended family, starting with computer games.

Computer games

By the early 1980s computer games (or video games as they are often called) had become firmly established as a new and significant mass cultural form.[9] As we begin the new century games have come to rank alongside cinema in terms of market size and cultural importance. Whether in the arcade or the home, the computer games of recent times are complex in their formal make-up, engaging players in various modes of real-time hands-on control of, and response to, technically sophisticated images, action and sound. Most current games' imagery is in colour, it is figurative, and – depending upon the genre – usually highly detailed and realistic; increasingly, it is likely to involve three-dimensional animation.

The story of the evolution of computer games as a visual cultural form since the 1960s is partially tied to the developments in digital imaging already sketched in relation to the emergence of digital cinema. Clearly, the headway made in the domain of computer imaging has fed into the growth of computer games since their commercial appearance at the beginning of the 1970s. Yet there is far more to the historical development of the form than this. Certainly, the computer game emerges as a historically discernible mass cultural industry a good decade earlier than its cousin digital cinema.

The hacker

The early or prehistory of games coincides roughly with the emergence of computer imaging (i.e. the 1960s). However, it was not from within the graphics milieu discussed earlier – not, at least, in any obvious or direct sense – that the first games emerged. There is something of an anecdotal element to the early history of the computer game. The first games are invoked as the diversions of a certain type of computer scientist who – in the early 1960s – was otherwise occupied in more 'serious' (if still somewhat idiosyncratic) pursuits (see, Brand 1972; Levy 1984; Haddon 1988). It is one type of programmer – the so-called 'hacker' – who has been most consistently associated with devising and playing the prototypes of commercial computer games.

Hackers are people who have developed extraordinary programming expertise. They have a monomaniacal relation to computers and what they can be made to do if the right instructions are fed into them. Hackers are to be distinguished from other programmers mainly by the way in which they make programming an end in itself. The hacker is often characterised as a perfectionist; involved in either attempting to right those parts of his program that are not functioning as smoothly as they might, or, alternatively, adding elements that are designed to improve what is already there. Levy refers to this phenomenon as 'making tools to make tools' (1984: 142). It is interesting to read, alongside Levy's enthusiastic and colloquial account of hackers, the somewhat different though highly informative accounts of hacking and hackers by Turkle (1984) and Weizenbaum (1984).

The hacker's approach to computer programming has been characterised as 'playful' rather than utilitarian; in this way hackers are to be distinguished from other technicians (see, for example, Turkle 1984: 2–11; Haddon 1993: 126). Certainly, this rather curious conception of a compulsive yet 'playful' approach to programming *per se* is seen as predisposing the hacker towards the creation of games. *Space War* – the first game to emerge within MIT that got any exposure outside of its birthplace – is seen as typifying the hacker's predilection for highly formalist aesthetic modes (see Brand 1972; Turkle 1984).

Whereas divergent currents were involved in the first stages of computer image exploration, the same cannot be said of computer games: games it appears were created within a mileu that was highly uniform in terms of its affiliation and the practical and cultural interests of those affiliates. Indeed, in certain respects computer games were from their very beginnings grounded in preoccupations, notions and practices which to this day – despite other quite phenomenal developments (see pp. 28–30) – have remained remarkably constant. Certainly, descriptions of that 'first' game, *Space War*, seem extremely familiar. The game usually involved two players who each had real-time responsive control of manoeuvrable spaceships and the missiles that they fired at each other. The 'action was continuous, leaving little pause to stop and plan. It called on physical reflexes as much as on strategy' (Haddon 1993: 132). *Space War* is the archetypal battle or shooting game; the original of what has subsequently come to be known, in its myriad arcade and home computer variants, as the 'shoot-'em-up'.

It is important, however, to note that these early games involved primitive forms of real-time interactive graphics. *Space War* was created at the same time and in the same institution that computer graphics pioneer Ivan Sutherland was completing his doctoral dissertation ('Sketchpad: a man-machine graphical communication system' (MIT Lincoln Laboratory, 1962)). Were those hackers responsible for *Space War* aware of Sutherland's work in the area? Certainly – at the level of programming or 'hacking' a game – lie the very same problems of *interactivity* and *simulation* that were preoccupying those operating in the domain of computer animation and cinema at the end of the 1960s. Initially, it is the aspect of real-time response – what subsequently comes to be known within the form as 'gameplay' – that most interests these first computer games producers. However, it is not long before the visual dimension assumes a much greater prominence within the form – particularly as the computer game progresses through its commercial history and as graphics capabilities develop in sophistication.

A new visual form

The computer game sprang 'almost fully formed' from the powerful minicomputers and mainframe machines that occupied the computer research centres in the 1960s. Driven by a certain technological obsession, technological in make up, and at the same time firmly rooted in form and content in popular genres – science fiction, Tolkienesque-fantasy and pinball – the first computer games also clearly locate themselves from the first within the space of commercial culture.

There are two facets to the rise of the computer game as a digital visual form: its development as a public form of entertainment via the arcade or coin-operated machine, and its development as a private form of entertainment through machines and software designed for use at home. The first commercial development took place in arcades at the beginning of the 1970s, though home development was to follow closely on its heels. Indeed, after 1972 the two strands evolve in parallel and relations between them are extremely close from the very beginning, not least because the dominant company of the early period – Atari – produced both hardware and software for both spheres. This link has continued unbroken right up to the present. Only the emergence of the personal computer introduces a certain discontinuity. Though, even here, links are quickly asserted at the level of software, for eventually games initially played in the arcade are converted for both home consoles and personal computers (PCs).

On one level the character of the connection between arcade games and home games is easy to describe: traditionally the arcade with its machines dedicated to the repeated delivery of one specific game, has always had the edge in terms of computer processing power. Thus in terms of the complexity and sophistication of 'game play' and audio-visual elements, the arcade machine has always held an advantage. The home computer game – continually hamstrung by price considerations – has until recently struggled to emulate the constant advance of its public and more technologically powerful relation. Things are not quite so simple however.

Arcades and consoles

The advances made in microprocessor technology led to the appearance of the first commercial games outside of the research laboratories. Dedicated games machines could now be built which combined both the TV screen and the player control of the image afforded by the computer. And, if the first stage of computer games history is that of the hackers and the 1960s, then the second commences with *Pong* and the beginning of the commercial exploitation of the form in the 1970s. During this period computer games slowly develop and grow in the arcades until, at the end of the 1970s, there is an explosive growth in interest in the form. The game that initiated this period of intense popularity was the prototype 'shoot-'em-up' *Space Invaders*. When this game was first released in Japan – which is where it was developed – its rapid rise in popularity had been quite phenomenal. And the release of the game in the US and Europe had a similar impact, prompting a sharp escalation in arcade game development and manufacture. During this period of video game fever, a host of new games were released into the arcades. Many of them were variations of the *Space Invaders* combat theme, indeed, the majority of them were 'shooting' or 'battle' games – 'twitch' games as they came to be known. Such games required high degrees of concentration, hand–eye coordination and rapid reflexes.

Visually, these early games tended to be highly schematic, with flat geometrical figures composed of dots or vector lines, action which took place against a flat two-dimensional background, and an increasing, though variable, use of colour. Sound effects were beginning to play more of a part in the experience, and a range of monaural noises were attached to the various on-screen opponents and to actions. The shooting game – and among the many to emerge at this time were *Galaxian, Asteroids, Defender, Battlezone* and *Pleiads* – was consolidated as the staple of the arcade, a position which it holds to this day; in fact it is one of the main kinds of the whole computer game form.

From the first there had been attempts to build games around flight and driving simulation technology, and these continued to appear during the first video arcades boom, as did some of the first games based upon attempts to produce a simulated experience of sports such as soccer and golf. At the same time, other kinds of game such as *Pacman, Lunar Lander* and *Donkey Kong* moved away from the shooting theme in various ways, thereby prefiguring subsequent genre developments. The arcade game *Donkey Kong* is significant as an early example of an enormously successful type of game that has subsequently come to be known as the 'platform' game. In this kind of game the player usually controls a character whose ultimate objective involves progression through a particular location filled with a variety of obstacles.

Alongside these developments there was a parallel process under way with respect to home computer games, or 'video games' as they are called. Throughout the period under discussion this took the form of TV games which were played via consoles attached to the domestic TV set. Initially, these consoles were limited to playing only those games that were encoded on its fixed chips. However, since the semiconductor manufacturer Intel had already announced in 1971 that it had developed a 'micro-programmable computer on a chip', it was not long before such technology was installed in home games consoles. Once it was – from the mid-1970s on – games machines became 'potentially "software players" like hi-fis and other home based delivery systems' (Haddon 1988: 66). Most of the successful games first produced for the coin-ops were copied for home consoles, though for those familiar with the original versions the home games were only a pale reflection of their more sophisticated because more powerful relatives.

Games on the first PCs

One important upshot of the transition to microprocessors in the middle of the decade was that it encouraged a greater separation between software and hardware development and manufacture. By the end of the 1970s it was not just the huge companies like Atari who were designing games software. Independent companies had begun to emerge and, through licensing agreements, were developing game software for the machine manufacturers. As the decade drew to a close these client manufacturers were not just producing software for dedicated games machines but increasingly for personal computer manufacturers such as Apple, Commodore, Tandy and even Atari itself.

For the 1970s are also the period in which the microcomputer (or PC) begins to take shape in the US. It was mainly computer hardware enthusiasts and program 'hackers' who initially pursued the idea of converting the new microprocessing technology into programmable general-purpose *personal* machines (see Freiberger and Swaine 1984). As these prototype home computers began to emerge in the second half of the 1970s – to be bought for the most part by computer 'hobbyists' – a preoccupation with software applications designed to display what such novel machines could do, took hold. Programmes centred on games were a central component of this process of demonstration and exposition. However, hobbyists apart, the new companies were already beginning to capitalise on a distinctive and fast growing kind of consumer, one who merely wanted to use the home computer as a delivery system for pre-programmed software.

Whereas the arcade and home console's reputation was built mainly around action genres – shoot-'em-ups and simulations – home computer game playing enabled the pursuit of the more cerebral puzzle-solving and map-making adventure genre. Ultimately, it would seem that the reasons for this have to do with time. For these games do not rely on rapid physical reflex, on the contrary, they often require long periods of reflection and information assessment before options are acted upon via the key board – indeed, they are designed that way. Clearly, both practical and financial (profit) considerations militate against these kinds of game appearing on arcade machines. Of course, the new independent games software companies also converted many of the arcade games of the time for the personal computer. However, one of the main contributions of these companies was the development of the fantasy/adventure as a distinctive game type.

home vs arcade [game genre]

The emergent independent games industry based around the microcomputer and founded largely on the interest of hackers and hobbyists operated largely along artisanal lines. Throughout the boom period of the early 1980s and beyond, both in the US and Europe, this hobbyist element of the young independent games industry encouraged a production process based around individual programmers working on a commission basis. Game writers worked in relative isolation on the conversion of an existing game or the development and perfecting of a new one.[10]

All of this was to change during the 1980s. If the 1970s and early 1980s had been the time of the 'coin-op' and the home games console, the rest of the 1980s was the decade of the home computer as far as game playing was concerned. During this period home computer hardware advanced from cassette to floppy disc, thus speeding up the time it took to load games on to the machine. At the same time the power of the machines themselves increased, which meant faster response times when playing, increased sound and image capabilities, and/or more elaborate or complex games.

Gradually, the dedicated player or user superseded the hobbyist who had been concerned to build machines (from kits) and to program as well as play. As the software companies began to cater for this kind of consumer, as the capacities and capabilities of the machines advanced, and as the market form itself matured, then so, inversely, did the maverick or independent programmer begin to recede. For, as the computer games industry grew and began to show a potential for stable profit making, so, slowly but surely, did the giant multi-media corporations become more centrally involved, investing in both hardware and software development and in lucrative licensing agreements with Hollywood and TV. Marketing (management of research, promotion and advertising) became more closely tied to production schedules. By the end of the 1980s, regulated teams of programmers, sound engineers, graphic artists, animators and so forth had largely superseded the freelance programmer.

This eventual regulation of the industry is also of course centrally related to the development of the form itself. In ways that closely resemble the industrial development of Hollywood and pop music as cultural forms and institutions, computer games have settled quickly (much quicker than either of the former) into a stable form with a limited number of 'genres' or game types. Like the mainstream cinema before it, computer games production appears to involve a process of refining, improving and 'innovating' within a set of formal parameters which remain stable from the outset, only changing, if at all, extremely slowly and over a relatively long period. Increasingly, as we shall see, the element of producing a novelty-effect within the repetition of a well worn game format, has rested upon the production of a greater sense or impression of realism within the game experience.

The return of the console

Having – to an extent at least – effectively seen off consoles dedicated solely to computer games playing in the 1980s, the personal computer sees them return with a vengeance in the 1990s. Perhaps one reason for this largely successful challenge to the growing supremacy of the home computer rests with the fact that it was becoming a general purpose machine – more and more people were using the personal computer for practical pursuits such as word-processing, accounting, publishing and so forth.

Yet, what also appears to have helped to re-establish the dedicated home games console, was the cartridge-based character of its software and the relatively low cost of the consoles themselves. Cartridges meant virtually instant playability, plus they could hold more information, which meant that a player did not have to wait for the game to be loaded, nor did s/he have to swap disks during play as was often the case on the microcomputers of the day. Certainly, the console – tenaciously promoted as a superior delivery system in terms of response and playability – triumphed in the long run. For, with the development of more powerful systems (which entailed smoother interfacing, improved response, more realistic characters, smoother motion and so forth), consumption of such machines and the games they play has grown enormously (see Hayes and Dinsey with Parker 1995).

The first years of the 1990s is a period of near-monopolistic manoeuvring between two companies – Nintendo and Sega – for leadership of the home console computer game market. In conjunction with carefully managed and hard fought publicity and advertising campaigns both sides systematically refined, restyled and increased the capabilities of their hardware. Of course, the games themselves had been 'upgraded' and 'reinvented' and a host of new ones had been released to display these improvements in delivery capabilities. Central to each were their particular versions of the popular platform genre based upon the numerous *Mario Brothers* games for Nintendo and *Sonic the Hedgehog* games for Sega. However, the other major action genres are all strongly represented on their consoles, and the two companies have been at the forefront of the 'innovation' which has taken place in the form of these games (see pp. 30–1). Though others have entered the market to challenge their monopoly (see Hayes and Dinsey with Parker 1995).

However, the 1990s are only partly the story of the rise to supremacy of the console – important though this undoubtedly is. The playing of games in arcades has continued to evolve. One of the functions of the arcade is to premier new games before their release on home platforms, which are now beginning to deliver comparable experiences in terms of graphics and interactive response. In addition, the dedicated 'one game only' machines of the 'coin-op' have concentrated upon enhancing even further the experience of *as ifness* that is central to the game-playing experience. Which is to say, they refine the elements of a single game experience along the lines of increasing the illusion of participative engagement. Thus we see arcade games where the interface no longer involves mock-ups of racing car interiors, but rather the cars themselves with a response to the screen to match. In addition, many games now include elements of so-called 'virtual reality' technologies; that is to say, machines which incorporate head-mounted display helmets, and/or synchronised movement. Similarly, the home computer has continued to grow, evolving in its latest manifestation into a powerful multimedia system. PCs now operate CD-ROM, have the capacity to link up to the Internet (for multi-player games) and – with greatly improved sound and image reproduction – are just as capable as the dedicated console of playing the most sophisticated games.

The ascendancy of the personal computer in the 1980s brought with it a certain re-balancing of games genres, such that the 'slower' games of exploration, fantasy and puzzle solving achieved something approaching parity with action genres in terms of popularity.[11] Yet, it is the 'twitch' games – the 'shoot-'em-ups', 'beat-'em-ups', 'platforms' and 'racing' games – that continue to be the most popular. And the rise of the dedicated home console in the 1990s has further underlined this dominance. The majority of the games made for and played on the 1990s home consoles have been action games, latter-day examples of *Space War* and *Space Invaders*.

Yet, though the recent action games share the fundamental characteristics of real-time control, fast hand–eye coordination, strategy and shooting, as their early predecessors in other respects they could not be more different. Thus in extremely popular mid-1990s examples of the shoot-'em-up game, such as *Doom*, *Hexen* and *Quake*, the player's viewpoint is first person, with the screen representing a direct view of the scene as if seen through the player's own eyes. If the player turns, runs, leaps, stops, then these actions are synchronised and matched accordingly with changes and movements on the screen, producing the sensation of being there. The environments of these games are rendered in extraordinarily realistic detail, with naturalistic surface texture, dramatic lighting effects and subtle use of colour. Nowadays the majority of adversaries – monsters, zombies, aliens and so forth – are rendered and animated with the same high levels of surface accuracy and increasingly this is combined with a persuasive anthropomorphism.

The institution of computer games

Less than a decade after it was originated the computer game became a new culture industry. Barely twenty years later is has become one of the major institutions of contemporary visual culture. The rise of this industry has produced new kinds of manufacturer, dedicated to the production of machines for game playing and to the production of games themselves. New companies have grown up around these different, though interconnected areas of production, and as the industry has grown so has interest in it from producers and distributors in older and well established areas of popular visual entertainment. Many of the original games companies have either disappeared or been incorporated in larger conglomerate concerns with their own computer games divisions.[12]

In the field of software production – the life-blood of the industry – similar developments have taken place. There is now both in-house software design by the hardware manufacturers who control distribution and numerous third party software houses that operate through licence agreements. In addition, most of the Hollywood studios now have computer game production subsidiaries, as do many of the established computer animation companies.

In the case of Hollywood, licensing film titles to computer game manufacturers for tie-in productions has long been commonplace. However, it is at the level of game design and development that a confluence is occurring in terms of underlying aesthetic ideals. Unsurprisingly, the dominant visual aesthetic of verisimilitude is now viewed as the main sign of success and progress within the form. This shares much in common with the prevailing aesthetic of digital cinema, especially in terms of the illusionist goals fuelling the endeavours of those involved. In this respect, the main difference between the two lies with the fact that, unlike cinema, games involve the element of so-called 'interaction'. This means that the player has an element of control and – within certain limits – is able to act upon that which appears within the audio-visual field of the screen. In the case of the computer game, this defining element of the form has become an additional and vital factor in a constant striving for greater and greater levels of illusion. Only now, the illusion is not just the impossible photography of digital cinema (*just as though* it had been photographically recorded), but rather of producing an experience that is *as if* one were actually taking part.

Given the above, then perhaps it is not surprising that the current character of games production is one of increasing cooperation and integration between other sectors both of the traditional and the digital imaging domains. Nowadays, the research, development and production of games can take up to two years or more and cost as much as several million dollars. Both digital and traditional forms of animation play a central role in games imagery: and the techniques of classical animation are being married with those attached to the digital cinema, such as, 3-D modelling, ray-tracing and motion-capture. Indeed, as data storage technologies become more powerful, traditional live action imagery is being incorporated into interactive programs. Although this has happened in the domain of CD-ROMs oriented towards reference and educational uses, software companies are already producing so-called 'interactive movies': hybrids of movies and computer games where the spectator selects options to determine the way the plot unfolds.

Special venue attractions

Terms such as 'special venue', 'special attraction', 'ride film' and 'simulation ride' have become common currency in the past decade, particularly in the context of mainstream cinema and the popular criticism surrounding it. The terms are used to refer to a range of phenomena which collectively make up a distinctive dimension of contemporary audiovisual entertainment, one which has grown rapidly since the 1980s – a fact that is related to many of the developments in the digital cinema described above. Special venues are exhibition spaces that are dedicated to showing a variety of non-traditional forms of cinematically related spectacle entertainments. These range from purpose-built theatres to specially adapted exhibition sites in locations such as theme parks, shopping malls, urban centres, hotels, amusement arcades and the like.

The term 'special attraction' is used to refer to what is exhibited at such

31

venues. Currently, the two main categories of special attraction are Imax films and the 'simulation ride'. Significantly, however, there are variations and hybrid forms of both of these emerging all the time (see pp. 33–5). Motion simulation-based attractions employ a hydraulically moveable platform (which supports the, usually seated, audience); the pre-programmed movements of the platform are synchronised with projected moving images and sound to fabricate the sensation of travelling. Imax (and Omnimax) films are shot and projected via specially designed film recording and projection systems. The original cinematography uses 65 mm film stock and this then gets printed on 70 mm for projection, the resulting image is ten times larger than conventional 35 mm film. Imax films are projected on to giant rectangular screens and Omnimax films on to giant spherical screens. The sheer size of the screen causes the spectator to lose sight of its edges and this produces a sensation of proximity and 'engulfment'.

Imax and motion simulation

Fundamentally, Imax cinema is a variant of traditional analogue cinematography. It does not depend upon digital techniques – though there are several reasons why it is important to the background history being sketched here (see T. Wollen, 1993). In the first place, Imax is a pioneer of the special venue attraction. Second, it has evolved in its own manner under the same aesthetic rubric of 'realism' that is central to the two broad areas of digital culture already introduced. Finally, in the same way as mainstream cinema, Imax systems are themselves succumbing to the lure of the digital, and simulation rides are now being produced in the Imax and Omnimax formats. Imax films operate within a perspective of both perfecting and augmenting the dominant ideal of visual realism already encountered with regard to digital cinema and computer games. They do this through their own technical modification of the existing apparatus of the cinema: attempting to improve upon prior registers of surface accuracy by combining magnification with high fidelity, thereby intensifying the spectator's illusion of 'being there' by engulfing him or her in the image. This project has an affinity not just with the modes of visual digital culture already alluded to, but, more importantly for present purposes, with those slightly more recent digitally based attractions which revolve around the simulation ride. The character of this kinship is both aesthetic and technical: technical development and innovation provides the basis for the production of novel image-centred forms based upon illusion and special effects.

Undoubtedly the immediate technical predecessor of the simulation ride as an entertainment form is the simulator used for professional training. Specifically, it is the oft-cited flight simulator, introduced to train pilots during the Second World War and intensively developed in both military and civil contexts ever since, which lies at the technological heart of today's simulation ride attractions. The flight simulator has three fundamental components: image, motion and interaction (hands-on control). Most flight simulators consist of a detailed mock-up of the cabin of a specific aircraft replete with instruments and seats but without the rest of the plane. This is:

> enclosed by a visual surface on which the visual scene is shown. To simulate the motion of the plane the cockpit is mounted on a platform that can be moved up and down and from side to side as well as tilted. As the pilot operates the controls of the aircraft both the visual scene content and the sensation of aircraft motion change.
>
> (Haber 1987: 90)

Of course, the digital computer is central to such a sophisticated technical apparatus. The computer enables the simulator to produce real-time synchronised changes both in the visual field and on the motion rig in response to the trainee operating the controls.

As we have seen two of the elements of the flight simulator – graphics and joystick control – are central to the computer game. With simulation rides however, whilst the visual aspect and the motion component remain central to their basic formal make-up, the element of being able to directly control or affect what one sees disappears. Simulation rides have developed around the impression of propulsive motion that the flight simulator is able to convey to passengers. Meticulously choreographed to repeatedly unfold in an unvarying manner, in this sense, the form has more in common with the sub-genres of digital cinema than with computer games.

Establishing a new spectacle form

Among the first people involved in the development of the simulation ride was Douglas Trumbull who, seeking the kind of 'liquid realism' he had only been able to glimpse looking at *2001: Space Odyssey* embarked on a project to produce a commercial film system with a similar visual quality. Trumbull is credited with the creation of the celebrated 'Star Gate' sequence on *2001*. This was produced utilising techniques pioneered by John Whitney Snr in the 1960s (see Whitney 1981). In the 1970s he and his associates developed a large format (70 mm) high definition (60 frames per second) film process called Showscan that was similar in many respects to the Imax system which had been introduced a few years earlier. In the early 1980s the Showscan system was used in the production of *Tour of the Universe* one of the first simulation rides. Other specialist production companies have emerged around the form, particularly in the United States. In addition to producing large-scale rides several of these companies are also involved in exhibition (for further details of this history, see Pourroy 1991; Huhatamo 1996).

The form has developed and expanded greatly since the 1980s. Such attractions are no longer confined to the large theme park and similar locations, smaller versions of the simulation ride can be found in amusement arcades, funfairs and shopping malls. It is, however, the theme park and the specially designed 'ciné city' type of exhibition site which houses the most technically sophisticated and spectacular rides.[13] These tend to be large-scale productions, realised through some kind of large-format film system such as Showscan, Vista Vision or Imax. Such rides are installed in large theatres, which have either been specially built or specifically adapted for the purpose. Usually, they are located in a limited number of sites.

Traditionally it has been at the theme park locations of large corporations such as Disney and Universal – where attractions are designed both with expectations of longevity and in terms of being at the leading edge of the genre – that the most effort has gone into formal development and innovation. One of the clearest examples of this was the production of *Back to the Future: The Ride* (1991) by Universal Studios for its Florida and Hollywood theme parks. Whereas, the majority of simulation rides involve a platform situated in front of a flat screen which acts as the 'windscreen' for the ride one is experiencing, *Back to the Future: The Ride* departed from this convention and utilised a hemispherical screen. The attraction was shot for exhibition in a specially constructed building that contained a giant Omnimax surround screen. In this instance the motion platform – which carries eight passengers – is an open-topped DeLorean car. As those familiar with the film *Back to the Future* on which the ride is based will know, the car doubles as a time machine (for more detail on the technical problems encountered in the production of this ride see Pourroy 1991).

Digital technology is a vital component of *Back to the Future: The Ride*. It is crucial both to its kinetic aspect and to its audiovisual dimension, though it is not deployed in the direct rendering of the visual imagery. Increasingly however, computer animation and image synthesis are finding their way into special venue attractions. For example, in a ride entitled, *In Search of the Obelisk* (1993) located at the Luxor Casino in Las Vegas, computer graphics and computer animation begin to figure more prominently. Here computer images augment scenes involving miniature backgrounds by adding computer generated flying vehicles, smoke and so forth; and at least one sequence was entirely computer generated (see Abrams 1995). Even the traditional Imax medium has succumbed to digital image effects and computer generated imagery. In *The Journey Inside* (1994), an Imax film about the production, use and workings of microchips, the film climaxes with a computer generated 'ride-like' journey into a computer chip.

At the more technically sophisticated end of the special venue form there have also emerged hybrids such as Universal Studio's theme park attraction, *Terminator 2: 3-D* (1996) and Walt Disney World's, *Honey, I Shrunk the Audience* (1995). Costing as much as blockbuster special effects films to produce and install, these special attractions, based – as so many are – on tie-ins or sequels to successful feature films, are an amalgam of formats and techniques. Thus large format 3-D cinema, special effects, computer manipulated, composited and generated 3-D moving images, live theatrical performance and 'elaborate in-theatre effects' are all present – though neither involves a motion platform. Both use large, high definition film formats in an attempt to match the clarity of normal vision and, at the outset at least, to produce the impression of actually being present at a live event. Innovative 3-D processes are used, partly to intensify this high definition illusionism, partly to exploit the impression that people and things can leave the screen and enter the personal theatrical space of the audience – usually to exhilarating effect. In the case of *Terminator 2: 3-D*, one way in which this is achieved is by the use of live actors who are seamlessly integrated into the cinematic action and space. In *Honey, I Shrunk the Audience* in-theatre special effects carry over the action taking place on the stage/screen to the space occupied by the audience. For example, the sneeze of a giant dog is not just seen and heard, it is also *felt*. In a manner that parallels the attempt to produce the illusion of propulsion in the simulation ride, these attractions are attempting to produce the illusion that the distinction between screen space and the space of the audience itself has dissolved.

One thing which remains unchanged whatever the size of the attraction is the relatively short duration of the ride experience itself. Indeed, this is a definitive characteristic of the special venue form. Even Imax films are far shorter than the 90 minutes plus running time of the average feature film and average out at about 40 minutes apiece. Simulation rides and related special venue attractions are shorter still. A major ride such as *Back to the Future: The Ride*, is a mere 4 minutes long, whilst *Terminator 2: 3-D* – with a running time of a full 12 minutes – becomes an epic of the genre. Moreover, the majority of the smaller arcade simulations and medium-sized rides last no longer than 5 minutes. Of course these attractions are technologically dense and require a great deal of painstaking development and laborious production time before their release. What is more, such high concentrations of technological prowess do not come cheap. This applies particularly to the larger-scale instances of the genre but is also a factor that is present in the smallest examples. Undoubtedly, this goes some way towards explaining the brevity that characterises the form, but it does not totally account for it. For it also seems that there is something in the aesthetic character of the genre itself which dictates the short duration of its particular attractions. Douglas Trumbull says his rule of thumb is, 'as you increase the power of the medium, the audience wants to shorten the experience. The more immersive the experience, the more compressed it should be in time' (quoted in *In Camera* Autumn 1994: 10). He may well have a point, yet one wonders if there is not more involved in understanding what is occurring here than this. However, these are questions we shall explore in subsequent pages.

As this overview of the recent emergence of the forms at the centre of this book shows, the development of the computer is having a significant effect on mass visual culture. New technology centred upon digital microprocessing and computer programming is transforming the ways in which visual culture is produced and received. It is doing this, as we have seen, both at the level of technical modernisation and at the level of formal developments. In a period of barely twenty years, digital techniques have left the research laboratories and integrated with established means of production and exhibition. With the emergence of the computer, entirely new ways of making images, together with ways of assisting and augmenting established methods and techniques have become commonplace within contemporary forms of visual cultural production. Moreover, this process has also given rise to the emergence of distinctive genres and forms within the sphere of mass visual culture. Among these, two in particular – computer games and simulation rides – appear to be unprecedented. New-sprung concepts such as 'simulation', 'interactivity' and 'immersion' have emerged to describe what is seen as unique and different within these new forms, whilst older-sounding terms like 'realism', 'illusionism' and 'spectacle' still appear to play a crucial part in the discursive practices which constitute them.

Clearly a new aesthetic space has opened up within contemporary culture, one which owes its existence to digital technology. It is important to stress, however, that this debt is by no means absolute. The computer is vital to understanding the make-up of the forms whose development we have just sketched, yet it is not the only agency explaining what they are and how they have come to be that way. The computer has not shaped the aesthetic character of these forms all by itself, as – taken on its own – an account such as the one above might be mistaken for suggesting.

2

GENEALOGY AND TRADITION
Mechanised spectacle as popular entertainment

This chapter employs history in a different manner to the more straightforward way it is used in chapter 1. I now embark upon a consideration of the forms and genres of visual digital culture introduced above, from two quite different historical perspectives. Chapter 3 will concern itself with the particular character of contemporary *aesthetics*, exploring shifts which have occurred there in the late twentieth century, and relating these to the emergence of the forms in question. I begin, however, by contemplating the forms of digital culture at issue within a more expansive history of popular entertainments, and in particular those that are technologically based (though not only them). The discussion revolves around forms, institutions, contexts and modes of reception associated with pre- and early cinema. I return to this earlier context because, as I contend below, both in terms of important analogies and direct historical lineage, such an approach throws considerable light on visual digital culture as I am defining it here.

I shall suggest that the new digital forms signal a kind of reawakening or renaissance; a return to and a continuation of preoccupations, practices, forms and experiences that were part of an earlier phase of popular entertainment. Though these were ever-present in twentieth-century popular visual culture, they have, nevertheless, existed as a marginal or secondary dimension: a tradition which was less theorised and less lauded, and that was overtaken by narrative (particularly the cinema) and further displaced by the advent of television. In many respects the forms of visual digital culture at the centre of this discussion constitute a resurgence of this dimension: they are both continuous with it and at the same time distinctive.

Popular entertainments and the cinema

Digital cinema, computer games and special venue attractions: what can an exploration of the history of earlier modes of entertainment tell us about these latest forms and their genres? I believe that it can explain a great deal. It can establish that these forms are not nearly as novel as many would have us believe. For, although clearly they do exhibit extremely distinctive properties – and it

37

will be important to elucidate what these are – there is, nevertheless, a very real sense in which they are part of a distinct lineage. This lineage is not entirely uniform and straightforward and it requires a little work if it is to be fully uncovered, nevertheless, it exists as a kind of genealogy of the forms in question. Revealing something of the nature of the ancestral background involved here can also begin to give us clues and cues to understanding the formal make-up of these latest forms, thereby telling us much about how and why people enjoy them. Despite all this talk of the importance of continuity and lineage, however, the history I am going to explore here – albeit, somewhat briefly and schematically – is by no means one of simple succession and progression.

The fulcrum of the discussion in this chapter is the cinema. That the cinema itself should form the fulcrum of a discussion of the history of technologically based popular entertainments ought to surprise no one. Of all the forms of aesthetic visual representation based around the new technologies that were to emerge during the period of industrial modernisation, the *cinématographe* appears to be both culmination and emblem: not only the most advanced in terms of its technological sophistication, but the synthesis of the past two centuries of technological invention in the service of visual representation. It was the eventual emergence of the cinema as a (heterogeneous) cultural institution, which established that the distinctive modality of visual representation for the future would be the moving image. The cinema may well have lost some of its hegemonic power as a form of popular entertainment, challenged by television, video and now, of course, recent digital forms – yet the cinema still seems to resonate in all of these later entertainment forms. The question, however, is which cinema and in what ways?

It is, I believe, through looking at the history surrounding the cinema's birth and development that we can begin to get more of a purchase on the character of the contemporary forms under consideration. I take my lead and inspiration from recent work undertaken by scholars of the cinema who have been concerned to re-visit the moment of the cinema's emergence. Though authors such as Noël Burch (1990), Tom Gunning (1989) and Miriam Hansen (1990) often take very different approaches to their subject, they all appear to agree on one thing: the early cinema is far more complex and heterogeneous than has generally been allowed. Although such work is not directly related to understanding the contemporary forms with which this book concerns itself, it seems to me, nevertheless, that much of it is highly suggestive in this regard.

Far from seeing the first films as merely the starting point for narrative development, scholars such as Burch and Gunning, are concerned in their different ways to show that early cinema was a distinctive kind of cinema; a cinema that can only be properly understood by examining it not just in relation to the subsequent history of the form, but to forces (cultural, social, political, ideological) that were operating at the time of its emergence, and by looking backwards to the (similarly determined) forms and practices which had helped to shape it (see, for example, Burch 1978/9). Picking up from here, I shall begin this exploration by returning to the period before the rudimentary cinema (camera, film, projector, exhibition space) existed as such.

My initial focus is on two key aspects of nineteenth-century cultural development. The first involves the character of popular entertainments and amusements during the period, and the second considers a parallel development, the extraordinary growth of optical and other technologies and devices dedicated to the production of a variety of forms of visual representation. I shall not be overly concerned with the precise chronological progress of these increasingly interconnected spheres of nineteenth-century culture. I want, rather, to consider them in relation to two broad, but nevertheless, crucial aesthetic concepts: spectacle and realism. Neither of these are simple terms, but they are central to understanding the evolving character of popular visual culture, both in the nineteenth century and in the present.

Spectacular entertainments

By the end of the eighteenth century popular culture had entered a period of transition. Whilst the traditional rural or 'folk' forms and genres did not completely disappear, they were being rapidly supplanted by commercial forms of popular entertainment. The shift appears to have moved decisively towards the growing urban centres as the locus of performance-oriented entertainments. These forms did not necessarily displace older modes of performance, such as juggling, clowning and acrobatics. They did, however, begin to challenge the itinerant character of traditional forms by locating their performances in fixed exhibition sites.[1] Increased marketisation also led to larger and more businesslike organisations. One example of the entrepreneurial spirit that increasingly came to pervade the sphere of popular amusement is the case of Philip Astley, who is credited with founding one of the pillars of modern commercial popular entertainment – the circus. Astley's claims in this direction have much to do with the fact that within a few years he had greatly increased the scale of his organisation and had begun to put on seasons with highly varied programmes. No longer simply an equestrian act, by 1773 Astley was augmenting this attraction by hiring the services of diverse performers such as acrobats, clowns, strong-men, balancing acts and animal trainers (see Speaight 1980). Within a few years Astley had stopped presenting seasons of attractions in different venues and had constructed his own theatres, among them Astley's Amphitheatre Riding House, which opened in London in 1799, and the Cirque-Olympique, which Astley founded in Paris in 1782.

Like the circus itself, these theatres had their origins in the great fairs of seventeenth-century Europe. The Boulevard du Temple district in which the Cirque-Olympique was located is interesting precisely as a site of transition from the old to the new; a place where the older itinerant forms of performance existed side by side with the new and developing commercial popular theatres. As the great Parisian fairs such as Saint-Laurent and Saint-Ovide were closed in the second half of the eighteenth century, the entertainments and entertainers which the fairs had housed began to relocate in Paris itself, specifically on and around the Boulevard du Temple (see Carlson 1974: 26; Speaight 1980: 16).[2]

Commercial popular entertainments were largely based around live performance, and by the late nineteenth century had come to include the circus, several kinds of variety entertainment such as vaudeville and burlesque shows, the pantomime, the fairy play, melodrama, farce, magic shows and spectacle theatres (hippodromes). All of these forms were based firmly in spectacle: the emphasis was on performances which were designed to elicit intense and instantaneous visual pleasure; the production of imagery and action which would excite, astound and astonish the audience. This explains the form of a large number of such entertainments, where they are made up of some kind of variety format, consisting of a collection of separate or independent acts or attractions (see McNamara 1974).

Clearly, popular entertainment forms of the late eighteenth and nineteenth centuries diverge greatly from conventional or classical models in terms of aesthetic properties. Designed to stimulate and capture the eye and, often, the gut (viscera) as well, rather than the head or intellect, by comparison with the mimetic or representational preoccupations of establishment culture, such forms seem to exist for their own sake, with conventional external reference at a minimum. Often appearing ephemeral and superficial, when they do relate to something beyond themselves it is more than likely to be to such things as the ludicrous, the grotesque, the exotic or the fantastic. Like conventional drama, the forms of popular entertainment depended upon highly skilful modes of performance, though these skills differed greatly, for example, acrobatics, conjuring and illusionism, high-wire acts, escape acts, puppetry and ventriloquism. They also frequently – more so as the nineteenth century wore on – rely upon stage contrivances, elaborate props, and mechanical and optically based special effects and trick techniques. Even within a relatively conventional (and relatively late) genre such as melodrama, the greatest attention was paid to introducing moments of trick-work and special effects. Indeed, it was on such aspects of productions that the most money and attention was lavished, 'since it was the sensational and spectacular that invariably brought crowds into the theatre' (McNamara 1974: 20).

Optical illusions: Phantasmagoria and diorama

By the turn of the century, commercial entertainment and amusements had lost none of their spectacular character, though they had altered somewhat. However, before we explore the character and conditions of late nineteenth-century popular entertainments, I want to turn to another crucial strand of visual culture that had been advancing since the late 1700s. The two centuries which precede the first public projection of films by the Lumière Brothers in Paris in 1896 attest to an extraordinary growth in optical and other technologies dedicated to the production of a whole array of forms of visual representation, beginning with the magic lantern show. Most of these forms, along with their numerous variants, share the common feature of being *spectacle* forms: which is to say, their overriding characteristic is that either by accident or design they produce striking visual stimulation; they astonish the spectator. Significantly however, they do this in rather different ways.

The Phantasmagoria was a type of magic lantern show. It rose rapidly to success (and infamy) in the 1790s first in Paris, then a little later in other European capitals (see, for example, Barnouw 1981; Clarke 1983). Its exhibition space contained a diaphanous screen, on one side of which sat the audience. This screen was hidden behind a black gauze curtain, and was only uncovered once the audience had assembled and the lights had been extinguished. On the other side of the screen, hidden from view, was the lanternist who projected specially painted images on to the screen using slides. Other hidden effects involving mirrors and lenses, lights, sounds and braziers formed part of the attraction, as did the important use of assistants who were there both to help with the technical operations and as audience plants or confederates (see Barnouw 1981; Clarke 1983; Hecht 1993). The key distinguishing feature of the Phantasmagoria, however, lies in the character of the illusions and stage tricks which it presented, for these were used to produce 'seance-like' events in which spirits and ghosts were conjured up before the awe-struck spectators.

It would appear that the Phantasmagoria constituted a distinct improvement upon earlier efforts with the magic lantern. For one thing it was altogether more sophisticated both as an apparatus and with regard to the presentations which it staged and, indeed, these were so elaborate that at the time they merited their own dedicated exhibition spaces. It is difficult to establish the life-span of the Phantasmagoria proper. Certainly at the beginning of the nineteenth century they had proliferated greatly and, although they seem to have lost some of their immediate attraction fairly quickly, their direct influence on other similar forms continued throughout the 1900s.[3]

Whilst the Panorama and the diorama produced similar effects to that of the Phantasmagoria, the kind of images they produced and the character of their spectacle were quite different. If the Phantasmagoria was attractive and astonishing insofar as it rendered the 'supernatural' and the fantastic with new levels of convincing visual illusion, then the Panorama was successful because of the extraordinary realism it brought to depictions of the natural world – its astonishing degree of verisimilitude (see Gernsheim and Gernsheim 1968: 6).

By the early 1800s Panorama buildings designed to contain the necessary cylindrical viewing space had been constructed in many major European cities and in the United States. Barely twenty years later these would be followed, and to a great extent supplanted, by the construction of buildings to house another kind of visual attraction which, though clearly related to the Panorama, constituted an advance on the latter in terms of verisimilitude or the rendering of surface accuracy, principally via the use of elaborate lighting effects. It was two French painters, Daguerre and Bouton who first developed the diorama for commercial exploitation.

In their book, *L.J.M. Daguerre: The History of the Diorama and the Daguerrotype*, Helmut Gernsheim and Alison Gernsheim produce a deft description of the diorama explaining that the 'great diversity of scenic effect was produced by a combination of translucent and opaque painting, and of transmitted and reflected light by contrivances such as screens and shutters …' (1968: 20). The addition of lighting coupled with the translucent screen enabled the introduction of a new dimension into the naturalistically depicted scenes: a sense of time could be conveyed, the realistic effect could be heightened, and Daguerre perfected elaborate techniques of combining painting and lighting in order to display in a scene the passage from day to night. An effusive contemporary response to one of the most famous of these so-called 'double effect' dioramas, *A Midnight Mass at Sainte-Etienne-du-Mont* (1834), concludes by exclaiming that it was 'magic' (1968: 34).

Magic, indeed – though it was of a different order to that of the Phantasmagoria. For, although the Phantasmagoria and the diorama both use visual illusion to astonish and visually confound – trading on the conviction that the images the spectator is seeing are 'real' when s/he knows that they are not – they do, nevertheless, differ with respect to the character of the ways in which they take possession of the eyes. The reliance of each on novel ways of combining light and image to produce their captivating effects clearly unites them. Still, it would appear that the Phantasmagoria sits firmly within a representational tradition of fantasy and magic (convincing images of the supernatural), whilst the diorama is closely associated with representational realism (convincing images of the natural).[4]

Indeed, although these two differing attitudes to representational illusionism can be traced through the line of technological developments – photography, 'persistence of vision' techniques, rapid photography – which lead to the *cinématographe*, it was clearly the realist strand which was predominant here. For, arguably, it was the struggle to produce a verisimilitudinous visual replication of reality rather than the production of diversion through spectacle, which provided the greater impulse to these technological endeavours.[5] However, having admitted this much, one still must acknowledge that these novel inventions whether intentionally or otherwise, contributed significantly to the production of spectacle. Indeed, many of them were moulded to produce amusement and entertainment – even if this was supplementary. It was not just the Panorama and diorama that became cultural institutions, for apart from the many variations (close relatives) of the latter which sprang up around the same time, we might also mention the fascination with the image produced by photography itself in the first years of its commercial exploitation in the middle decades of the nineteenth century. Indeed, many of the devices produced in the course of serious scientific study into the phenomenon of the 'persistence of

vision' during the nineteenth century – devices that were crucial to the technological development of the cinema – were later turned into parlour toys and
amusements (see, for example, Neale 1985).

Illuminating here is the work of the nineteenth-century scientific current
engaged in attempts to investigate the world of movement through its photographic representation. Utilising and building upon intensive and ongoing work
into optics, the notion of 'the persistence of vision' and photography, it was
scientists such as Muybridge and Marey who – in the pursuit of the means to
analyse human and animal movement which escaped the naked eye – made
some of the crucial technological breakthroughs which led directly to the
cinema. Despite the fact that Muybridge's experimentation with rapid photography and its projection was oriented solely towards reproducing movement in
order to better understand it, the projection of these images provoked 'astonishment and pleasure' in those who first saw them. Neale cites a description
written by one of those present at one of Muybridge's demonstrations: 'the
most striking of all the demonstrations was that of the wing motion of a large
white bird (a cockatoo, I believe) … I well remember the murmur of astonishment and pleasure … and the persistent demands for the repetition of what was
as beautiful a picture as I have ever seen on a screen' (1985: 38–9).

Clearly, even work which has little, if any, aesthetic pretensions, work which
has not been specifically calculated to produce spectacle, can astonish and
produce intense scopic pleasure. Indeed, this illustrates a further facet of the
fascination and wonder generated by such endeavours at this time, for one
strongly suspects that it was not just the moving image which caused the astonishment here, but also the apparatus which was producing it.

Cinema and the Luna Park

Machines that produce distinctive (astonishing) kinds of realistic illusion,
thereby eliciting a fascination and wonder at their workings and power, and
forms of live popular entertainment which are designed to produce intense
levels of sensation and astonishment: how are these two lines of nineteenth-
century spectacle related? During the course of the nineteenth century these
two lines of technological optical experimentation and popular visual entertainments begin to converge, though the manner of their meeting – especially in
the case of the cinema – is by no means a case of simple amalgamation.

It is, arguably, the (early) cinema and the amusement park that most clearly
represent the prevailing character of contemporary popular entertainments at
the turn of the twentieth century, and each displays in its own way both the
continuities and the changes that have occurred in popular forms in the decades
which precede them. The early cinema and the amusement park emerged
together at the end of the nineteenth century, the latest manifestations of a
tradition of popular entertainment – now commercially and technologically
informed – whose fundamental aesthetic properties turned upon modes of

direct spectacle and sensation. Indeed, these forms may be considered representatives of a commercial popular culture which at that time could be characterised as involving a veritable frenzy of spectacle and sensation. Undoubtedly, this is intimately connected to a particular historical context or moment in the maturation of processes of industrialisation and urbanisation that were under way in both Europe and America; processes that were bringing about significant changes in social and economic conditions; processes that had encouraged the kinds of research into technologies of visual representation to which we have already made reference; processes that were creating the basis for new forms of culture and cultural experience.[6]

Although both the early cinema and the amusement park extend the spectacle-oriented aesthetic ethos of popular entertainment, there are certain distinctions to be drawn between the two in terms of the ways in which they each manifest this ethos. Let us turn first to the amusement park – which began to appear across America at the turn of the nineteenth century. Among the newer technologically inspired commercial forms of mass entertainment, it is this distinctive mode of 'institutionalised carnival' that most boldly expressed the element of instantaneous spectacle and sensory stimulation associated with earlier commercial performance-based popular entertainments. In his lucid and evocative account of the first amusement parks, John Kasson explains that the most distinctive feature of the popular attractions which the amusement park gathered together was, 'the new mechanical amusements and the exotic settings they provided ... [for, whereas] in most entertainments of the period the public remained in the position of spectators ... at Coney Island and other amusement parks ... audience and activity frequently merged .... Customers participated intimately in the spectacle about them' (1978: 8).

The mechanised rides and attractions in the turn-of-the-century amusement parks were part of an immense and enveloping spectacle. From the moment they entered the park and for the duration of their visit, spectators were systematically enticed and excited into active participation, becoming themselves performers in, and contributors to, the overall display. The amusement park was an entertainment of attractions, but its attractions were both diverse and many: the roving visitor could choose to mix the pleasures of a variety of separately staged spectacles and diversions with a host of rides all of which entailed a more directly physical experience. Alternatively, s/he could simply enjoy the spectacle of others undergoing the giddying thrills and spills of these pervasive pleasure machines.

The rides which were so central to the amusement park experience, were based upon devices such as the Ferris Wheel and the water slide or Shoot-the-Chutes. The 'Flip-Flap' Railway 'propelled daring twosomes rapidly down a track and through a twenty-five-foot vertical loop ... [whilst] the "Leap-Frog" Railway thrilled passengers by sending two electric cars, each filled with forty people, toward one another on the same set of tracks ...' (1978: 77–8). Disaster spectacles comprising both mechanically constructed simulations and live performances were regular attractions. Thus, in the live disaster spectacle 'Fire and Flames', 'a four-story building was repeatedly set ablaze, the fire battled by heroic firemen while residents leaped from upper windows into safety nets below' (1978: 71–2).

The amusement parks were places of enveloping spectacle and intense kinaesthetic experiences. Kasson describes the visitor's encounter with such a space, as the entry into 'an environmental phantasmagoria, combining characteristics of the beer garden, county fair, Chicago Midway, vaudeville, and circus' (1978: 49). Here, clearly, was a form commensurate with the times, a form that continued the sensational and spectacular dimensions of established popular entertainments, yet which also intensified them: through exaggerations of scale and design, certainly – but more than this, through the diversion of contemporary mechanics and engineering to recreational or playful (i.e. non-utilitarian) ends. The amusement park does not itself directly marry the new techniques of (moving) image production to the prevailing popular ethos of spectacle – we must look to other forms for that: the magic theatre, but above all the *cinématographe*. Although its attractions certainly included forms which display such couplings, ultimately, the technological reach of the amusement park is broader; its principal referents are mechanised modes of transportation and production (trains, trolleys and milling-machines), and beneath these the new conceptions and experiences of speed and space which they were engendering.

It is the early cinema, of course, which most immediately displays the nineteenth-century fascination with technologies of spectacle. The cinema is in a sense the culmination of these preoccupations. Both the Phantasmagoria and the diorama have a latent presence in early cinema, but then so too do other elements of nineteenth-century popular entertainment, most notably stage magic, special effects and the exotic. Indeed, it is not only the so-called 'trick-film', associated most notably with the films of George Méliès – crucial though this is – with its continuation of the illusionism and visual display associated with the magic theatre, which links the nascent cinema to the tradition of popular spectacle. Just as significant is the way in which 'realism' in the form of Lumière-style actuality films and the phenomenon of Hale's Tours conforms to the popular aesthetic.[7] In the same way that the new levels of verisimilitude which were evident in the diorama produced astonishment and visual curiosity in the spectator, so too did the moving, realistic images presented by the likes of Lumière. Here, a novel kind of 'realistic illusion' becomes fascinating; and, once again, it is not just what is being shown that creates the spectacle, but how it is being shown; the cinematic apparatus itself is being wondered at.

Film historian Tom Gunning has argued precisely this point about the early cinema in general (1989). In his attempt to characterise the distinguishing properties of the early cinema, he casts doubt on the commonly held myth that early spectators were so convinced by the realism of these first moving images, that they fled the theatre in panic at the filmic representation of an approaching train. Gunning argues that the first audiences were not so naive as to confuse the image for reality. Instead, he accounts for the 'shock and astonishment, an excitement pushed to the point of terror' caused by the first film shows in another way. Reminding us that the early screenings began with still images which only subsequently began to move, he argues that, 'rather than mistaking the image for reality, the spectator is astonished by its transformation through the new illusion of projected motion. Far from credulity, it is the incredible nature of the illusion itself that renders the viewer speechless ... less the impending speed of the train than the force of the cinematic apparatus' (1989: 24). Gunning goes on to suggest that this 'new illusion of projected motion' parallels experiences that spectators of early cinema were already familiar with through the extraordinary illusions produced in the magic theatre. Arguing further that early cinema is defined by an 'aesthetic of attractions' he suggests that it is a spectacle form: a form which, 'solicits a highly conscious awareness of the film image engaging the viewer's curiosity. The spectator does not get lost in a fictional world and its drama, but remains aware of the act of looking, the excitement of curiosity and its fulfilment' (1989: 36). In so doing Gunning looks backwards and sideways to the extraordinary process of modernisation which is the context of the cinema's emergence, regarding the rapid growth of urbanisation, consumerism, visual display and colonial exploration, as contextual stimuli for the imagery of the cinema of attractions.

Gunning is correct to view the early cinema as in a sense the latest form of illusionist spectacle – a form that was wondered at just as much for what it could do, as for what it did do. Clearly, also, the character of the early cinema is peculiarly modern – shaped by and reflective of the new experiences of late nineteenth-century modern life. However, I should like to stress again that the early cinema's particular aesthetic character also owes much to earlier modes of popular entertainment: in terms of formal make-up the early or so-called 'primitive' cinema has a much closer affinity with the tradition of popular entertainments than it does with painting, literature or the theatre; in effect, the early cinema is itself a popular entertainment.[8] This is confirmed both by its decidedly popular contexts of reception – the fairground, the circus, vaudeville and the nickelodeon – and by the character of its representations. Gunning himself neatly summarises the aesthetic form of this early 'cinema of attractions' in the following way:

> [It] ... directly solicits spectator attention, inciting visual curiosity, and supplying pleasure through an exciting spectacle – a unique event, whether fictional or documentary, that is of interest in itself. The attraction to be displayed may also be of a cinematic nature, such as the early close-ups ... or trick films in which a cinematic manipulation (slow motion, reverse motion, substitution, multiple exposure) provides the film's novelty .... Theatrical display dominates over narrative absorption ...
>
> (1989: 58, 59)

The cinema and the amusement park emerged together, the latest manifestations of a tradition of popular entertainments – now commercially and technologically informed – whose fundamental aesthetic properties turned upon modes of direct spectacle and sensation. Clearly, the early cinema differs from the amusement park in the sense that its spectacular aspect is far more proscribed. This is most evident, perhaps, in the way that early cinema's impact depends far more on a singular optical experience wherein visual illusion – be it 'magical' or 'naturalistic' in orientation – is a far more important, if not *the* vital, element. If the astonishment and excitation elicited by the cinema had a more straightforward relation to the image and its manner of reproduction, the visual astonishment of the amusement park is mixed with more directly visceral sensations or thrills.

At the beginning of the present century it was still the case that the cinema was one form of popular entertainment among many. As I have already indicated, the context of reception of the first films was decidedly located within the exhibition sphere of popular entertainment. As often as not, films took their place as separate attractions within a mixed programme of diverse entertainments, in what may be termed the space of 'variety theatre' (see McNamara 1974). True, technological experimentation and development had imposed itself during the preceding century. Whilst (industrial) advances in mechanics and mechanical engineering fed directly into the vehicular and kinetic forms of the amusement park, the emergence of distinctive techniques of visual representation helped to constitute novel visual forms (of which the cinema is but one). Technologically based forms such as the praxiniscope, the stereoscope, the diorama, Pepper's Ghost, dissolving views and the kinetoscope, constitute new ways of producing spectacle which had a clear propinquity with that already central to popular cultural forms; indeed, these later forms were already rivals to live forms of traditional popular entertainment. Still, the latter continued to thrive through forms such as the circus, the magic theatre, melodrama, vaudeville, funfairs and, as we have seen, the more recent, amusement parks and the cinema itself. Increasingly, the technological and live forms had begun to coexist within the same exhibition contexts. Thus, by the turn of the century the amusement park involved a happy mix of mechanically based, optically based and live attractions; stage magicians had imported many of the latest techniques of visual illusion to augment their conjuring acts; Hale's Tours were combining the realistic illusion of the cinema with the desire for thrilling motion so obvious in the amusement park; and films were projected alongside live acts in variety theatres and the burgeoning Nickelodeons (see Merritt 1976: 61, 62 for a description of a typical Nickelodeon show). What is distinctive here is the manner in which these vibrant popular entertainments were founded upon modes of visual representation that were meant to excite visual curiosity, to thrill and astonish the spectator.

Spectacle displaced

How different this was to the literary and theatrical modes of establishment art, where psychological motivation, a coherent story and a credible fictional world were among the most important guiding principles. It was not direct stimulation of the senses (particularly the eyes) which counted here, rather identification, recognition and the suspension of disbelief. It is now a commonplace of film history that it was such principles as these that informed the subsequent development of the cinema, at least in its predominant commercial form. The early cinema exemplifies and extends the spectacle-oriented aesthetic ethos of popular entertainment, but it was to be precisely the cinema's subsequent development that formed a powerful agent of displacement of these traditional popular forms and their peculiar aesthetic. Indeed, it could be argued that the early cinema had itself already begun the inexorable assimilation of live popular entertainment forms, if only because it was by definition a means whereby such forms could, in large part, be *re*presented and *re*produced.

Of course, the rise to dominance of a style of film based upon narrative principles was by no means simply a case of the straightforward transposition of one set of aesthetic precepts on to a new medium. In the formative development of narrative cinema as an aesthetic style, the new medium itself offers up possibilities (and constraints) of its own which both alter and augment prior models of dramatic storytelling. Thus, whilst certainly perpetuating aesthetic principles that were attached to nineteenth-century art – particularly the late nineteenth-century theatre – the classical Hollywood style, when it was eventually consolidated (in the second and third decades of the twentieth century), nevertheless does so within a mode of representation which at the formal level is quite distinct from preceding forms.

One crucial way in which the classical narrative cinema differs from the theatre is in the way it solicits the spectator. If a certain kind of voyeurism was already an element of the pleasures derived by spectators of the bourgeois stage, then film narrative greatly amplifies this aspect of spectatorship. The fictional worlds of the stage and the narrative film are both constructed and apprehended in very different ways. Through the movie camera the spectator of the narrative film is assigned a delegated mobility which provides anonymous 'entry' to the fictional space or world of the story and its characters. The fixed viewpoint of the theatre spectator is replaced by the multiple points of view of the cinema viewer as s/he is 'taken' into the world of the story and through the story itself. When one adds to this the pictorial verisimilitude of live action film, the camera and editing conventions that allow it to produce the illusion of continuous space and time, its fixation with representing the psychology of characters, and the binding of the story to the revelation and eventual resolution of character-centred problems – then, as countless commentators have pointed out, the pleasures attached to this mode of representation are considerable.

48

Clearly, the classical narrative film is a highly distinctive way of telling stories, the power of which can be gauged by the fact that for fifty years, or thereabouts, it was not only the dominant form of cinema itself, but also the dominant form of popular entertainment. Its contrast with the kinds of film constituting the early cinema as described above is marked. The enjoyment of coming to know characters and following their adventurous – and, frequently, amorous – exploits as they attempt to resolve a problem of some kind, the voyeuristic pleasures of identification and desire, which are attendant upon unacknowledged looking within and upon a realistic fictional world, these entail a very different kind of viewing experience to that of the spectator of popular entertainments and the early cinema.[9] It was, however, the narrative cinema that displaced the heterogeneous forms of early cinema: the trick film, the actuality film, Hale's tours – all were supplanted by the narrative film. The display of realistic representation as astonishing in and of itself disappears. The kind of fascination with the apparatus, which was apparent in the early audiences, gives way to a certain familiarity and the narrative film fortifies this by striving to produce stories which are highly transparent and involving, hiding the marks of their construction as far as possible. The trick film is superseded by the story film, the fantastic and the marvellous gives way to realism and characterisation.

Of course, the element of spectacle, which is central to the definition of modern forms of popular entertainment, did not entirely disappear from the cinema with the rise to predominance of the narrative style. Spectacle may have been tamed by narrative, but it persisted as a more or less latent dimension of classical Hollywood cinema; one can glimpse it in the highly staged performances of the musical, the special effects of the science fiction and horror genres, and the visual display and trickery of many animated films. However, there is another way in which we can look at this issue, for it could be argued that the hegemony which narrative cinema achieved within the domain of popular entertainment itself, was far greater in terms of its implications than an exclusive focus on cinema history itself can reveal. For narrative cinema did not simply displace or subordinate the spectacle modes of early cinema, but, in addition, its emergence and phenomenal industrial growth also had a profound effect on live or performative modes of popular entertainment.

Although spectacle forms such as the circus, the magic theatre, the music hall or variety theatre, the amusement park, the waxworks and so forth, did not disappear as a result of competition from the rise of narrative film, they nevertheless suffered a severe aesthetic and commercial challenge. As the century wore on, the Hollywood cinema developed technically (and aesthetically) with the introduction first of sound and then of colour. By the middle of the 1930s it had developed economically into what has been described as a 'mature oligopoly' (Balio 1976: 213). At the end of the 1930s, though not ranked particularly highly relative to other industries in terms of its gross income, when the motion picture industry was compared to other branches of the entertainments field, it far outstripped them. The film industry, with its enormous

49

economic power – based in large part on the vertical integration of production, distribution and exhibition – had a virtual stranglehold on the sphere of popular entertainment. In America at least, though the rest of world was not far behind, the movies were by far the preferred form of entertainment (Huettig 1976).

Of course, the hegemony of Hollywood as a form of popular entertainment in the decades stretching from the 1930s and into the 1950s involves more than just economic ascendancy. It also meant the dominance of a specific mode of representation: during this period most people sought amusement at the cinema, and by and large the cinema had become a dedicated exhibition site, a place given over for the exclusive screening of films. As I have already indicated the kernel of film production was the narrative, though this had settled into a number of specific genres. Thus the films that people flocked to see told a story, though they did so in their own unique and highly pleasurable manner. For the most part, such films entailed that the spectator give him or herself over to a certain kind of reception or viewing which entails absorption or a kind of rapt attention to the actions of characters and to the gradual revelation of their story through the unfolding of the plot. This quiescent, contemplative and 'anony-mous' mode of following and making sense of actions and events whilst simultaneously (and, perhaps, sporadically) attending – through the complex interplay of various modes of looking which operate in such films – to other aspects of the fleeting images on view, has held sway within popular modes of spectatorship for most of the present century.[10]

It is clear also – in tandem with this powerful regime of realistic narrative illusion – that radio, the emergence of which was contemporaneous with that of Hollywood, also operated to marginalise further the once central space occu-pied by modes of direct spectacle and stimulation. Even more than Hollywood, radio provided a form of entertainment or amusement that was immediate, easy to access and (relatively) inexpensive. Further, it removed entertainment from the public to the private domain, providing distinctive modes of story telling (the serial, the 'radio play'), the series, the quiz, the variety show, music and sport, as well as information in the form of news, reportage and current affairs programmes. Whilst the convenience and programming scope of radio posed a certain challenge to the dominance of cinema, given the latter's position in the 1930s and 1940s as the most popular form of *visual* entertainment, this threat was never particularly pronounced.[11] Nevertheless, radio did introduce a defi-nite element of diversity into its programme schedules, and undoubtedly its adventure series, westerns, mystery shows, melodramas (prototype soap operas), comedies, variety shows and so forth, posed a real additional threat to estab-lished forms of live popular entertainment. Beyond this, of course, the non-visual character of this growing popular form put it at odds with the spec-tacular aesthetic almost by definition.

However, if radio's acoustic serials and dramas, its aural modes of informa-tion relay, constitute distinct rivals to popular spectacle, things were not nearly so clear with the arrival of its close relative – television. For one thing, TV was from the first a direct threat to Hollywood, precisely because it had moving images along with its sounds. Television had the sense of immediacy of radio – it could show things as they actually happened. Further, it appropriated all of the programme genres of radio, and not long after it had begun to get established it had started to broadcast movies. Crucially, television brought moving pictures with synchronised sound into the home: television was as *convenient* as radio but it had the advantage of moving images.

Somewhat in the manner of Hollywood, though in its own distinctive way, early television contains vestiges of spectacle forms. Its appearance constitutes a reintroduction of spectacle in two senses: first, it represents as part of its programming schedules extant popular visual entertainments such as the circus, the music hall and the magic theatre, thereby reintroducing the visual dimension that had been missing from the relays of the radio. Second, early television's own visual character – a variety of programmes, segmented and punctuated by advertising, and increasingly operating over a number of simultaneous channels – bears a certain similarity to the formal organisation of early popular amusements.[12] Thus, modes of drama, music, variety, comedy, discussion, game shows, films, news and documentaries appear to offer the viewer a regular stream of varied visual attractions, much in the tradition of the popular variety theatre. But how are we to assess such traces and suggestions of a different tradition of popular visual amusements?

Television in the 1950s and 1960s may well have incorporated hard-pressed forms of live popular entertainment such as stage magic, the circus and variety theatre, into its schedules, but this hardly constituted a revival of the spectacle that these forms rested upon. Indeed, far from reasserting the spectacular character of such forms, it could be argued that this serves rather to demote it even further. For not only is the important impression of presence lost to the mediation of the small screen, but these convenient representations – part of the still novel experience of television itself – operate to displace and further discourage experience of the original forms. Early television is congruous with Hollywood in this respect: if the latter tamed spectacle through the institution of a narrative style, then early television contained it through a more literal domestication. Spectacle does not disappear but it exists in a more regulated and – especially in the case of television – a far more muted form. Arguably, drama and realism may not have played the central role in television that they did in Hollywood (despite their importance to the form), but even setting this aside, television's assortment of light entertainment and diversion was still a poor substitute for the immediacy and sheer visual power of earlier forms. If anything, perhaps, the fascination which this novel form of visual culture produced in early television owners, had to do with its apparent instantaneity. It purported to put worlds at one's fingertips; not only the everyday world of social and political events, but also those of art, education, religion, entertainment and so forth. The distracted kind of viewing which gradually came to characterise television-*watching* contrasts quite markedly with the enthralled *looking* of the mainstream cinema.

Nonetheless, both, in their different ways, contribute to the diminution of spectacle as pure stimulation, astonishment, the pursuit of sensation and illusion for their own sake.

Extending a tradition: *fin-de-siècle* digital forms

The dimension of direct spectacle and stimulation – such a major aspect of popular entertainments throughout the nineteenth century – was eclipsed in the twentieth by the enormous popularisation of narrative. The spectacle modes that had flourished throughout the nineteenth century and which became so resonant at the beginning of the twentieth century – so strikingly evident in early cinema and the amusement park – are overtaken and supplanted by forms of dramatic and realist meaning-making (along with fresh and similarly engaging modes of information dissemination).

Today, however, we are witnessing something of a resurgence of spectacle within the sphere of popular entertainment and amusement.[13] Among the main promoters of this revival are the mainstream cinema (late Hollywood) and television themselves – or certain kinds of them at least – whilst one of its key determinants has been the emergence of digital imaging technologies. Indeed, for the most part it is the expressions of an emerging visual digital culture that are at the forefront of this return to spectacle and stimulation: the ways in which this is occurring display both direct continuities and striking parallels with the earlier popular cultural tradition outlined above.

The aesthetic character of these new forms is analysed in more detail in coming chapters. Here I shall do no more than sketch the main lineaments of these continuities. One of the clearest illustrations of this relates to what occurred within the cinema itself in the 1980s and 1990s. We saw in chapter 1 the way in which contemporary mainstream cinema has developed within itself a significant (and growing) dimension – what I have termed 'digital cinema' – that is given over to the production of rapidly paced and action packed 'blockbusters'. These films are essentially vehicles for displaying special effects (which are themselves undergoing a period of intense rejuvenation with the advent of the new technology).

As the corpus of films attached to this rejuvenation of special effects has developed and expanded – from *Star Wars* to the likes of *True Lies* and *Titanic* – so has the narrative element of such films distinctly receded in favour of the stimulation, impact and astonishment that can be produced by new and revamped techniques of image-capture and fabrication. The verisimilitude of the diorama and the 'primitive' actuality film on the one hand, and the 'supernatural' or 'magical' illusionism of the phantasmagoria and the early 'trick film' on the other – each of these modern kinds of visual illusion is apparent in the images of late twentieth-century spectacle cinema. For, typically, the scenes in such films involve a kind of deception that is akin to that of stage magic –

outlandish and thoroughly impossible events and actions are depicted – yet such portrayals are realistic to a fault (see chapter 5). Certainly, these images of preposterous actions, fantastic events and bizarre beings are staggering for *what* they depict. However, the astonishment involved here parallels that experienced by the early spectator insofar as it appears to turn on the question of *how* it is possible to produce such high degrees of surface accuracy in such patently unattainable scenes. Part of the wonder is caused by the distinctive capacities of the apparatus itself: digital imaging is directly analogous in this respect to the *cinématographe*. The technology itself is the message.

But if the cinema itself has recently begun to rediscover and revive once vital aesthetic aspects of its original forms, it is also possible to see this return to modes of direct spectacle in some of its more recent siblings. TV advertising, for example, stands out in this regard. One of the principal differences between the latter and recent spectacle cinema is that it relies far less on narrative anyway. A highly rhetorical form, advertising involves a type of communication which is not literal, prosaic and naturalistic in the way that mainstream cinema (or even television itself) is. Relying more on symbolism and metaphor, advertising must constantly strive to produce texts that grab and hold the viewer's attention, and appear – for a while at least – distinctive, fresh and memorable amongst the constant flow of similarly oriented images in which they appear. Accompanying the phenomenal growth of advertising and its gradual passage from language-based to more and more visual or iconic forms of mediation has been an extraordinary increase in its use of special effects and sophisticated modes of image manipulation. Many TV advertisements employ the kinds of devices and techniques that are producing revived spectacle in the cinema for their own ends. Thus new levels of surface accuracy and image brilliance, novel or augmented forms of image combination, distortion and alteration, all are utilised within these brief, playful and pictorially compressed texts (see chapter 4). The aim is to take possession of the eyes, to surprise and hook the viewer to a brief yet intense image display.

Special venue attractions are particularly interesting here because in many ways they appear to be the mode of digital visual culture that most clearly manifests the spectacle ethos in contemporary forms. Like late twentieth-century Hollywood cinema, special venue attractions and simulation rides have a direct connection with the nineteenth century's tradition of popular entertainments. Indeed, the so-called 'special venue' of today has roots both in the early cinema and in the amusement park (in the case of the simulation ride itself, it is the Hale's Tour that forms its early prototype).

The principal site of the recent revival of this idea of the special attraction, and in particular the notion of the 'ride film', was the theme park. Of course, the theme park itself – associated most closely with the name of Walt Disney – distinctive though it may be, has its origins in the earlier amusement parks. It was amusement parks that consolidated the concept of mechanised attractions having themselves first borrowed this idea from the world's fairs. The latter having maintained a primary interest both in displaying new technological developments and in applying them to entertainment purposes (see, for example, Nelson 1986; Weinstein 1992). If anything, the Disney version of the amusement park strengthened this focus on technology and technologically grounded entertainment forms, making it a fundamental feature of the theme park ideal. The fascination with technology both as a producer of spectacular diversions and as spectacle in and of itself, is carried over from the early cinema and the turn-of-the-century amusement park and reproduced as a key facet of theme park entertainment. Perhaps the exemplification of this in the theme park begins with the early Disneyland rides in which the spectator was transported through three-dimensional theatrical settings and dioramas involving animatronic characters acting out historical or fictional scenarios.

The recent manifestations of such entertainments – located both in theme parks and in special venues outside them – have usually involved a direct return to the cinema apparatus itself, particularly to its enhanced capacity for generating startling illusion and larger-than-life images. Thus the concern has been with large-screen formats, special visual effects and, similarly, for the new possibilities introduced into sound production with the arrival of digital techniques. However, this is not all, for along with this have come further concerns involving various ways of marrying these enhanced image forms with performance modes and with computer programmed and controlled mechanical technologies. It is among such integrated forms – some of which resemble latter-day examples of the hippodrome – that the most spectacularly engaging instances of this mode of amusement are to be found. Thus, a simulation ride such as, for example, *Back to the Future: The Ride*, is a short but extremely intense experience involving actors, sets, props, images, sound and movement (both real and imagined). The manner in which these basic elements are brought together produces extraordinary degrees of spectacle and visceral excitement. Indeed, this attraction might be described as a latter-day hybrid of the roller-coaster, the magic theatre, the trick film and the Hale's Tour.

The sheer thrill and visual stimulation that such attractions produce largely bypasses all but the most elementary (and necessary) of classical cinematic signification processes and motivations. It is an experience revolving, perhaps, around vision, though one that brings all of the senses into play; an experience where meaning in the classical (cinematic) sense is overtaken or hijacked by sensations of sheer delight, visceral thrill and near-vertigo.

One of the most striking features of this partial return to an earlier popular visual aesthetic is the *displayed* character of these contemporary productions and representations. Much of the time, as we have begun to see, such forms rely upon intensified kinds of visual illusion. The ends of this heightened illusionism, however, no longer appear to serve the purposes of achieving a 'reality effect' for character-centred story telling. Hollywood empathy has very little part to play in the reception of the new forms. Of course, as I have just pointed out, one has to be convinced – the 'suspension of disbelief' or, at any rate, the attempt to encourage the impression of *as ifness* is important. Ultimately though, this is not to be taken too seriously: the ever greater levels of realism in the imagery and interactivity of computer games, the new heights of seamless visual illusion achieved in the presentations of the special venues and the cinema – all tell us that we are being tricked, that what we are seeing and experiencing is, precisely, an effect of fabrication, an illusion. Being tricked is the whole point. Signification does not run very deep here: for the most part the plots (if they exist all) are extremely basic, involved meaning non-existent. We are at the magic show, where being fooled is enormous fun, and although we are not sure precisely how it was done, we are amazed at the cleverness of it all.

Of course, I do not want to suggest that illusionism is all there is to contemporary spectacle modes. This clearly is not so. Thus, for example, in a form such as music video – as in the digital cinema generally – montage is a central technique of aesthetic production. However, the character of montage in the music video tends to differ markedly from that associated with spectacle cinema and the special venue attraction – if anything it has a closer affiliation with the manner in which it is used in TV advertising. Pop promos have no specific ties with any particular or established way of putting images together, and, like adverts, their ties with narrative forms of meaning construction are not particularly pronounced. In part at least, such relative autonomy, coupled with the imperative to produce visually arresting tapes which also capture the style of the performer (whether or not s/he actually features on the image track) as well as the mood of the music, has encouraged the release of all manner of visually diverse texts within the genre. It would be fair to say that within this output the tendency to produce work that forgoes visual transparency – foregrounding or displaying, instead, the constructed character of the images – has taken precedence. Of course in this way the manner of display differs from that of mainstream spectacle cinema, for it is not so much that the images display photographic impossibility (though they may), rather that they expand and push the register of eclectic combination (see chapter 3). Unsurprisingly, in the competitive quest for greater novelty and individuation, music video was quick to turn to new imaging technologies. For the most part these technologies have been used to further intensify ways of combining (through montage, collage, editing, superimposition and the like) different kinds, styles and forms of imagery within the same text. The result has been to heighten even further what was already an extremely eclectic visual genre: a genre, moreover, which produces dazzling image effects without paying much attention to conventional notions of meaning-making (chapters 5 and 6).

What of the computer game? How, if at all, might it be related to the heritage of direct spectacle and stimulation so often invoked in this chapter? We might begin to answer this question by observing that, unlike the other forms of visual digital culture at issue in this book, the computer game does not have quite the same kind of direct ties with the cinema. What needs to be kept in mind here – for this is crucial to the definition of the form – is the so-called 'interactive' dimension. For the most part – and I am thinking here particularly of predominant game genres involving action and simulation – playing a computer game differs quite markedly from that of watching a traditional movie (though *not*, significantly, as much from its digital cinema cousins – the spectacular blockbusters – introduced above).

Interaction in computer games entails rapid decision-making tied to direct hands on control – no matter that the extent of this control is predetermined and limited. In fact, the player is aware of this, s/he knows or comes to know which are the legitimate moves or things to try and do and which are not. Indeed, such skill acquisition is one important facet of the game-playing experience: one is playing *against* something (and this involves more than on-screen fictional opponents – ultimately it is the game program itself). This competitive or agonistic form of play takes place in real time in relation to events represented in a surrogate on-screen world. The player has the power to intervene – indeed s/he is compelled to do so – and thereby to affect directly the course of the events and action. The length of time spent playing a game (even the same game) varies. To an extent it is under the control of the player and is dependent upon factors such as familiarity and playing skill.

Clearly, the playing or participatory aspect of computer games is central to the form and the experience it produces (chapter 7). Like the other forms discussed here, indeed, perhaps even more so, computer games comprise a fundamental de-centring of narrative. Perhaps the significant difference between narrative and computer games is that the space and time for depth of meaning does not exist to anything like the same degree in the latter, where the spectator is involved in a mode of usually intense surrogate performance of their own. Playing a computer game is as much a physical as it is a mental activity. Active participation, competing in a contest which – despite its *as if* character – is taking place in the present (happening in real time), involves a certain urgency, immediacy and physical stimulation. It is an experience which is more akin to the transitory diversions of the amusement park: mechanical rides and such participatory exhibits as the 'test your strength' booth and the shooting gallery.

What I have been concerned to do here is argue that the forms of visual digital culture – though not only them – share something of the same cultural space with an earlier tradition of popular entertainments. What they are doing in terms of aesthetic practice bears direct comparison with prior forms of popular entertainment that operated with the same overall principles. Broadly, what these latest forms share with their earlier counterparts is their primary concern with procuring and possessing the eyes, with exciting, shocking or charging the senses. Technique and skill is central to producing such affect. Acrobatics, legerdemain, stage effects and so on, these all have their complements within the forms of the new space of spectacular display which opened up in the late twentieth century. Whilst we marvel at the spectacle itself we are also marvelling at the skill or technique of the producer (or the production) of the effect as well as the apparatus which is able to deliver it.

Today, as we know, the skills of visual display, magic and illusion, which already in the nineteenth century had been changed by technological developments, are increasingly delivered – mediated, so to say – through technologies of reproduction and representation. While these distinctive techniques and the skills they manifest preserve and intensify the tradition of popular spectacular entertainment, it is also here with digital technologies that we begin to glimpse what might distinguish the past from the present, the new from the old. It is not so much by attending to the techniques themselves that the differences – both of manner and substance – of the new spectacle forms can be illuminated. Rather, it is by casting these new forms and the techniques that help support them within the broader aesthetic context of early twenty-first century culture. For then we can begin both to refine more precisely the character of their particular mode of spectacle and, at the same time, explain how they differ from their nineteenth-century counterparts.

3

SHAPING TRADITION
The contemporary context

In terms of their aesthetic character, the digital genres and expressions at the centre of this book are part of a certain tradition of commercial popular amusements that have their origins in the nineteenth century. Yet despite this continuity, these latter-day forms and expressions are also highly distinctive. They share a propensity to spectacle and sensation with their ancestors, yet there is something quite different about the mode of their spectacle: they return us to spectacle but in a different guise.

Of course, the *means* utilised today are distinctive, and it is tempting to attribute the particular or peculiar character of this spectacle to them. Yet, as I have already indicated, these means – this technology or apparatus – no matter how new, is not autonomous: its development and deployment takes place within and draws upon an entertainment tradition that precedes it. In other words, it is being contained and in some measure shaped by the aesthetic parameters of the tradition to it which belongs.

At the same time, inordinate and far-reaching changes have taken place in the sphere of visual culture since the end of the nineteenth century: changes that have had a corresponding conditioning affect upon the spectacle tradition. As I pointed out in the last chapter, the rise of the cinema, radio and television as commercial cultural forms – modes of mass reproduction and mass consumption – had the effect of displacing the spectacle forms of popular entertainment. If this tradition is enjoying a renaissance then certainly this may have something to do with the appearance of enabling new means of production. However, as I shall suggest below, it is also bound up with a prevalent background cultural-aesthetic that both supports and bolsters such developments. Any attempt to specify and account for the aesthetic complexion of these new forms and the role of digital technologies within them also must consider the particular character of the contemporary context in which they are emerging.

In this chapter I shall look in more detail at the character of contemporary visual culture itself: the broader framing aesthetic of the genres and expressions under consideration in this book. How does the background framing aesthetic of contemporary culture affect the idea advanced so far that the visual digital expressions explored in these pages are spectacle forms? In what ways are the new digital techniques related to the particular character of contemporary visual culture?

During the last decades of the twentieth century, debates among cultural commentators centred upon a perceived change in the character of cultural/aesthetic practices. The sense has been that from the 1960s onwards – perhaps even earlier – a shift has been under way in the general aesthetic character of culture, certainly in the developed countries of the West. The main concern has been with what is perceived as a move away from modernism – a term that was used to characterise the cultural/aesthetic practices of the late nineteenth and first decades of the twentieth century – towards quite distinctive aesthetic dispositions in the second half of the century. There has been considerable discussion as to whether or not this transition should be understood as a new phase of modernism itself – a late (or later) modernism – or, as a decisive move to something altogether different: a veritable postmodernism. Trying to resolve this issue is something that need not concern us here. What I want to do, rather, is endorse the idea of a shift in cultural and aesthetic practices themselves. Given the phenomenal developments in the twentieth century in the ways in which culture is produced and distributed, it is difficult not to see this having a profound affect on the aesthetic character of contemporary visual culture. I shall introduce an account of the changed character of the framing aesthetic of contemporary culture. It is an account that in many respects is both suggestive and persuasive as a description of what is occurring at the level of *visual aesthetics*, despite the sense that the transformations it describes are not as absolute as some of its proponents argue.

On formality in contemporary visual culture

Let me begin by looking at the work of Jean Baudrillard, concentrating particularly on those influential aspects of his work that relate to visual culture (images). What is already apparent in Baudrillard's early work on the rise and influence of modern systems of signification and representation is a preoccupation with *form*. This manifests itself in many areas and in different ways, though nowhere more so than in his thinking about the media and aesthetic questions. By looking at specific discussions of the media and images within Baudrillard's broader discourse on representation, it becomes possible to see how certain of his insights have found a distinct echo in the theories of others. Despite its extreme and often exasperating character, Baudrillard's work has had a profound impact on our understanding of contemporary culture, in particular the visual aesthetic sphere.

Benjamin and McLuhan

Baudrillard's thinking has been greatly influenced by the work of Walter

59

Benjamin and Marshall McLuhan (see especially McLuhan 1968; Benjamin 1973).[1] In 'Requiem for the Media', one of Baudrillard's first attempts to look specifically at the media themselves in the context of the consumer or semiological order, he introduces Benjamin's notion of 'reproducibility', endorsing the latter's insight that the technically reproduced work increasingly becomes the work designed for reproducibility (Baudrillard 1981). In the same essay, McLuhan's formula, 'the medium is the message', is privileged above neo-Marxist critiques of the media as purveyors of ideology. Here, Baudrillard endorses the notion that it is the character or the form of the medium itself (how it communicates), rather than its contents (what it communicates) that is important to an adequate understanding of the current state of things.

Baudrillard consistently returns to these two theories, elaborating and building upon them and, eventually, bringing them both together, viewing McLuhan's theory as, in certain respects, a continuation of Benjamin's insights (see Baudrillard 1983b: 98–102). According to Baudrillard it was Benjamin (later McLuhan), who first understood that technique is important, not so much for its productive potential, as for its mediating power: 'the form and principle of a whole new generation of sense' (1983b: 99). Technology, and the various forms it assumes, is viewed as 'structuring the world directly'. In the sphere of culture this implies a theory that privileges the particularities of a technological form and how it induces certain relations, experiences and effects, over, say, looking at the content or meanings contained in its various mediations.

Baudrillard views the advent of technical reproducibility as *the* major aspect of late industrial society. On the one hand, he argues that one important upshot of evolving reproducibility lies in the speed, the excess, the *overproduction*, of information or messages. Constantly concatenating one upon the other, these serve not the cause of meaning but the opposite: its diffusion and obfuscation, and the abolition of any time for contemplation. On the other hand, he views the tremendous upturn in the proliferation and distribution of products, replicated through industrial manufacture, as beginning to dominate and stamp itself as the crucial (and key) dimension which is constitutive of a new reality. It signals the onset of a new era where things are 'directly conceived as a function of their unlimited reproducibility' – reproducibility assumes precedence over production.

Benjamin's observation (1973: 226) that 'to an ever greater degree the work of art reproduced becomes the work of art designed for reproducibility' is developed and takes on wider and more momentous implications today when the stage of serial production has 'mutated' into 'generation by means of models' – when, that is, the very fact of serial reproducibility comes to influence and precede production, establishing models that function somewhat analogously to the genetic code; fixing in advance, so to speak, and despite specific variations within each form (i.e. 'marginal difference' and 'difference within repetition'), all future production, be it of fashion, advertising, or whatever media genre. According to Baudrillard, our lives are now regulated by 'the perpetual reactualisation of the same models' (1983b: 100).

In this sense mass reproducibility can be seen to underlie Baudrillard's characterisation of contemporary culture as instantiating new kinds of cycles: an idea anticipating the importance that fashion (conceived both in a specific and broad sense) comes to have within the context of the simulational society. Recycling is one of the main ways in which the increasingly uncoupled or autonomous signification systems of consumer society function as a mode of fascination and control. This involves a kind of feeding-off, a mode of rediscovery of 'obsolescent cultural ingredients and signs', which are used as a means to reproduce a peculiar modality of novelty, one which reuses the old to produce distinctiveness in the present (see, for example, Baudrillard 1990: 65). In its fully developed form, such recycling involves a play with modulation and alternation: at regular intervals there is a certain modification of the object, an updating occurs, and a novelty effect is produced afresh. Use value or content in the traditional sense are demoted here, for Baudrillard claims that it is precisely the institution of *forms* such as those of modulation and recycling which are important to the activity of (cultural) consumption and, as well, to an adequate understanding of it.

Baudrillard believes that 'digitality' or the binary system is the defining characteristic of the new code of the third (present) era of simulation (for his theory of the development of simulation, see Baudrillard 1983b). Digitality:

> haunts all the messages, all the signs of our societies. The most concrete form you see it in is that of the test, of the question/answer, of the stimulus and the response ... we live by the mode of the *referendum* precisely because there is no longer any *referential*.
>
> (Baudrillard 1983b: 115–16)

Again, an aspect of Benjamin's theory is invoked to support this claim. Baudrillard refers to Benjamin's observation that the photographically recorded screen actor is 'subjected to a series of optical tests' and that consequently cinema spectators, in adopting the position of the camera, themselves adopt the stance of testing. Baudrillard says that before the screen:

> no contemplation is possible. The role of the message is no longer information, but testing and polling, and finally control ... . Montage and codification demand, in effect, that the receiver construe and decode by observing the same procedure whereby the work was assembled. The reading of the message is then only a perpetual examination of the code.
>
> (1983b: 119–20)

Thus, the technology itself imposes a model of response, and even though further 'sub-codes' such as montage and its associated codes and conventions appear to liberate 'response mechanisms', they do so, 'only according to stereotypes and analytical models' (1983b: 120).

This reading of Benjamin is in turn interpreted as prefiguring McLuhan's famous dictum that 'the medium is the message'. Thus, says Baudrillard: 'it is in effect the medium – the very style of montage, of decoupage, of interpolation, solicitation, summation, by the medium – which controls the process of meaning' (1983b: 123). In Baudrillard's second order of simulation, medium and message had not collapsed one into the other, despite the fact that serial production carried within itself the seeds of the disappearance of (traditional) reference in its progressive abolition of the notion of the original. Only when the model has itself become the 'signifier of reference' – floating completely unattached to any reality – does McLuhan's dictum take on its true descriptive power. Today there is not only the implosion of the message in the medium, but as well, '*the implosion of the medium and the real* in a sort of nebulous hyperreality where even the definition and distinct action of the medium are no longer distinguishable' (Baudrillard 1983a: 44).[2]

What is more, McLuhan's understanding of the electronic media as involving a kind of 'tactile' communication is also wholly appropriate as a description of the function of the media in the present era of simulation.[3] This is because the notion of tactility as opposed to visuality (of touching as opposed to seeing), more closely approximates the controlling or manipulative function performed by the new media experience: 'tactile' implies a denial of the distance or 'reflection' which is 'always possible' in the 'visual universe'.

Formality and resemblance

In the twenty years (or thereabouts) that it takes for the full development of his theory of simulations, Baudrillard constantly stresses visual aspects and modes of representation (see, for example, Baudrillard 1981: 102–11, 1987, 1988b, 1990: 63–97; and Gane 1993: 67–71). 'Technological images', by which Baudrillard means those images which issue from photographic, cinematographic, televisual, (and now) digital processes and systems, are central to the theory of 'simulations', through which he understands our contemporary world.

Two crucial aspects of Baudrillard's thinking about images are his preoccupation with questions of *formality* and *analogy*. In keeping with his notion of the manipulative/regulative semiological order that has come to constitute contemporary systems, he argues that images today are of minimal importance qua image, for what is more important are the formal structural relations which govern or control their production and circulation (see Baudrillard 1981: 102–11). Thus, in terms of modernist art Baudrillard argues that more and more the move has been away from looking at or contemplating a work in terms of its form, content and meaning, and towards recognising it as part of a differentiated but related series. A key moment in this was the emergence of Pop Art and Super-realist painting which take the already-reproduced as their image object: a return to figuration, perhaps, but one which involves reduplication: the copying of a copy. Pop Art signals the end of art as representation (see Baudrillard 1990: 81).

At the same time as this is occurring, however, Baudrillard also acknowledges the increasing 'analogical nature' of technological image development, by which he means the increasing verisimilitude (photo-realism) of contemporary images. It appears therefore, that just as images are becoming more and more 'convincing', so also, are they becoming increasingly detached from traditional representation, and more and more caught up in modes of serial equivalence, modulation and self-referentiality. The images of *trompe l'oeil* have a privileged status for Baudrillard. He believes he can discover in them a capacity that leads to the total destabilisation of the (Modern) notion of and belief in reality: they constitute 'a kind of game with reality' – they are examples of what he terms 'enchanted simulation' (Poster 1988: 154). This fascination with *trompe l'oeil* images is bound up with his concept of 'seduction': that is to say, they constitute perfect examples of his conception of seduction as a transgressive or subversive category. Seduction is both the reaffirmation of appearances, the domain of 'the play (artifice) of appearances', and at the same time it is the defining principle or strategy of this surface play, what Baudrillard has termed 'the superficial abyss' (Baudrillard 1988a).[4]

Trompe l'oeil defines itself according to Baudrillard as 'anti-painting'; it stands outside of history and art.[5] However, it is its (re)emergence during the Renaissance which most engages Baudrillard's attention. In this context what Baudrillard means by anti-painting begins to take on a much clearer meaning. For, when set against what were at the time exciting new departures in art, the *trompe l'oeil* images of this time escape from the role of representing the 'theatre of the natural' which has now become the world. At the same time they test the axiom lying at the very heart of the system: the privilege accorded to the gaze of the individual actor/spectator in such a world which is inscribed within the invention of perspective.

Baudrillard cites as one of their most distinctive features, the banality of the objects that are depicted in *trompe l'oeil*: they are everyday – and almost without exception – inanimate objects; objects that are always themselves already the result of artifice (i.e. non-natural). As 'minor signs of culture' such artefacts, when set against the vertical (flat) background (yet another of the features defining the 'pure form' of *trompe l'oeil*), not only approach zero in the amount of meaning they connote, but they also eliminate the discourse of painting: 'no fable, no narrative. No "set", no theatre, neither plot nor characters' (Baudrillard 1988b: 53).

The question how can something appear so real and yet not observe the 'rules of depth', is for Baudrillard the key to the seductive power of *trompe l'oeil*, for it reveals to us that, ' "reality' is never more than a world hierarchically *staged*'. Without recourse to perspective, the images of *trompe l'oeil* still manage to fool the eye, in so doing, they undermine and expose, as itself simulation, the Renaissance model of vision, without in any way attempting to insinuate themselves as a replacement. *Trompe l'oeil* not only relativises, it moreover begins to make notions of reality volatile. It constitutes a playful challenge to the then dominant principle of reality.

For Baudrillard the *trompe l'oeils* – despite their minor status – are images of simulation, playing a game with the real and revealing that reality is constructed, fragile, unstable and relative. They also anticipate the more prevalent images produced by technologically based media (photography, cinema, television), whilst at the same time diverging significantly in their effects or in the conditions they induce. For 'technological images' are central elements in the production and maintenance of a general condition of 'disenchanted simulation', that is, of the 'hyperreality' which everywhere has come to constitute the contemporary world.[6]

Indeed, I would argue that computer imaging has a privileged relation to Baudrillard's conception of *trompe l'oeil* images. Though reluctant to endorse all of the claims that Baudrillard makes for them, I do accept that *trompe l'oeils* can be considered paradigmatic instances of super-realism: meticulous copies (simulations) of circumscribed portions of phenomenal appearances. I also agree that, as a form of visual representation, *trompe l'oeil* images constitute a radical reduction of the significatory/symbolic dimension. They can also be construed as instantiating a kind of ironic game with dominant perspectival visual representation. Characteristics not dissimilar to these are attached to current forms of computer image text. In this case however, the simulation taking place is of a secondary nature: that is to say, it is no longer phenomenal appearances (and the dominant conventions of their representation) which forms the ground for such work, rather, the realm of the already represented itself.

The transparent image and frenzied reception

The Evil Demon of Images (1987), ostensibly a discussion of cinema and television, and *The Ecstasy of Communication* (1988a) are Baudrillard's most concerted attempts specifically to address the role and functioning of images within his conception of today's society as a world of simulations. Here, he sets out to discuss 'the perversity of the relation between the image and its referent, the supposed real; the virtual and irreversible confusion of the sphere of images and the sphere of reality whose nature we are less and less able to grasp' (1987: 13).

Although the 'immense majority of present day photographic, cinematic and television images are [still] thought to bear witness to the world with a naïve resemblance and touching fidelity' (1987: 14), Baudrillard argues that modern media images have themselves actually come to instantiate the disappearance of meaning and representation. The real and the reality principle are today denied or confounded by the images of the system itself, there is no longer any space left for the play of illusion that constituted the challenge of *trompe l'oeil*. This is Baudrillard's by now familiar thesis that, whereas media representations (images included) were once held to refer to an objective reality, today as their techno-logically based proliferation, reproducibility, mobility and 'realist capabilities' intensify, so they come to compete with, to confound and eventually to volatise reality, replacing it with a new mode of experience which he terms 'hyperreality' or 'the more real than the real'.[7]

Baudrillard characterises television (pace McLuhan) as a 'cool' medium: 'the cold light of television is inoffensive to the imagination (even that of children) since it no longer carries any imaginary, for the simple reason that *it is no longer an image*' (Baudrillard 1987: 24). Cinema on the other hand, though increas-ingly 'contaminated' by television, is still an image – 'that means not only a screen and a visual form but a myth, something that belongs to the sphere of the double, the phantasm, the mirror, the dream ... ' (1987: 24). Unlike McLuhan, Baudrillard argues that cinema is essentially a much more involving medium than television. Cinema, especially in its heyday, was still a medium that was identifiable as such and could be distinguished from the messages and meanings it contained. Moreover, these meanings and messages constitute what Baudrillard calls an 'intense imaginary'. Speaking of the mid-career films of the Italian director Luchino Visconti (*The Leopard*, 1963, *Senso*, 1954) Baudrillard says that in such films it is still possible to find 'meaning, history, a sensual rhetoric, dead moments, a passionate game ... ' (1987: 30). He believes, however, that the same can hardly be said of today's cinema, and that it most certainly does not apply to television. The establishment of television signals the definitive end of the idea of representation, the expulsion of the space of the game of illusion, and the inauguration of the era of what Baudrillard calls 'obscenity', when literally nothing is left to the imagination. And where, as a consequence, the imagination itself (along with memory and affection) is fast disappearing. 'The dissolution of TV into life, the dissolution of life into TV ...' (1987: 26).

Television, thus conceived, functions somewhat like a processing program that we are all wired or patched into. As the medium of 'obscenity', television is non-spectacular, non-theatrical and the denial of illusion. It functions, rather, as a medium of immediate transparency, exposure and visibility. It does not involve us in a game of meanings, truths, myths, fantastical or phantastical projections, on the contrary, it fixes or conditions us within a reception mode that Baudrillard quite simply describes as one of 'brute fascination'. Modern media images do not function in the same way as traditional images; they are rather, 'the sites of the disappearance of meaning and representation', they tend more and more to be totally transparent, they hide nothing, they display everything, they constitute a 'state of radical disillusion'. In this way they thereby prevent and preclude genuine looking. And this is because for Baudrillard looking at images (genuine images) always involves one in a kind of oscillation ('a game of emergence and disappearance'). He says, 'in an image certain parts are visible, while others are not: visible parts render the others invisible, a rhythm of emergence and secrecy sets in, a kind of watermark of the imaginary' (Baudrillard 1988a: 33). The latter describes the site and the functioning of meaning and representation with respect to images which the superficiality, the 'pornographic objectivity' of the hyperreal world has now replaced.

The implications of this closing down of the space and distance that once existed between the world and the world represented (i.e. 'the game of the scene, the mirror, challenge or otherness … ') have profound effects for the subject: 'the simple presence of television transforms our habitat into a kind of archaic, closed-off cell, into a vestige of human relations whose survival is highly questionable' (1998a: 17–18). The mass media is producing a new form of generalised narcissism, a withdrawal of the individual into an ever more isolated and isolating private world of the all-too-visible, a world to which we have unlimited access via our screens and the networks into which they are plugged. The implication Baudrillard wishes to draw from such a definitive capture, is the dissolution of the subject/object distinction; the individual is conceived of as terminal point or nexus of media networks, the point of the collapse of the former distinction between public and private, interior and exterior spheres as these become more and more blurred in our heads, and are substituted with the media-produced hyperreal.

An important upshot of the fascination induced by the 'promiscuous' character of contemporary media images is what Baudrillard views as a kind of heightening of their empty or arid character through what he terms 'the perfection of models'. Ultimately this can be seen to hinge on the significance he attributes to the emergence of seriality and reproducibility. For what the evolution of these notions have led to, is 'not merely an exponential, linear unfolding of images and messages, but [also] an exponential enfolding of the medium around itself' (Baudrillard 1987: 28). This is Baudrillard's mutation, to a higher level of abstraction, of the way the reproduction of images and the seriality this involves leads to the reproduction of already reproduced images; the effect of reproduction leads to images beginning to feed upon themselves. And this happens increasingly, not only in terms of the images themselves, (e.g. Warhol's reproduction of the image of Mao or Marilyn), but also in terms of the forms or models in and through which images are reproduced. Baudrillard takes the example of contemporary cinema, which he views as being caught up in an attempt to perfect its own model. According to Baudrillard:

a whole generation of films is appearing which will be to those we have known what the android is to man: marvellous, flawless artifacts, dazzling simulacra which lack only an imaginary and that particular hallucination which makes the cinema what it is.

(1987: 29)

The promiscuity of detail, both in terms of the image itself (transcriptional transparency, close-up detail, nothing left uncovered) and in terms of the refining of a prior model (genre, narrative, *mise-en-scène*), come more and more to constitute the parameters of fascination for both film-makers and audiences alike.

> Our desire reaches out to these new kinetic, numeric, fractal, artificial and synthetic images, because they are of the lowest definition. One could almost say that through a technical excess of good will they are asexual, like porn images. However, we don't look for definition or richness of imagination in these images: we look for the giddiness of their superficiality, for the artifice of the detail, the intimacy of their technique. What we truly desire is their technical artificiality, and nothing more.
>
> (Baudrillard 1988: 43–4)

Eco and Jameson: repetition and surface

Insofar as they concentrate on questions of form, both Umberto Eco and Fredric Jameson advance theories that are extremely close to those of Jean Baudrillard in their reflections on contemporary cultural developments (see Jameson 1984; Eco 1985).

Eco is in no doubt that a shift to a new aesthetic is under way. His analysis revolves around conceptions of the series, repetition, redundancy and formalism. For Eco it is serial production which provides a key to defining the difference between modernism and both (what he terms) post- and pre-modern aesthetics and theories of art. He entertains the possibility that repetition and modulation have figured at least as much, if not more, in the history of (Western) culture, than have notions of novelty. From this perspective, the idea that a new aesthetics is developing out of mass cultural production which, though most certainly representational or 'figurative', nevertheless carries with it an indifference to content, information, meaning and reference, is made to seem not such a strange or unlikely eventuality at all.

This emphasis on the centrality of seriality within contemporary cultural production is shared with Baudrillard. Eco introduces and discusses a new and currently prevalent theory of art, what he terms 'postmodern aesthetics'.[8] Eco homes in on what for him is a more interesting variant or sense of repetitiveness and seriality from the point of view of contemporary culture: that repetitiveness and seriality which 'at first glance does not appear the same as (equal to) something else' (Eco 1985: 167). Here Eco comes extremely close to Baudrillard in his discussions of the concepts of 'modulation' or 'the precession of models' and his related idea of 'difference within repetition'. Indeed, Eco's much more specific concentration on art and the media, attempting to elucidate the different types of aesthetic *repetition* and *seriality* that have existed in the past and which predominate today, helps to bring into much sharper focus what Baudrillard was intending.

Eco believes that, today, there is in operation a sense of aesthetic repetition involving a radical conception of seriality: one that 'wholly escapes the "modern" idea of literature and art'. This involves a new concept, 'the infinity of the text', whereby 'variability' as a *purely formal principle* becomes the object of aesthetic pleasure and interest.

> Variability to infinity has all the characteristics of repetition, and very little of innovation ... the era of electronics – instead of emphasising the phenomena of shock, interruptions, novelty, and frustration of expectations – would produce a return to the continuum, the Cyclical, the Periodical, the Regular.
>
> (1985: 179)

Eco explores this idea by drawing upon the work of Omar Calabrese which sketches the outlines of a 'neo-baroque aesthetic' of the era of mass communications involving types of difference or variation within repetition (see Calabrese 1992). We are back again to Baudrillard's concept of modulation, or one which is strikingly similar, appearing to share several of its defining features: the importance placed upon industrial replication, that is, the '*serial* repetition of the same object', and more recently, out of this, the development of models, which is to say the periodic production of 'new' (re-fashioned) instances of the same type.

Both Eco and Baudrillard produce similar considerations about the implications of the emergence of such a regulatory principle. 'Redundancy', Eco's concept, is a case in point. For Eco redundancy is the antithesis of information, which is associated with notions of meaning and content in works. He argues that with the advent and development of industrial serial production, redundancy – as a direct function of the development and extension of seriality in cultural production – has increased in inverse proportion to information. Of course (as I have already pointed out) one of Baudrillard's central claims is that an important constitutive characteristic of late twentieth-century culture is precisely the disappearance of meaning and the increasing preponderance of what he terms '*superficiality*'. For Baudrillard, the accelerated production and circulation of meaning achieved through media proliferation is only a mirage, for, in effect, 'information is directly destructive of meaning and signification, or neutralises it' (see Baudrillard 1983a: 95–110). Eco would not, perhaps, want to claim so much. He is careful not to essentialise or reduce texts and textual production to media technologies themselves (it is, for example, the television series *Dallas* that he discusses, not television *per se*). It is by presupposing an audience that, in the first instance, is relating to the pleasure of the 'reiteration of a single and constant truth', that Eco is able to 'conceive of an audience also able to shift onto an aesthetic level and judge the art of the variations on a mythical theme' (1985: 183). Typically, Baudrillard goes much further. Meaning cannot be 'rescued', even in the minimalist way that Eco suggests. Media growth has resulted in an oversaturation of information, an overloading or overexposure. This has switched people (the masses) away from meaning; attention is transferred instead into pure fascination with surface spectacle, and the movement and play of detail and forms (the passage from a 'scenic' to an 'ecstatic' sensibility).

Echoing Baudrillard, Jameson claims that the reason why it has been questions of culture that have most often been addressed in discussions of postmodernity is because 'aesthetic production today has become integrated into commodity production generally'. He continues, 'the frantic economic urgency of producing fresh waves of ever more novel-seeming goods (from clothing to airplanes), at ever greater rates of turnover, now assigns an increasingly essential structural function and position to aesthetic innovation and experimentation' (Jameson 1984: 56–7).

Jameson sets out the central features of late twentieth-century culture (his 'postmodernism') at the beginning of his discussion:

> a new depthlessness, which finds its prolongation both in contemporary 'Theory' and in a whole new culture of the image or the simulacrum; a consequent weakening of historicity, both in our relationship to public History and in new forms of our private temporality, whose 'schizophrenic' structure ... will determine new types of syntax or syntagmatic relationships in the more temporal arts; a whole new type of ground tone – what I will call 'intensities' – which can best be grasped by a return to older theories of the sublime; the deep constitutive relationship of all this to a whole new technology, which itself is a figure for a whole new economic world system ...
>
> (1984: 58)

Nowhere is Jameson's theory more in accord with Baudrillard than when he is considering the 'new depthlessness' that permeates both culture and theory. Jameson's own articulation of this new phenomenon in the realm of culture, involves a discursive comparison of a work of modernist visual art, Van Gogh's *Peasant Shoes*, and a more recent work, Warhol's *Diamond Dust Shoes* (viewed as an instantiation of postmodernism). Of the former, Jameson reproduces two readings, which he describes as 'hermeneutical', in the sense that each takes the painting as an object which stands for another 'vaster reality', one which only interpretative reading can disclose or reveal. It is a definitive feature of the modern work, not only that it demands that we should speak to it, ask it questions, but moreover that such work should be able to answer back. *Peasant's Shoes* does this, whereas *Diamond Dust Shoes* does not. The content of the latter is no longer a reference to a wider 'life-world' within which it exists, and upon which it figuratively comments. Given the fact that Warhol's work 'turns centrally around commodification' then, according to Jameson (1984: 60), its content ought to refer to and foreground the commodity fetishism of late capitalism, something which it patently fails to do. The image, itself already 'second generational' ('debased and contaminated in advance by ... assimilation to glossy advertising images') before Warhol reproduces it, is 'flat', 'depthless' and 'incomprehensible'.

Jameson's way of connecting the *superficiality* he believes he detects in contemporary culture, with the disappearance of reference or depth in relation to theoretical perspectives, is through what he sees as the specific 'disposition' of the contemporary subject: evident in what he calls the 'waning of affect' and the 'deconstruction of expression'. Significantly, however, Jameson holds that it is not the case that all subjectivity has vanished from contemporary imagery. Returning to the example of *Diamond Dust Shoes*, he muses suggestively about 'a strange compensatory decorative exhilaration' which the painting exudes, due solely to the 'spangling of gilt sand, which seals the surface of the painting and yet continues to glint at us' (1984: 61). Clearly, it becomes possible to glimpse, in Jameson's view of the 'gratuitous frivolity of this final decorative overlay', what he considers to be a more general characteristic of late twentieth-century cultural consumption, namely, a fascination and pleasure in *surface* and *the superficial* (1984: 60).

For Baudrillard too, contemporary audiences no longer 'look for the richness of imagination in [contemporary] images; [they] look for the giddiness of their superficiality, for the artifice of detail, the intimacy of their technique'. Indeed, Baudrillard also connects this to the disappearance of affect for, as absolutely everything, including desire and imagination, is 'realised' in, and 'exposed to view' through mediation, there is a concomitant withdrawal or dispersal of expressive subjectivity (see Baudrillard 1988a: 42–3).

The connection between this and 'the poststructuralist critique of the hermeneutic', that is, of theories which rely on what Jameson calls 'depth models', is related by Jameson to the fact that 'the very concept of expression presupposes ... some separation within the subject, and along with this a whole metaphysics of the inside and the outside ... ' (1984: 61). But just as the concept of aesthetic expression (externalising, attempting to share ideas, feelings and emotions) is disappearing, so too, Jameson argues – in the wake of poststructuralist critique – are those theories which depended upon some concept of an 'inner and an outer': historical materialism, psychoanalysis, existentialism, structuralism. What replaces them is *surface*. 'Surface', according to Jameson, emerges in theory too, in the 'conception of practices, discourses, and textual play' (1984: 62). Once again, Baudrillard is one of those theorists, influenced by – if not directly of – post-structuralism, who launches a frontal attack on the notion of depth, on the idea that there is something (the genuine reality) behind appear-ances, or latent (authentic or true) meaning underneath the manifest one. As I have already indicated, Baudrillard erects a whole metaphysics of appearances, under the sign of 'seduction', as an alternative to what he views as the discred-ited depth model.

Jameson follows Baudrillard, at least insofar, as his insights appear to accord empirically with developments in contemporary culture. Furthermore, the radical questioning of the whole idea of an autonomous centred subject or psyche, something to which, again, Baudrillard, unreservedly subscribes, bears closely upon the problem, as Jameson understands it, of 'expression' or the 'waning of affect'. For Jameson, a de-centred subject is very much part of the waning of affect that he believes he can detect in contemporary society. The implications of the death of the 'bourgeois subject' for the question of express-ivity, which for Jameson lies at the heart of modernist aesthetics, are profound indeed. Among other things, it signals the beginning of the end of personal style and the emergence in its place of mechanically reproduced works together with 'the well-nigh universal practice today of what might be called pastiche' (1984: 64).

Formality endorsed

The idea of 'pastiche' as Jameson defines it has strong affinities with Baudrillard's central concept of simulation. For Jameson, 'pastiche is, like parody, the imitation of a peculiar mask, speech in a dead language: but it is the neutral practice of such mimicry, without any of parody's ulterior motives, amputated of the satiric impulse … ' (1984: 65). Like Eco, Jameson thinks that we are witnessing the end of a modernist ideology that was centred upon an aesthetic of innovation, however, for him this turned upon stylistic invention premised upon individual expressivity, rather than metaphor. Jameson is led thereby to what is, in certain respects at any rate, a different understanding of what this implies with respect to the aesthetic paradigm which – like Eco – he believes is coming to replace modernism. Eco's historical dialectic of repetition and innovation enables him to conceive of our present cultural predicament as constituted by a new aesthetic of the serial. For Jameson, after the death of stylistic innovation, the producers of culture have 'nowhere to turn but to the past: the imitation of dead styles … ', the idea here being that of culture feeding off itself. The extent of Jameson's coincidence with Baudrillard in this respect is apparent in the following:

71

The hyperreal is the first moment in which there is a game played with representation nowadays. One plays parodically with photographic resemblance, with things that one doesn't believe in anymore. One knows quite well that there are no longer any exact images of the world, no more mirrors – there are only tricks with mirrors ... a game with the vestiges of what has been destroyed.

(Baudrillard 1984: 25)

This idea of a 'cannibalistic culture' is also very close to that of Eco, especially in the sense that it implies a certain notion of repetition. Indeed, all three of the thinkers under discussion produce as a principal example of the functioning of late twentieth-century culture the idea of the *remake*, and all three discuss this phenomenon in conjunction with another central idea, called by Eco 'intertextual dialogue'. Jameson's discussion of this is built around an analysis of what he calls 'the nostalgia film'. The conclusion he draws from this is that 'we are now ... in "intertextuality" as a deliberate, built-in feature of the aesthetic effect, and as the operator of a new connotation of "pastness" and pseudo-historical depth, in which the history of aesthetic styles replaces "real" history' (Jameson 1984: 67).

Eco also understands *intertextuality* as centrally involving 'the phenomenon by which a given text echoes previous texts'. And he makes the same point as Jameson when he argues that a prevalent aspect of contemporary cinema is that it puts 'into play an intertextual encyclopedia. We have texts that are quoted from other texts and the knowledge of preceding ones – taken for granted – is supposed to be necessary for the enjoyment of a new one' (Eco 1985: 172). Both Jameson and Eco here are discussing what Baudrillard, more poetically perhaps, terms 'the exponential enfolding of the medium around itself ... this endless enwrapping of images (literally, without end, without destination) which leaves images no other destiny but images' (Baudrillard 1987: 28).[9]

Jameson's discussion of the new mode of what he terms 'nostalgia film', is part of an attempt to explain what he understands as 'the disappearance of the historical referent' (1984: 71). Baudrillard's discussion of the cinema, typically, goes much further, and treats it as an example of the disappearance of the more inclusive 'real as referential' (1987: 31). Nevertheless, both draw strikingly similar general conclusions. Jameson says that:

if there is any realism left here ... it is a 'realism' which is meant to derive from the shock of ... slowly becoming aware of a new and original situation in which we are condemned to seek History by way of our Pop images and simulacra of that history, which itself remains forever out of reach.

(1984: 71)

Baudrillard argues that it is 'reality' itself which remains forever out of reach: 'cinema attempting to abolish itself in the absolute of reality, the real already long absorbed in cinematographic (or televised) hyperreality' (1987: 31).

Résumé

I have made frequent allusion to Baudrillard's preoccupation with questions of form, suggesting that he is not alone in this. Though it would be inappropriate to call Jameson's approach formalist, nevertheless, in his discussion of the emergence of 'a whole new culture of the image' he is at pains to draw attention to precisely those features that Baudrillard himself highlights.[10] According to Jameson, these features involve, 'depthlessness' and a concomitant concern with surface (superficiality and spectacle); a generalised 'intertextuality', in the sense of an ever increasing practice of imitation and self-reference ('pastiche'); and a retreat from originality, 'expression' and meaning, evident in the repetition (remakes) and 'nostalgia' of many contemporary forms.

Eco, similarly, focuses on formal features as the most important aspects of contemporary culture, pondering the end of innovation and metaphor (definitive of modernism). This is being replaced today by increased redundancy (a thinning down of meaning), forms involving 'intertextual dialogue', and a new involvement with a kind of circular formal play of difference within repetition. Eco says little about how this new culture has developed, being more concerned to describe and analyse its principal characteristics. Jameson and Baudrillard (though in very different ways) both view developments in technologies of reproducibility as a central, ultimately perhaps *the* central, determinant in the process of the development of a general preponderance of form over content.[11]

There seem to me to be two important dimensions to this new focus on formality. First, there is the tendency – most clearly in evidence in Baudrillard, but also apparent in different degrees, in other theorists of 'postmodernism' – to collapse the world into culture: all that we can legitimately say exists are texts (intertextuality). One important consequence of this has been the demotion of traditional domains of the social world such as the economic and political, and the promotion of concern with the cultural. It is almost as if the former somehow cease to exist once the post-structuralist challenge to representation has been admitted.

Second, there is the more cautious and less absolutist analysis of a new situation. Such a position, though fully cognisant of the fact that things are quite drastically changing, and that old categories and ideas no longer appear to apply as neatly and cohesively as they once did, is nevertheless, much more reluctant to accept the idea of a total break with the past. This amounts to a more specific analysis of the nature of the changes taking place within cultural development itself, still viewed as only one aspect or dimension of a far larger, differentiated, more complex whole.[12]

It is this position that I adopt here. In ways that will become clearer in the pages that follow I endorse and pursue Baudrillardian-inspired insights into the character of the contemporary cultural context only insofar as they illuminate the *aesthetic dimension* of digital cultural genres and their expressions. Unlike Baudrillard, I do not think that these new features now constitute the whole of (visual) culture *per se*, only that they are now so prevalent as to constitute a new and significant dimension of representation within it. Other (and older) orders of representation exist alongside and in contention with this newer one, though they may well be increasingly compromised by its expansion.

All of the above provokes the long-standing question as to what is more important, the medium or the message, the form or the content? Perhaps the best response to this is to refuse to accept the choice thus presented as spurious, arguing instead that both continue to be relevant. In this way it is possible to recognise that the aspect of *formality* – in the senses introduced – has, whether we like it or not, come to take on a more central significance in today's consumer society. That is, some such culture, involving forms of seriality, repetition, self-referentiality and spectacle is currently emerging, rising on the back of sign proliferation and enabled by continuing developments in mass production techniques. Moreover, this culture does appear to involve a 'new depthlessness', i.e. a demotion or negation of the idea that we are able to distinguish between signifier and signified, or, to use another of Jameson's phrases, a 'whole new culture of the image as simulacrum' (Jameson 1984). At the same time, and though one might want to admit that there are significant questions concerning the demotion of content or meaning in today's media, one does not have to follow Baudrillard the whole way, admitting thereby that meaning or the possibility of representation has disappeared altogether. Clearly this would be wrong.

Yet, I shall pursue the claim that the forms of visual digital culture at the centre of this discussion *are* striking exemplars of current trends to formality and surface within the domain of mass culture. Continuous with an earlier tradition of popular entertainment that operated through modes of spectacle, a clear kinship exists between the tradition of popular entertainments outlined in chapter 2 and the cultural trends described here. Both share the same aesthetic leaning towards visual modes that are the opposite of classical theatre, and – in most respects – opposite, also, to the forms and practices of modernism, both mainstream and avant-garde. The tendency here is one that is more inclined to redundancy and visual or physical diversion (spectacle, technique, style) rather than to the significatory depth of classical narrative modes, or the originality and difficulty associated with metaphorical challenge.

I have suggested that what distinguishes the spectacle of these recent forms is their historical location. They are situated at the end of a long period that saw the development and proliferation of visual media that are tied to different kinds of technical reproducibility (part of the advanced commodification of culture). In the actual cultural context in which digital processes are operating and developing – and for reasons discussed above – there exists a strong preoccupation with the production of representations of a *second degree* or *second order*, a preoccupation – unconscious though much of this may be – with the simulation of prior or already existing modes and forms of representation. Indeed, this is particularly pronounced and begins to reveal itself precisely within the visual digital practices associated with forms and genres of mass culture. Here, it would seem, computer imaging looks not so much to the world itself, as to already existing techniques of mediation, together with their attendant forms and styles. Prior forms, genres and works constitute a referential basis or ground for copying, acts of manipulation and recombination, and efforts aimed at further 'perfecting' and simulating the already mediated.

Both the latest digital cultural entertainments themselves and the new techniques that support them are fashioned by the presence of such an aesthetic, increasingly absorbed with formal matters – although, clearly, a multitude of forces help to shape the forms these techniques are coming to assume. For example, in addition to a prevailing technological legacy of objects and means and established aesthetic techniques and devices, we must also take account of institutionalised forms and practices. At the same time however, the new techniques themselves *do* (as we began to see in the first chapter) involve distinctive elements and possibilities that push for or enable certain developments rather than others. Indeed, the recent development of the computer in relation to image manipulation, image synthesis and simulation processes, might be viewed as broadly congruent with a visual order that involves such practices as recombination and pastiche. The former constitute some of the most recent techniques to emerge in the course of the developments in technological reproducibility. It is *not* coincidental that such techniques – which involve a further perfection of the means for both (re)producing and manipulating ever more *divorced* or *uncoupled* visual (and other) signs and representations – emerge at the very moment that such practices (intertextuality, hyperrealism, simulation, etc.) have themselves come to occupy a distinctive place within mass visual culture.

In the course of this chapter, I have referred to and introduced a host of related terms. Among those that have cropped up most frequently are notions such as reproducibility and repetition, self-referentiality and intertextuality, simulation and pastiche, and superficiality and spectacle. All have been used with cultural and aesthetic senses and references in view, that is to say, as concepts that explain, designate and describe distinctive practices, processes, forms and conditions within late twentieth-century (visual) culture. As such, they might usefully be set against another group of terms, terms which they are displacing or challenging. This set includes concepts such as signification and meaning, realism and narrative, originality and authorship, metaphor and depth, and reading and interpretation.

Plainly, it would be rash to claim that the terms in the first list now more accurately describe or define contemporary culture as a whole. Not even mass culture is as uniform as this. Having said this, however, I do suggest that with respect to certain domains of mass visual culture the terms in the second list above no longer do the work of describing and defining that they once did. Increasingly, the practices and generic expressions associated with digital visual forms elude their explanatory grasp.

It is becoming harder to discover mass cultural practices that are not referring back in some way to past styles. Whilst using the forms and genres of the past as a source of intertextual reference is not the same thing as developing or extending an aesthetic tradition, these two things clearly coincide in the forms of visual digital culture. The aesthetic tradition, which the latter falls under, is a spectacle tradition, a tradition that revels in sensation, astonishment, ephemerality and diversion. Correspondingly, 'intertextuality', standing in here for a host of related senses, brings with it – as we have seen – formal excitement and encourages aesthetic practices that promote the play and allure of surface and the reflex response. Not only is there a high degree of correspondence between these two phenomena, but it *is* difficult to reconcile the kind of aesthetic that they suggest with the ideas of significatory depth, originality, reference and so forth, inherent in the second set of terms listed above.

Certainly, ideas such as depth of meaning (manifest *and* latent) and reference (to 'the real' *and* to 'the imaginary') – no matter how much they have been contested and argued over – have an affinity with aesthetic modernism and the critical discourses which have surrounded it. Such ideas invoke questions to do with representation, realism, ideology and interpretation. These, in their turn, recall activities – both practical and theoretical – associated with them: Hollywood, counter-cinemas, and a variety of critical approaches both to understanding the practices, forms and contexts of meaning-making and the processes of signification involved in meaning made. At the centre of all this work – indeed, its very *raison d'être* – lie conceptions of a (more or less) complex world represented. Ultimately, what are at stake are issues of how a world is being articulated and how this measures up to perceptions (and conceptions) of the world itself. A rich field of symbolic representation is at the heart of such work, whether it is that of practical or critical production.

However, as I shall show, the forms under consideration here do not share these features. They lack the symbolic depth and representational complexity of earlier forms, appearing by contrast to operate within a drastically reduced field of meaning. They are direct and one-dimensional, *about* little, other than their ability to commandeer the sight and the senses. Popular forms of diversion and amusement, these new technological entertainments are, perhaps, the clearest manifestation of the advance of the culture of the 'depthless image' of which Jameson speaks. As such, they would seem to be prime sites for a more concerted exploration and testing of the shift to increased formality in mass visual culture that has been introduced in this chapter. What, specifically, do new concepts such as simulation, hyperrealism, pastiche, interaction and immersion designate? How do they manifest themselves in cultural practices? What are the implications with respect to questions of aesthetics and spectatorship? What

76

is the significance of the changes that are involved and how are we to make sense of them? To begin answering these questions the next section of this book shifts the methodological focus away from historical contextualisation and onto the forms themselves.

Part II

AESTHETICS

4

SIMULATION AND
HYPERREALISM

Computer animation and TV advertisements

The second part of this book looks in more depth and detail at the particular aesthetic character of the digital genres introduced and historically contextualised in Part I. As we have seen, a tradition of popular amusement relates the new forms to an aesthetic that turns upon modes of spectacle and sensation. However, as the latest expressions of this tradition these genres are quite distinctive. The manner in which they continue this tendency to spectacle is subject both to the enabling powers of the digital technology that supports them *and* to certain moulding pressures operative within the encompassing visual culture of which they are a part. The aesthetic character of this culture is itself rather particular – indeed, many of its defining characteristics or traits manifest a marked resemblance to those of the spectacle tradition itself. It is a culture that, in a growing number of its practices and expressions, endorses form over content, the ephemeral and superficial over permanence and depth, and the image itself over the image as referent.

The expressions of visual digital culture at issue here are exemplary instances of this proclivity to form and spectacle. In the following chapters I look directly at their distinguishing characteristics, examining particular genres, citing specific examples, exploring the actual role of the computer in the production of their visual aesthetic, and describing and analysing their status as part of a new aesthetic preserve of visual representation within contemporary culture. The intention is to produce a more tangible examination than is usually attempted of some of the new aesthetic concepts now being used to describe contemporary visual culture (introduced in chapter 3). How do these ideas manifest themselves in concrete expressions of contemporary aesthetic practice?

I shall begin by looking at computer animation and television advertisements. The discussion of computer animation will refer in the main to the work of the computer animation firm Pixar (see chapter 1). Their films are among the best-known within the genre, and their work is typical of the aesthetic trajectory of digital animation within the visual cultural mainstream.

Whereas computer animation exists as a form or genre in its own right, TV/cinema advertising is different. With respect to digital techniques in advertising, we are talking of a rapidly growing and increasingly influential subgroup within the genre, a growing corpus within which digital imaging techniques and technologies – ranging from image synthesis to image manipulation – have been decisively integrated into the production process.

When addressing questions of digital imaging and their associated forms 'realism', as we have begun to see, is never far away. As I shall show, realism is connected to these visual digital forms in ways that are frequently both complicated and novel, nowhere more so than in the realm of computer animated films. For it is here in particular that we can acquire insight into what the idea of *simulation* might mean in practice. We are able to see how this term is related to certain conceptions of representational or mimetic realism, whilst at the same time transcending them to help produce a rather different kind of film and film text.

Similarly, digital techniques are providing the means for television (and cinema) commercials to develop conceptual possibilities that are changing the formal and aesthetic character of the genre. Imagery and image forms are emerging that display new levels of surface accuracy and image brilliance: heightened kinds of photographic and cinematographic illusion. Accompanying this is an intensification of the tendency, already well established within advertising texts, freely to borrow from and to recombine other forms and styles of image production. Indeed, together with music video – its more recent cousin – advertising is perhaps the prime site of the intensification and augmentation of *montage* that the advent of electronic imaging has spurred (see chapter 6). If we want to see how the idea of *hyper-realism* might function in contemporary visual practices, then we need look no further than advertising centred upon digital techniques.

Computer animation: second-order realism

'Computer animation' has two senses: it refers to a particular way of producing the illusion of movement, and it refers to a genre or type of film so produced. Plenty of mainstream films employ computer animation as part of their production process, but they do not become, thereby, examples of computer animation. In the mainstream culture at least, this title is usually reserved for films synthesised entirely by digital means and it is these which form the focus of interest in this chapter.

Toy Story (1995), the first feature-length computer synthesised film is, perhaps, the best-known of such movies. From one perspective, *Toy Story* is the culmination of an intensive research and development programme: one that has taken place within the digital animation domain of new Hollywood. Its aim has been to develop the technical power and the apparatus necessary for the production of detailed and sustained character-centred story telling that could rival that produced by established means. Thus, the celebrated short computer animated films produced by Pixar between 1985 and 1990 were preparatory works for the more sustained and commercially oriented *Toy Story*. Among these 'trail-blazing' films – acclaimed winners of many awards within the film and computer graphics industries – are *Luxo Junior* (1986), *Red's Dream* (1987), *Tin Toy* (1988) and *Knick Knack* (1989). The kinds of objects, sets and props rendered and animated in the anthropomorphic manner familiar to Disney and the classic cartoon tradition in these accomplished preliminary exercises, all reappear in more developed form in the feature film itself. The technical groundwork of the 1980s is capitalised upon in the 1990s.

Establishing the means to produce a novel mode of entertainment cartoon was the overt goal. However, Pixar's work is also clearly motivated by the ✓ extraordinary realist thrust that has pervaded the commercial (and military) spheres of computer imaging since the middle of the 1970s. Looked at from this point of view *Toy Story* is only partially successful. Yet it is still an excellent example of what I call 'secondary' or 'second-order' realism. As with all the other films with which Pixar have been involved, and in keeping with the prevailing attitude within the computer animation industry generally, *Toy Story* involves an attempt to produce old ways of seeing or representing by other means.

Of course a new technique of image origination is involved here, and it is tempting to attribute the unprecedented forms of imagery that are present in this and related films solely to this fact. Clearly, the techniques of digital animation and image synthesis are central, as I shall show. However, the distinctive imagery and the novel formal character of such films as a whole can only be properly understood when one begins to look at what is being attempted with this new means of image production. In other words, computer imaging does not produce these new forms of image all by itself. We must also explore the particular kinds of contact it has with established aesthetic conventions and forms. When this is undertaken, it becomes possible to see computer animated films such as *Toy Story* in a new light. I shall suggest that these films are specific examples of a generalised shift towards forms constituted through hybridity and simulation. Examples of a new level of preoccupation with signifiers at the expense of signification (and reference).

Illusionist realisms: continuing a tradition

In certain respects the films emerging from the computer animation mainstream – this certainly applies to Pixar – are continuing a tradition of cartoon realism stretching back to the early efforts of Disney and his animators. What they attempted (from the mid-1930s onwards) was to produce films that combined certain of the existing codes of live action narrative cinema, integrating them in a more rigorous fashion than previously with those of the animated cartoon. The culmination of these efforts, of course, was *Snow White and the Seven Dwarves* (1937), a feature-length cartoon. However, the same drive is evident in countless other Disney animation shorts produced both before and after the latter. A classic in this regard is *The Old Mill* (1937) one of the *Silly Symphonies* series. What Disney achieved by this was a heightened sense both of naturalism and illusionism within a form that was usually viewed as inherently non-realistic.[1] The computer generated animation of Pixar furthers this approach, taking it to new levels of sophistication. Nowhere is this more apparent than in the degree of surface accuracy and the greatly enhanced illusion of three-dimensional space and solidity produced in their films by the computer animation itself.

At the same time, however, there are significant differences at the aesthetic level between a film such as *Toy Story* and its Disney predecessors. These have little or nothing to do with content or meaning. It may well be true, especially since Pixar's involvement in the field, that character animation and story telling has finally caught up with traditional animation in the computer animated film – a technical achievement, no doubt, for those involved, though the stories and characterisations themselves are hardly exceptional. It is, rather, at the level of *form* that this work distinguishes itself. Of course, I am not claiming that these films fail to signify in any important way – clearly, this would be fallacious. My point is that it is at another level entirely that they display aesthetic import and much of their spectator interest.

In the first instance, this is discernible at the level of the image itself. In terms of plasticity, texture, look, weight and movement, films like *Red's Dream*, *Tin Toy* and *Toy Story* certainly produce the impression of a much higher degree of surface accuracy than has hitherto been the case in the animated cartoon. More than this though, a certain sense of ambiguity haunts the imagery of such films. This is related to uncertainty as to the status of the imagery in terms of origination: is it cartoon animation, three-dimensional (puppet) animation, live action or, perhaps, a combination of all three? One becomes fascinated with the imagery precisely because of this uncertainty, seduced by the ways it recasts, amalgamates and *confuses* familiar techniques and forms. Such fascination comes to define a significant way in which these films are received. Indeed, I shall dare to suggest that it is *the* primary element of reception, entailing a displacement away from concentration on narratives (such as they are) and towards the allure and fascinations of the image itself.

Accounting for the features that ultimately mark these films as aesthetically distinctive with respect to previous examples in the tradition involves an attempt to understand the ways in which the new means of image origination figure in their production. Two of the crucial factors shaping any emergent form of cultural production are existing or prior techniques and aesthetic conventions or rules. The *means* responsible for the production of films like *Toy Story* are clearly radically different from traditional film and cartoon. In their case, the actual process of image origination and construction did not involve the usual paraphernalia of either live action or cartoon film production. Instead, camera, lights, locations, sets, props, actors, cels, paint, puppets and so forth, physically disappear – replaced by their virtual or surrogate counterparts within the programs of computers.

At the level of aesthetic conventions, what we appear to have here is a further extension or development of the preoccupation with heightened realism first displayed by Disney. The crucial difference, however, is that the new digital techniques are employed in an attempt to achieve this goal through complex forms of image *simulation*. Indeed, the historical form of animated realism associated with Disney – itself already something of a hybrid – becomes a partial model and reference for attempts at simulation by other means.

It is the impulse to simulation or imitation underlying Pixar's computer animated films that not only continues the realist course of Disney, but, at the same time, leads to altogether new forms of image. The production of this distinctive imagery occurs through an original way of combining images, an original form of image hybridisation made possible by digital techniques. The mode of combination involved is indirect. It happens at one remove from the kind of manipulation of final imagery usually associated with established ways of combining and linking (i.e. through practices such as superimposition, collage, in-frame or between-shot juxtaposition and the like). In the films at issue here the combination is not of already produced images – raw material awaiting some kind of work of combination. It is, rather, a question of the synthetic blending or *fusing* via the computer of certain prior image forms. Thus, Disney-style animation, live action cinema and three-dimensional (puppet) animation, each of these kinds of film provides a partial *model* for the programmers to aim for in the search for heightened illusionism. The computer eventually brings them all together (fusing them) in the process of synthesising the final simulation or image.

The digital animation in *Toy Story* does not just involve the traditional cartoon form as the model for emulation. It is crucial also to recognise the way in which this form has been made to combine or become coextensive with the conditions obtaining on and within the live action set. In this case, of course, the set is *virtual* or latent – itself a simulation created and existing in the program of a computer. Such programs are now able to simulate three-dimensional spatial and temporal conditions, natural and artificial lighting conditions and effects, surface textures, the full spectrum of colours, solidity and weight, the movement of objects and, as well, the complete range of movements of a camera within and around their virtual space. When cartoon characters – and, just as important, cartoon tropes such as anthropomorphism – are imaged through this studio simulacrum, then new registers of *mimetic* imagery are achieved within the cartoon: a consequence of this peculiar *crossing* or *fusing* of traditionally distinct forms of film.

The unusual mode of hybrid imagery that emerges from this process helps us to understand its ambiguous quality. The new techniques of image and textual simulation at work in *Toy Story* produce *not* a simulation that is wholly indistinguishable from its model(s), rather, a relatively unprecedented kind of image (and text). Indeed, even the most innocent of spectators must suspect that these films are not like the cartoons they are used to watching. What contributes to producing this response is the extraordinary detail of lighting, colour and texture – akin to cinematography, yet different somehow, because it is just too *pristine.* In addition, there is the peculiar substantiality of figures and objects, the novel way they appear to occupy (and move around in) three-dimensional space even though this is represented on a 2-D screen. The way the imagery looks *exceeds* that which is normally associated with its models (i.e. live action cinematography, realist cartoon, and model or puppet animation). There is an intensification or exaggeration (a certain kind of display) at the level of the (moving) image of the analogical or mimetic aspect of these prior models.

Simulation and hybridisation

One way of further illuminating the *excessive* character of these films, is to draw a comparison with a mode of painting that emerged in the United States in the 1960s: so-called 'Super Realism' (see, for example, Battock 1995). Such painting takes photography itself as its model or subject. Indeed, it is more direct than the kind of image simulation by computer under discussion here, for it involves the meticulous copying of a photograph (which the painter may or may not have taken himself). What is important about such painting for present purposes is the excessive nature of the resulting imagery. The painting process produces an intensification or exaggeration, and thereby a kind of *fore-grounding* or display, of the mimetic/analogical character of its model – the photographic medium. Moreover, and just as significant, Super Realist painting involves artifice – in this case simulation through copying – of a second order.

Of course, there is a difference, at the very least at the level of technical reali-sation, between these two modes of image generation. Super Realism produces its simulacra using the meticulous and painstaking method of painting (usually, with an airbrush) a slide, projected (and thus enlarged) on to a canvas. This is very different – both technologically and technically – to producing a simula-tion of a particular kind of cartoon film by the procedures involved in digital image generation (a practice that uses extremely powerful computers and highly complex programs). Yet, purely at the level of the image, a similar effect is achieved. And, although the computer generated images of films such as *Toy Story* have, subsequent to their synthesis, been recorded on to film, this only minimally modifies what may be described as the *Super Realist* character of those images.

Indeed, a further parallel may be drawn here. Despite the obvious differences between their respective models – stills photography on the one hand and film on the other – that is, despite the different aesthetic conventions variously established within each mode, the simulation, both in computer animation and in Super Realist painting, involves the reproduction of these conventions. In the case of the latter, this follows simply from the act of copying a still photograph. Thus, cropping, focus, film-stock, lighting, printing and iconography (subject matter) itself – elements that are mobilised and differently codified depending upon the kind of photography taken as subject – are transposed as part of the meticulous reproduction. In films such as *Toy Story* the simulation does not involve direct copying, rather, the production of a copy without an original, an instance of a certain kind (or kinds) of film realised through other means. Nevertheless, this also entails a transposition of aesthetic codes into the simulation itself, no matter that this transposition is less direct, given the more abstract nature of the models and the origination involved in the simulation in this instance.

Unlike Super Realist painting however, Pixar's computer animated films are second-order simulations that are far more continuous with the illusionism contained in the aesthetic forms they take as their model or subject of simulation. There are factors at work in Super Realist painting which clearly distinguish it from its model, the still photograph: scale is perhaps the most important example, though viewing distance when confronting the painting itself is also crucial. Both photographic quality (image) and photographic conventionality (kind of photograph copied) are present in the Super Realist work, yet it is clear that no one is going to confuse the painting with a photograph, the simulation with its model (except, perhaps, if s/he sees that painting as a photographic reproduction in a book!). Films such as *Toy Story*, on the other hand, are ultimately reproduced precisely in the medium they are attempting to simulate.

The nub of the difference between computer animation and Super Realist painting, is that, whilst both are clearly primarily *about* realism – that is to say, about two different techno-aesthetic modes, forms and styles of realism – unlike Super-Realism, computer animation tends to dissimulate this concern. *Toy Story* does not disclose the realism and illusionism – the transparency – underlying its aesthetic model, in the same way that Super Realist painting does. If anything, it promotes the continuance of it. The computer animators and technicians working within this tradition appear to be striving for simulations that are indistinguishable from their model, whereas Super Realist painters do not. They know that this is an impossible goal and, besides, it is never the object of the exercise anyway, only a means to other ends.

Ambiguous imagery

This does not mean however, as I have already begun to show, that computer animated films of the kind under discussion here actually *succeed* in their 'objective' of the perfect simulation of their model. Indeed, given that I am suggesting that this model is not one simple image, as is the case with the Super Realist work, but exists rather as several separate moving-image forms, it becomes hard to see how it could succeed in this sense. Formal *hybridity* lies at the heart of the simulation involved in *Toy Story*, and the excess and ambiguity produced by this unprecedented mode of image conjunction is precisely what constitutes the aesthetic novelty of this and similar films.

Toy Story and its immediate forerunners are important for the peculiar way in which they are *about* realist and illusionary qualities, not character and plot.[2]

For beneath the desire to produce successful entertainment ('more of the same') lies a deeper preoccupation with the computer synthesis of realistic imagery. This fascination with achieving the appearances of a prior mode of representation (i.e. cinematography) by other means is one of the central objectives of the film and computer graphics industries. A technical problem – the concrete possibility of achieving 'photography' by digital means – begins to take over, and to determine the aesthetics of certain modes of contemporary visual culture. Attempts – such as those focused upon here – to imitate and simulate, are at the farthest remove from traditional notions of representation. They displace and demote questions of reference and meaning (or signification) substituting instead a preoccupation with means and the image (the signifier itself) as a site or object of fascination: a kind of collapsing of aesthetic concerns into the search for a solution to a technical problem.

Of course, that it is prior or established modes of representation that are assumed as the model for these new techniques of reproduction is not coincidental. For this is tied to the non-indexical character of computer generated imagery. That the computer should turn more readily to simulating already established forms and modes of representation, rather than attempting first-order representations of events and things in the world, seems to be connected with its definitive difference from photographic recording techniques. The break is with direct analogue procedures, that is, with *recording* and the fidelities of recording. Computer generated images do not involve recording, except in the senses of indirect or secondary contact. Strictly speaking (and using Peirce's categories or elements of the sign), computer generated imagery is *iconic*, never indexical – no matter how photo-realistic it looks – in the sense that photography is an index (not necessarily reliable) of there having been something in the world (staged or not) previously (see Peirce 1931).

Like the paintings of Super Realism that precede them, the imagery in these computer animated films is highly arresting. In a similar way to the former, it is so, not so much for what it contains, as for what it *is*: an imitation via the computer of imagery characteristic of other (earlier) means of representation. In a sense it is precisely this attempt to originate through other means, texts containing types of imagery which are already of an extraordinary analogical or mimetic accuracy that tends to govern the object of looking. Everything begins and ends with the image and its relation to its prior model(s).

TV advertisements: neo-montage and hyperrealism

TV and cinema advertising are prime examples of the ways in which particular computer imaging techniques have been integrated into an established form of contemporary visual culture. This process of integration – which is still occurring – is enabling the development of conceptual possibilities that are changing the formal and aesthetic character of the genre. This involves the emergence to prominence within advertising of imagery and image forms that display fresh and heightened kinds of *photographic and cinematographic impossibility*. Tied to such developments are new levels of surface accuracy, image brilliance and spectacle. And this is invariably bound up with an intensification of the reflex – already an established constituent of advertisements anyway – to freely borrow from and to recombine other forms and styles of image production.

Advertising became one of the central cultural institutions of late twentieth-century society. Recent students of the subject have pointed out that advertising is primarily a 'discourse through and about objects' (see Jhally 1990; Leiss *et al.* 1990). It is a mode of communication in and through which ideas are produced and mediated about the objects and services those of us living in 'advanced' or late capitalist societies consume.

Broadly, advertising has evolved within the historical development of the so-called consumer society. Advertising is now a fundamental component of this society and its counterpart, consumer culture. As such, it has passed from being an informational form related more to an object's use value, and has come to constitute *the* realm of a vast symbolic mediation of consumer goods and services. It is a cultural space wherein, for the most part, non-functional meanings and connotations – related to personal and social status and values – are generated and arbitrarily attached to commodities of all kinds (see, for example, Ewen 1976, 1988; Baudrillard 1990: 63–97; Boorstin 1992).

As part of this evolution, itself closely tied to developments within modes of mass mediation and culture, a further shift has occurred. This involves the passage from advertisements that were largely language- or text-based to current forms that are increasingly image-centred. That is, late twentieth-century advertisements came to rest more and more on visual or iconic forms of mediation. In Sut Jhally's words, current advertising is 'characterised by the growing domination of *imagistic* modes of communication' (Jhally 1990: 22).

Something of the specificity of advertising as a visually based form of contemporary culture may be achieved by comparing it to Hollywood cinema or television. Although there are, of course, important differences between the latter, it is apparent nevertheless, that in terms both of formal characteristics and meaning production advertisements are to be distinguished from them both. For, unlike mainstream cinema and television, advertisements are highly *rhetorical* in their formal make-up. In other words, they involve a type of communication that is far less prosaic and naturalistic than the former: symbolism, analogy, allusion and metaphor are centrally defining characteristics of the way most advertisements work or communicate.

There is one further aspect of advertising as visual culture that should be highlighted here: its long-standing relationship with art, design and fashion. Of particular importance in the context of the current discussion, is the observation – made by numerous commentators on the area – that advertising has developed on the basis of the parasitical relation it has enjoyed with respect to other forms of cultural production (see, for example, Leiss *et al.* 1990: 49–89). Certainly since the 1920s – perhaps even before – advertising has looked for inspiration first to forms of still imagery and literature, and then additionally and increasingly, to forms of moving imagery and music.

Indeed, with respect to questions of the distinctive character of contemporary visual culture addressed in these pages, advertising might be seen to hold something of a privileged position. Advertising has continued – and with increasing voracity – to variously borrow from prior and other forms, recently making modes of pastiche, copying and simulation the very basis of its rhetorical aesthetic. Certainly, advertising forms an extremely important space within the contemporary visual aesthetic adumbrated here. The following examination of the now central use of digital imaging within the genre aims to provide further clarification and insight into the role of the computer both in the definition and in the production of this aesthetic.

Attempting to discuss texts such as TV advertisements is notoriously difficult. Unlike the 'universal' Hollywood feature film, it is not so easy to assume familiarity on the part of the reader with specific (and often short-lived) examples of TV advertising. Further, although some advertisements are produced for consumption across national borders, such ads are still in a minority – most advertising is designed for localised consumption on national or regional TV. Nor – for those interested enough to want to view particular ads that one may discuss – can one assume a ready or easy access to them outside of their normal screening context.[3] My chief examples are advertisements that I have viewed within the context of British TV and cinema in the 1990s (see Figures 4.1, 4.2).[4] Therefore, for the above reasons, when I do refer to particular instances in this discussion it is with a view to making points which invariably have a wider or more generalised applicability across the domain of advertisements involving digital means. I aim to point to and broadly describe some of the main ways in which computer imaging techniques are beginning to figure in the formal and symbolic systems of advertisements. I shall pay particular attention to the way in which the computer's production of realistic or transparent image forms is affecting the rhetorical aesthetic of TV advertising.

Most advertising now uses digital imaging techniques as a matter of course: these techniques involve both image manipulation (and image combination) and image synthesis (see chapter 1) – though not necessarily always together in the same advertisement. It is still possible to point to ads which merely use a digital technique – a motion control shot, say – within an advertising text that is visually mundane or ordinary. However, for some time now, TV advertisements – among the shortest moving image texts in existence – have increasingly turned to using the new digital techniques to produce altogether new levels of arresting visual brilliance and allure. For the most part, such techniques are enabling the production of high-resolution photographic simulations of impossible or virtually impossible shots, actions and occurrences. These – to the naked eye at least – perfectly sutured (i.e. realistic) image combinations are drawn directly and indirectly from other styles and genres. This is occurring within texts that strive to 'generate meaning by constructing schemas of well-being through associating images of people, products, and settings'. Indeed, the degree of technical skill and aesthetic artifice involved at every level of the construction of such ads – from conceptualisation and storyboarding, through cinematography and editing, to post-production – is highly accomplished. These 20- to 90-second *blasts* of imagery and action are meticulously choreographed: calculated to grab one's attention and to capture and delight the eye.

Hyperrealist Disney

On the increase (at the time of writing) are digitally produced advertisements that have adopted the computer animation technique *and* the formal/aesthetic style of films such as *Toy Story*. That is to say, the representational models of such ads are traditional cartoon animation of the Disney variety *and* the more recent computer animated films, which I have linked primarily to the work of the Pixar Company. Among the earliest of such ads to appear in the British context were a striking series produced for Yoplait's fruit yoghurts. Based upon individual scenes from Disney's film *Fantasia* (1940), their scenarios took place in a kitchen at night and involved the computer animation of objects such as spoons, refrigerators, cartons of yoghurt, crockery and suchlike. Most noticeable of all however, was their rendering, which involved an extraordinary level of anthropomorphism and photo-realistic accuracy.

Of course, much of what I said above about computer animation also applies to these texts. Such ads involve an intensification of Disneyesque naturalism, and this produces 'hyperrealist Disney' of a similar stamp to that which characterises films such as *Toy Story*. Such advertisements display how computer or digitally based imaging techniques are now able to produce (virtually) cinematically photo-realistic animated objects acting and moving seamlessly within cinematically photo-realistic three-dimensional space. A kind of visual impossibility is exhibited and is, perhaps, most apparent in the anthropomorphism which pervades the scenarios of such advertisements. Digital animation is able to impart extraordinary degrees of life-like movement and human-like behaviour to ordinary everyday objects: spoons, spectacles, milk bottles, spicejars, yoghurt pots, vegetables, personal computers – these are just a handful of the objects that have been 'brought to life' in recent advertisements. The three-dimensionality, solidity and weight, and the convincing rendering of surface texture and reflection imparted by digital synthesis combine to produce a new level of verisimilitude relative to the animated cartoon genre from which such figures are derived. Indeed, the three-dimensional aspect of these computer animated objects and characters is important. Such animated figures are – from their initial construction in the computer program – inherently three-dimensional and (potentially) infinitely manipulable. This lends itself to the reproduction of movements and actions, the naturalism or photographic-realism of which far exceeds that achieved by traditional 3-D animation (i.e. puppets, models and the like). The naturalistic cartoon is totally overhauled:

re-animated. The upshot, somewhat paradoxically, is the assimilation or domestication of otherwise disparate visual forms within the photo-realist (live action) mode of representation. Thus even cartoon forms and tropes (such as anthropomorphic spoons) take on a photo-realistic appearance. The *hyperrealism* manifest here stems as much from the intensification of a naturalism already tinged with contradictory tension – i.e. the realist cartoon itself – as from the sheer surface accuracy of the images themselves. Ordinary objects do appear to have 'actually', 'really' come alive – though not for a moment would anyone actually believe this.

Recorded or contrived?

The new levels of realistic-ness imported into cartoon animation via the computer is one way in which advertising is currently pursuing its constant search for novel and arresting kinds and forms of imagery. Far more prevalent, however, is another sort of advertisement – ostensibly, live action-based and displaying a predominant reliance on the new fashion for trick effects ushered in by computer imaging techniques. Such ads share much in common with the effects-laden blockbuster films of late Hollywood cinema discussed in the next chapter. However, although these ads employ figurative or representational 'photographic' imagery, the role or place of such imagery is rarely, if ever, straightforward, i.e. simply or only descriptive or denotative.[5] Their images are manipulated, combined or set in contexts and scenarios that deliberately set out – albeit rather gently in comparison to works of the modernist avant-garde, for example – to confound and scramble immediate referential meaning and sense. They provoke, rather, associative, connotative, allusive meanings – significantly though, responses of puzzlement, fascination or simple bedazzlement will do just as well.

In this brief exploration of such advertisements I shall focus on two examples: an ad called – by the makers – *Reflections* (Figure 4.1), one of the first of its kind to appear in the British context at the turn of the 1990s, and an ad called (again, this is a production title) *Liner*, which appeared on screens in the mid-1990s and was the first of a series (of three at the time of writing). Although these advertisements are exemplary instances of their kind, they are by no means untypical. Indeed, I have chosen them precisely because they so vividly illustrate the characteristics and features of the digitally produced advertisement of the late 1990s.

Reflections is a minute long and is made up of the sequential juxtaposition of eight dissimilar scenes: a communications satellite orbiting the earth; the taking of a wedding photograph; a glass-blower at work; a grandfather and grandson admiring trophies; a car in an automatic car-wash; a young woman arranging the interior of a new home; a diver working on a deep-sea platform; and, finally, a mother and child shopping in a far eastern city (old and new Hong Kong). Each scene ends by introducing the image of a flying eagle. This is integrated into the iconography of the whole as a reflection in the surface of an object

Figure 4.1   Stills sequence from the TV advertisement *Reflections* (1992)
Source: Courtesy of Eagle Star.

central to the scene itself (the one exception to this being the new home scenario, where the eagle is reflected as a mirrored shadow). A musical theme, catchy and atmospheric, both popular *and* classical (evocative of grandeur and security) accompanies the unfolding images. Several of the scenes have sound affects in addition to music. At the end of scene eight there is a concluding section in which a male voice-over speaks the words: '*Every minute of every day, Eagle Star opens eight insurance policies for people all around the world. Eagle Star covers your world.*' A spinning jumble of blue fragments combine to form the Eagle Star corporate logo: the silhouette of an eagle, wings outspread, perched on the peak of a mountain. Beneath this appears the legend 'EAGLE STAR COVERS YOUR WORLD', and the advertisement ends.

Such bald description, however, belies the sheer audiovisual intensity of this text, which has clearly been constructed for maximum visual impact. Despite its length the advertisement is both structurally complex and, in terms of its imagery, densely textured. A sophisticated visual logic at the level both of colour and graphic and spatial articulations operates throughout. The recurrence of circular/spherical and semi-circular/hemispherical objects in similar spatial locations within the frame, sometimes from shot to shot and scene to scene, sometimes in delayed visual 'echoes' of such spatial figures, is one example of the latter.[6] Whilst there is no tight symmetry to the pattern of colouring from scene to scene, there is a preponderant use of certain colours above others, and a complex hierarchical reorganisation and recombination of them occurs continuously. Gold, for example, clearly operates as a key colour throughout, both as an element in the formal rhetoric, and as a symbolic signifier, with connotations of security, warmth, maturity, wealth and so forth.

Such overall patterning or dispersed clusters of patterning bring a certain unity to the disparate scenes that constitute the ad. Through a systematic manipulation of colour (intensification and hierarchy); a certain editing rhythm (making the scenes more or less equal in length, controlling the direction of movement both within and between scenes); the repetition and play of certain spatial figures (the circle/sphere and the diagonal line); and through a direct play throughout on the theme of reflection and mirroring (always culminating in the repeated figure of the flying eagle), diverse and normally disconnected representations of various aspects of 'our' world are unified at a formal level.

Computer imaging is crucial to the extraordinary visual and rhetorical impact that is manifest in the ad overall, playing an important part in the fabrication of the scenes themselves. It contributes, for example, to the effect of heightened image brilliance through colour modification and image manipulation, the production of wholly convincing simulations such as the opening satellite scene and quasi-impossible shots such as that in the wedding photo scene. However, in this instance – as in so many other adverts of the same stamp – digital imaging adds a new dimension or register of visual interest and ambiguity. This occurs through the computer fabrication of the highly arresting images of the reflected image of an eagle in flight.

Fabricating the super-photographic

Here the computer becomes indispensable, not only with respect to technical realisation, but also in the sense of aesthetic and symbolic impact. Without these shots the ad would be severely impoverished, for they instantiate the *central* trope of the text at the level both of image and symbol. The flying eagle figure recurs in differing ways as the culmination of each scene; it is one further way of connecting or associating the otherwise dissimilar components of the ad. At the same time the eagle image provides a neat way of tying 'Eagle Star' directly, distinctively, and yet, not too obviously, into each of the disparate scenarios. Producing scenes in which the reflected image of a flying eagle appears, leads in every case to strange, impossible and near-impossible image conjunctions. In addition to the rhetorical or associative connotations with Eagle Star itself, this figure is also the text's 'unexpected' or 'magical' element, spectacular and fascinating in a number of ways.

There are clear echoes of surrealism in these meticulously fabricated conjunctions. Superficially, they are reminiscent of certain works by the painter Réné

Magritte, wherein a realistic visual style is used to depict scenes involving familiar, everyday images, and yet, because of the 'impossible', 'illogical' or 'irrational' conjunctions of these images within the paintings, a kind of subversion or confounding of recognition is achieved.[7] However, although the realistic character of the 'impossible eagle' image conjunctions in *Reflections* may be reminiscent of Magritte, the character of the conjunctions themselves are not. Whereas Magritte's work about painting and resemblance deliberately *encourages* reflection on the nature of visual representation, the ad *checks* the potential for such musings (for a fascinating discussion of this dimension of Magritte's work, see Foucault 1983). It does this by an overriding adherence to a realist logic of surface accuracy at the level of the image which strives to efface the illogicality of the scenes and, additionally, through a rhetoric at the symbolic level that ultimately ties it to the realm of mass consumption.

Yet there still remains a certain incongruity, and a peculiar *hyperrealist* aspect to these particular images. Although in one sense the recurrent trope of the reflected eagle is coextensive with the spectacular character of the rest of the imagery in the ad, at the same time it transcends this, coming to typify moments of arch-spectacle and visual stimulus. As a figure it is an extremely exotic manifestation: at its most potent, perhaps, in the reflection on the satellite antenna, though no less surprising when it occurs in extreme close-up on the visor of the deep-sea diver or in the mirrored glass of the skyscrapers in the Hong Kong business district.

Ambiguity attaches itself to these images in way that it could never do with, for example the computer imaged scenes in the Smirnoff ad, *Liner* (see pp. 97–9). For unlike the scenes in the latter, the shots in question here provoke the response, 'Are they recorded or contrived?' They *must* – so the viewer feels, and despite their photo-realism – have been *put* there somehow: certainly, one of the shots is impossible and could never physically occur to be cinematographically recorded in the first place. As for the rest, one cannot really be sure. The high fidelity of the imagery is there for all to see. Is this not a film of a *real* eagle and its reflected flight across the latticed face of the skyscrapers, or following in perfect perspectival distortion, the curved reflective surfaces of the car bonnet, windscreen and roof? Indeed, one might forgive the innocent spectator who decides that some of the shots are 'genuine', that is to say recorded, whilst others have a more dubious provenance.

Such *ambiguity* constitutes a particular instance of the quasi-cryptic character of the text overall. Indeed, one might argue that it is precisely the opposition of the recorded and the contrived, the genuine and the false – the paradox of the natural and the artificial which lies at the heart of this techno-aesthetic. The incongruent character of the eagle–object relation is the direct result of juxtaposing the image of an eagle with man-made objects and environments. An eagle, one of the rarest and wildest of birds, reflected in the mirrored-glass windows of a city skyscraper is without doubt an eye-catching image. Indeed, this is doubly so when the depiction is rendered with such perfect, that is to say, photographic, verisimilitude. Yet, it is precisely the virtuosity of the artifice involved in capturing such an unlikely occurrence that throws doubt upon the veracity of such scenes. Moreover, along with this visual hook and the uncertainties it carries with it, comes the knowledge that as the text is an advertisement, then playful, gorgeous, opaque or not immediately understandable imagery is very much to be expected.

Image simulations such as the eagle figure under discussion here would be impossible were it not for the novel techniques of 3-D computer modelling, texture mapping, digital matting and so forth. Of course, I am not implying that such 'impossible' image combinations have not been attempted before. Rather, what is so fresh about these images is their ultra-analogical character: the fact that they succeed in producing filmic imagery by means other than cinematography. And, the way in which, in so doing, they *surpass* their model medium, not only by beginning to 'photograph' the impossible, but also by being – to adapt an expression from Baudrillard – more photographic than the photograph, more filmic than the film. The implications inherent in this new means of image production, given the strong iconic character of contemporary advertising, becomes clear: the computer begins to offer a way of producing imagery that has both a powerful immediate impact and the potential for extended experimentation with new forms of visual rhetoric and stimuli.

Beyond this, one might claim that *Reflections* is a hybrid text, operating through borrowed rhetorical, formalist and realist codes.[8] Of course, when combined, these elements suffer some distortion and undergo certain transformations such that the resulting text – tied to the world of objects and consumption – functions in an extremely novel way. In *Reflections* the poetic aspect – a conjunction of symbolic and formal figuration – is hardly self-sufficient, reference to the world in the form of reconstructed scenarios taken from everyday life underpins its operation. These scenes may themselves be extremely idealised, in this case, heightened (even impossible) forms of the actuality shot or photographic image, but ultimately, nevertheless, they refer to the real world of commerce, domesticity, technology, work and so forth. The way they do so, however – hyper-realistically and through a complex rhetoric that is set in play within and around their imagery – does seem to point to something new in what may be termed the 'poetics of consumption'. Although this was developing well before computer imaging entered the scene, certainly, as this early example shows, the kinds of digital and computer assisted techniques now being employed have produced a qualitative leap in the iconic wrapping of such poetics. In other words, these new techniques are greatly aiding the production of rhetorical re-descriptions of the world that are simultaneously both more convincing and increasingly outlandish and bizarre.

Stylised hybridity or the tamed surreal

Liner – a much remarked upon advertisement for Smirnoff vodka and first seen some four years after *Reflections* – reinforces this claim. It also marks the continued trend to ever greater image-centredness in advertising – particularly that at the higher or luxury end of the consumer scale. In keeping perhaps, with the somewhat different character of the commodity being advertised here, *Liner* is a more markedly stylised text. In an attempt to produce the nostalgic evocation of an era of luxury and decadence, a kind of Art Deco retro styling – the image of an image of the past – is used to return us to life aboard an ocean-going luxury liner in the early decades of this century. The 60-second scenario which makes up the ad involves the movement of a steward as he carries a bottle and glasses on a silver platter through the ship to customers on the upper deck. This passage through the ship provides a platform for a series of startling and fantastical image scenarios, all of which are constructed around the same figure or trope. As the steward passes different people and objects the spectator is treated to a close-up view through the bottle he is carrying. The idea of distortions produced by viewing something through glass is here turned into a device for the production of startling metamorphoses and fantastic image shifts.

There are ten such moments in the ad: they involve a flower turning into a Venus Flytrap, a fox fur turning into a fox, a smoker turning into a fire-eater, a necklace turning into a snake, a trunk becoming a jack-in-the-box, a couple turning into a dominatrix and her client, two male passengers turning into penguins, galley stairs turning into the keys of a piano, a brunette turning into a blond and, finally, the ship's cat turning into a panther. A popular tune of the time – *Midnight and a Rendezvous* – is being sung over these scenes and there are several incidental sound effects (of a crowded bar, a glass being put down, a lighter being lit and so on). Apart from the words of the song, the only other verbal information comes right at the end when we finally see, in close-up, the label of the bottle itself.

Again, the main part played by digital imaging in this text is in the fabrication of the central device – the through-the-bottle image metamorphoses. These marvellous, 'impossible' transformations only work as such because of the possibilities for increased levels of imperceptible image fabrication (montage and image manipulation) that the computer has enabled within the realms of photography and film.[9] The opening shot sets the scene and arouses expectations of what is to follow. It involves the first of a series of meticulously choreographed motion-controlled camera movements. These enable close-up and unbroken camera movement past and around objects and facilitate the perfect compositing and subsequent manipulation of disparate imagery. In this instance, the camera pulls out from a close-up on an Art-Deco style image of an ocean going liner, revealing as it does so that the image is on a menu. The camera continues to travel – still in extreme close-up – past a vase of red flowers in front of which stands a bottle. Clearly visible through and beyond the bottle as the camera passes is one of the flowers, this then turns into a Venus Flytrap. As the camera pulls back from the bottle the Flytrap closes – the continued zoom out reveals that the bottle is standing on a tray on a bar and is about to be picked up by a steward.

Ultimately, what makes such ephemeral and otherwise trivial shots so spectacular is the manner of their rendering. The fact that the camera is moving as these surprising image substitutions are taking place and that they are always viewed in close-up reinforces their ironic (paradoxical) verisimilitude. However, just as significant in this respect is the transparent or undetectable nature of the image transformations – which are in effect novel forms of image combination or montage – as the camera passes in front of the bottle (and vice versa). The impression that all this is occurring photographically, which is to say *as if* in the real time and space of cinematographic recording (so-called 'profilmic space'), simply intensifies the absurdity.

Like the exhibited retro style of the ad itself, the central trope is put on display in a way that is reminiscent of the spectacle involved in early cinema. No one can doubt that trickery and special effects are implicated here, for the events depicted *as if* they had been recorded are for the most part physical impossibilities. Bound to the rhetoric of the text itself, which links drinking Smirnoff vodka to a challenging change in one's perceptions of the world and one's place in it, these astonishing *image-events* elicit both awe and delight.

This foregrounded use of digitally fabricated image effects has become progressively more self-conscious with each new ad that Smirnoff has commissioned in this particular series. The ad that followed *Liner* (production title: *Wedding Reception*) has an out of place and somewhat bored guest at a wedding reception livening things up for himself by deliberately using a bottle of Smirnoff to achieve similar effects to those produced in the earlier text. Thus, as the guest singles out other guests to look at through the bottle the viewer assumes his point of view and witnesses the amusing transformations that people undergo when perceived in this way. These images are in every way as remarkable as those they succeed; indeed, if anything, they tend to be more ambitious and nowhere more so than when the smug guest, catching sight of himself in a mirror, decides to apply the bottle trick on himself: the point of view shot reveals – to the surprise and horror both of the guest himself and we, the viewers – his transformation into a hideous, slavering ghoul.

The ultimate ad in the series – working title *Smarienberg* – involves a self-conscious reference both to the trick effects of the previous ads and, perhaps even more pointedly, to the current dominance of special effects in the cinema. It is a fast-paced, action-packed, non-narrative *pastiche* involving a range of references and allusions. These run the gamut from 'chic' thrillers of the Luc Besson variety, through Bond movies, to 'high-tech' effects-laden science fiction. A sly reference to the elliptical character of films such as *Last Year at Marienbad* underpins such reference at the level of overall form. Clearly, an inordinate amount of digitally based image production has gone into this technologically dense text, which from beginning to end is just one intense – and knowingly so – burst of dazzling special visual effects. Some of these reduplicate those used in the previous ads, though there are many additional ones.[10] Significantly, no matter how bizarre, the scenes are all rendered in the same seamless and photo-realistic manner: here hyperrealism is implicated not just in the representation of the fantastic, but also – in a manner resembling the doubling process occurring in *Toy Story* – in the representation of 'the already represented'.

Neo-montage

Unlike the Eagle Star insurance ad, the *photographed impossibility* involved in the Smirnoff series does not produce the ambiguity: 'Photographed *or* fabricated?' It is clear – despite their verisimilitude – that in the latter the scenes are contrived. Yet the central role of digital techniques here – as in countless other advertisements produced in the 1990s – revolves around the production both of seamless image combinations and of photo-realistic image simulations. At the aesthetic level these produce modalities of imagery which, though not altogether new, are, nevertheless, unprecedented in the qualitative leap that has occurred in the perfection of their production and rendering with the development of digital techniques. In particular, as we have begun to see, long-standing techniques of image montage are being overhauled and endowed with new capabilities (see chapter 6).

We are used to associating montage with modernist art practices, particularly those of the historical avant-gardes who were the first extensively to adopt and explore such techniques. However, the device was also subsequently incorporated into the burgeoning media forms of post-Second World War, post-industrial culture. Advertising was among the first to use domesticated forms of modernist montage, photomontage and collage, both in its 'still' and 'moving' image forms. At the end of the twentieth century, montage had received a massive boost through the emergence of digital imaging techniques. TV and cinema advertisements now rely on the extended forms of montage that the computer is able to effect to deliver condensed, meteoric, moving image texts with an extraordinarily high degree of visual impact and novelty. The splices and staccato edits of traditional montage still appear in such ads, although, vying for prominence, are elaborate shots and imagery that strive to hide their provenance in discrete or separate image elements. Thus, as we have seen, shots are constructed which, in spite of defying the logic of recording, nevertheless appear utterly naturalistic and fundamentally photographic. Similarly, ads are constructed upon the conceit of one continuous though impossible take. Here, it is *as if* the constantly travelling camera has been endowed with super-physical capabilities: zooming seamlessly from the microscopic to the life sized.[11] Much of the time this imagery far exceeds that from which it has been drawn (i.e. its original image sources or models): it is ultra-detailed, exaggerated – *hyperrealistic*. There can be no doubting the enormous power to arrest and delight the eye that such 'impossible photography' possesses.

In advertising – as elsewhere – the computer is increasingly being used because it is the technical means through which recombination, copying, pastiche, brico-lage can be most easily facilitated and achieved. Digital montage is introducing a new register of naturalism and verisimilitude to one of the most artificial and rhetorical forms of visual textuality in contemporary culture. As advertisements become more image-centred, so their essentially ambiguous character seems to increase in direct proportion. Having long since lost any importance as transmit-ters of hard information about the use-value of goods, advertisements have become more and more abstract in their representation and symbolisation (Jhally 1990 offers a persuasive account of how this has occurred). Persistently asserting themselves as representing the very core of our lives, ads remain highly appealing yet bewilderingly detached from real life experiences, for, ultimately, their images are impossible to live up to – forever beyond our grasp. The meanings they resonate are abstruse, indeterminate and vaporous.

However, whether or not contemporary advertisements contain such rhetor-ical messages, and whether or not viewers successfully decode these hardly seems to matter anymore. Excitement or captivation by a dazzling display of imagery produced by the latest means of technical alchemy may function just as well (see Figure 4.2). Much of this has to do not so much with the scenarios themselves, as with the ways in which the images were achieved, that is, with the dazzling virtuosity of the illusionism itself. In rhetorical texts of this sort, where meaning is allusive and frequently elusive too, the association with 'high-tech' imaging (special effects and its current connotations) and the product or brand name, may carry just as much importance for the viewer/consumer in terms of identification as the rhetorical meanings in the text itself. Indeed, the *association* of a service or product with the pleasurable *effect* – of delight, fasci-nation, bedazzlement – occasioned by particular instances of marvellous, fantastical, spectacular images and image forms, may well be the predominant way in which such image-intensive advertisements as those under discussion here do their work. Increasingly, advertisements – and this certainly applies to the growing corpus in question here – seem, as much as anything, to be about surface, style or form for its own sake. Significantly, it is frequently only at the end of such 'dazzling displays' that we learn the name of the product concerned. Of course, on subsequent viewing of the same ad, this can be trig-gered much earlier by the imagery itself. Yet, it is no accident that advertisements do not have titles. We supply our own – 'Saab', 'Renault', 'Persil', 'Yoplait', 'Smirnoff', 'Esso' and so on – the latter come to stand for the imagery in which the ads are wrapping them. In this respect digital imaging is (for the time being) a crucial new means of producing advertisements that stand out from others. An important consideration given the incessant stream ('flow') of images in which they reside and both the necessity and the problem of repe-tition: the ever increasing number (and choice) of images being broadcast, and the fact that (in Britain at least) advertisements are shown together 'back to back' in groups of five to ten in any one slot.

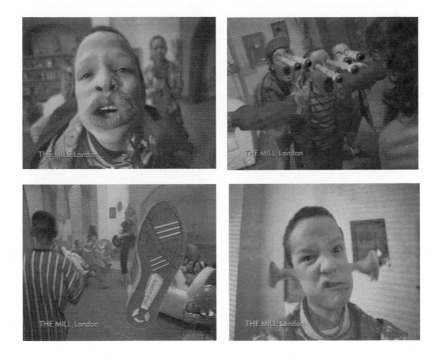

Figure 4.2 Stills sequence from the TV advertisement *Cool for Cats* (1992)
Source: Courtesy of BMP DDB/National Dairy Council.

Simulation and hyperrealism, in the senses in which these terms have been understood here, are not, of course, exclusive to digital animation and TV advertising. As we shall see in the next chapter, they have a continued presence in spectacle cinema and its cousin, music video. If, however, they are not as pronounced in the latter, where other elements are often more prominent in the production of diversionary spectacle, in the former their presence highlights yet another dimension of the importance they have assumed in contemporary visual culture. For, tied directly to the particular aesthetic of *realistic-ness* or verisimilitude that characterises live action Hollywood feature film, these terms help to describe a process of second-order imaging which is both continuous with and distinct from that involved in computer animations. Here, the photographic is not only the object to aim for, but rather the ground wherein such work takes place, and this, coupled to the conventional peculiarities of live action itself, alters the ways in which hyperrealism manifests itself.

5

THE WANING OF NARRATIVE

New spectacle cinema and music video

The clearest manifestation of the renovation of spectacle within late twentieth-century visual culture is the so-called 'blockbuster' film: technologically dense and laden with special effects, such films are, arguably, the principal emblem of the recent turn to image and form. The blockbuster has been firmly established as a deliberate and pivotal commercial strategy within Hollywood since the 1970s – with films such as *The Exorcist* (1973), *Jaws* (1975) and *Star Wars* (1977) cited among early examples (see, for example, Schatz 1993). However, it is from the mid-1980s that a clear trend, based squarely upon a revitalised resurgence in special effects techniques becomes discernible in the production of these high budget and intensively media-hyped movies. This impulse has, undoubtedly, been prompted and underpinned by various developments in digital image technologies. Such films, early examples of which include *Alien* (1979), *Blade Runner* (1982), *The Last Starfighter* (1985), *Robocop* (1987), *The Abyss* (1989) and *Total Recall* (1990), are texts that tend more and more to give spectacular imagery and action equal status with narrative content and meaning. As we start the new century the extraordinary growth of this kind of film shows no sign of slowing down. On the contrary, though such films still only constitute a small percentage of the overall output of mainstream cinema, they nevertheless invariably capture most of the pre-release publicity and continue to generate most of the profits.

This chapter comprises an exploration of the aesthetic character of current modes of spectacle through a closer examination of such mainstream digital cinema and one of its important correlates: music video. I shall suggest that both mass cinema and music videos – or, at any rate, the important groupings within them that concern us here – exemplify, in their rather different ways, a shift at the visual aesthetic level to formal preoccupations and excitations. That is, they involve the elevation to prominence within mainstream visual cultural practices of formal attributes in and for themselves: the prevalence of technique and image over content and meaning. The kinds of mass cinema and music video discussed below are primary examples of a distinct space that opened up within mass visual culture in the last decades of the twentieth century. In this space (introduced in chapter 3) the chief aesthetic *modus operandi* involves recursive modes of self-reference (both backwards and sideways) to already existing images and image forms.

The introduction of digital technologies into the production processes of the forms in question here is enabling the development of this new sense of *formalism*, and this is happening in ways that are both complex and diverse. In particular, different kinds of spectacle are manifest within each of the genres under discussion – a fact which, to some extent at least, is related to the different ways the same digital imaging possibilities are aesthetically deployed. Thus, positive reception of the films of mainstream digital cinema depends as much on a *fascinated spectator*, immersed in dazzling and 'spellbinding' imagery, as on identification with character and the machinations of plot and theme. Computer imaging techniques have assumed a central authority in this new mode or genre. Both directly and indirectly, they are introducing important and distinctive registers of *illusionist spectacle* into the cinema, as evidenced in such 'technological thrill' films as *Terminator 2: Judgment Day* (1991), *The Mask* (1994), *Speed* (1994), *True Lies* (1994), *Independence Day* (1996), *Starship Troopers* (1997) and *Titanic* (1997) (to name but a few). The modes of special effect or *trucage* mapped with such precision by Christian Metz in the late 1970s are now being stretched and overhauled with the emergence of digital techniques of image fabrication (see Metz 1977). Currently, the business of 'astonishing the senses', which Metz attributes to the 'avowed machinations' of special effects within classical cinema, is mutating. In so doing it threatens to overwhelm traditional concerns with character and story. In the kind of films at issue here, elevation of the immediately *sensuous* constituent vies with our usual means of entry to symbolic meaning, i.e. narrative. This does not mean that narrative content or ideological significance disappear in such films (see, for example, Tasker 1993), rather that this new dimension of visual display is now so distinctive that it requires recognition and analysis as a formal aesthetic element in its own right.

Music video shares with digital cinema (and computer animation and TV advertising – discussed in the previous chapter) the same thrust towards forms of textual production that are constructed upon an intensification and augmentation of modes of image combination or montage. In this respect, however, it is closer to TV advertising, for it is *hybridity* that defines the character of music videos at the level of cultural form. This is manifest at the level of individual texts through the pervasive manner in which tapes freely refer to and incorporate other styles and types of image, as well as forms and models from other media. Unlike the cinema, music video manifests its 'eclecticism', its 'intertextual references' through a veritable profusion of styles. The digital cinema tends to mask and contain its rediscovered penchant for montage and its recurrent recourse to borrowing from and referring to other texts within an illusionist aesthetic. Music video, on the other hand, does no such thing. Exultantly and overtly, it displays a diverse array of imagery and styles – frequently within the same tape. This tendency to capriciously copy, replicate and combine has intensified in music video over the relatively short period in which it has become established as a cultural form. Clearly, digital imaging techniques have been greatly enabling to this process. Indeed, they have begun to contribute new forms of imagery based upon image simulation and combination, delivering even greater visual intensity to these playful and ephemeral texts.

Spectacle and the feature film

The notion of spectacle is somewhat difficult to discuss precisely because of its non-verbal character. Nevertheless, in critical studies of the dominant cinema institution, centred upon analysis of classical narrative films, attention has most frequently focused on the 'tension' between the narrative dimension and the visual dimension, that is, between identifying with characters, being absorbed in a fictional world and following the plot on the one hand, and the pleasures involved in looking at images on the other. Of course, much of the pleasure of looking, particularly in the classical Hollywood cinema, is derived from the striking impression of hidden observation inscribed within its peculiar 'invisible' mode of story telling. The satisfying feeling of power involved in looking in, unobserved, on someone else's life-world; of being visually close to characters (even to the extent of seeing through 'their' eyes); of surreptitiously 'entering' their story space, safe in the knowledge that one won't be found out – this is certainly *one* source of pleasurable looking in the cinema (see Metz 1976).

However, although this pleasurable looking of the story space or of the world of the fiction may be predominant in classical Hollywood, it is not the only way in which looking is mobilised – even there. Within the development of the cinema it was narrative drama that eventually came to define its classical (dominant) model, not some other form based on a more sustained 'exhibition' of the visual itself. Yet, within the classical mode an array of tensions between narrative and the visual have been muted. If, ultimately, the spectacular aspect has always been viewed as subordinate to and in a sense subject to the control of a repressive narrative logic, this is precisely because spectacle is, in many respects, the antithesis of narrative. Spectacle effectively halts motivated movement. In its purer state it exists for itself, consisting of images whose main drive is to dazzle and stimulate the eye (and by extension the other senses). Drained of meaning, bereft of the weight of fictional progress, the cunning of spectacle is that it begins and ends with its own artifice; as such, spectacle is simultaneously both display and on display.[1]

It is variously argued that the visual aspect of narrative cinema is imbued with the potential to undermine or disrupt the spectator's primary subordination to narrative motivation. The sabotage of meaning through the sheer captivation of powerful images lurks beneath Hollywood's productions, threatening the cohesion of fictional or diagetic illusion. Most frequently, perhaps, this has been argued in relation to the problems posed by images of women in the films of classical Hollywood (see, for example, Mulvey 1975; Mellencamp 1977). However, it might analogously be argued – though far less specifically – that a similar propensity, one, moreover, with similar effects, has operated at the more general level of *mise-en-scène* itself.

Certainly, the technical virtuosity employed in the production of spectacle has constantly functioned to halt and disrupt narrative flow and – intentionally or otherwise – to draw attention both to the image and its fabricated character. The musicals associated with Busby Berkeley, wherein women are physically assimilated into the kaleidoscopic *mise-en-scène* of the lavish and elaborate camera-choreographed musical numbers, are clear and oft cited instances of this. Common, if somewhat more subtle examples of the same impulse include the extraordinary lighting and framing styles that occur in the films of so-called '*film noir*', or the 'artificial' (non-realistic) lighting and colour styling in a film such as *Written on the Wind* (1956) – indeed, the peculiarities of visual stylisation attributed to Hollywood melodrama generally. Similarly, historical films and biblical epics offer up the possibility for moments involving extravagantly staged panoramas and displays. Musicals, as already indicated, provide the chance for interludes or scenes containing highly stylised costumes and set design.

Undoubtedly, one of the clearest manifestations of this element has occurred through recourse to special effects.[2] Here, once again, technical expertise frequently functions to produce, precisely, both spectacle and recognition of artifice itself. The extraordinary character of such imagery no matter how 'invisible' and technically opaque, nevertheless calls attention to itself and to its place within a particular aesthetic system: it is astonishing both for *what* it portrays and for *how* it does so.

Along with the musical it is in genres such as the horror film, fantasy and science fiction that earlier forms of spectacle-based entertainments – part of the tangled heritage of Hollywood – resurface to disturb and trouble the narrative cause. I am thinking particularly of traditional forms of popular spectacle such as the circus and the theatre of illusion and magic. For here it is the *staged* combination and display of exotic, strange and incredible events, actions, objects and characters that takes precedence. True, the virtuoso display involved in the visual effects of horror and fantasy (then as now) operated under the particular regime of narrative realism that distinguished the Hollywood style generally. Still, as David Bordwell points out, such acts of '[s]howmanship' entail, 'to a considerable extent ... making the audience appreciate the artificiality of what is seen' (see Bordwell *et al.* 1985: 21). Special effects, particularly in the more *outré* of the Hollywood genres, frequently functioned both to produce astonished looking and to exhibit their own fabricated and conventional character. Indeed, we may surmise that this occurred even when the spectator remained puzzled as to the precise ways in which a particular image effect had been produced.

New effects, new spectacle

There are limits, however, to the use of overt visual display in Hollywood films of the studio era. For Bordwell – here discussing classical Hollywood generally, '*digressions and flashes* of virtuosity remain for the most part motivated by narrative causality ... or genre. ... If spectacle is not so motivated, its function as artistic motivation will be *isolated and intermittent.*' (Bordwell *et al.* 1985: 21, my emphasis). Ultimately, what is of overriding importance in the classical Hollywood film is the spectator's primary subordination to narrative motivation. However, in the Hollywood of the late twentieth century, so-called 'New Hollywood' – or a certain section of it to be more precise – this no longer seemed to be so. The notion of controlling or regulating the tension between narrative and image, as I have already intimated, has taken on an ever greater importance with the recent growth of special effects driven films. Indeed, particularly in recent 'technological thrill' films, where heightened forms of image and movement now figure so prominently, the conception that film equals narrative, which predominated in the classical era, appears now to have been all but superseded. No longer 'isolated and intermittent ... digressions or flashes of virtuosity', the new digitally licensed visual and action effects have now become the predominant aesthetic characteristic of such films. As such they elevate certain of the principles of the classical Hollywood style such as, 'mimesis, self-effacing craftsmanship and cool control of the perceiver's response ... ', whilst at the same time privileging motives of spectacle over those of narrative (Bordwell *et al.* 1985: 4).

Of course, these movies are still narrative in form, it is just that the story told is no longer the principal reason for going to see them.[3] Critics and reviewers may continue to appraise such films in terms of traditional narrative values such as depth of character, machinations of plot and narrative coherence. However, if, as is so often the case, they find them wanting in this regard, then this may well be because they are attempting to use evaluative categories that do not apply to the extent they once did. For in such films it is precisely new kinds of formal concern, tied to the emergent space of intertextuality (introduced in chapter 3), and centred upon the imaging of action, imagery and imaging itself that is at the forefront of their aesthetic operation. In this important strand of New Hollywood, traditional narrative containment of spectacle has crumbled in a manner that is quite unprecedented.

Spectacle cinema: digital effects

Let us take a closer look at that recent trend in mainstream live action film production which, from the mid-1980s, has based itself on a resurgence of special effects techniques: a revitalised resurgence that has been prompted and underpinned by various developments in digital imaging technologies. I shall concentrate on the path-finding films *The Abyss* (1989) and *Terminator 2:*

Judgment Day (1991) as well as more developed examples from the canon such as *The Mask* (1994), *Independence Day* (1996) and *Starship Troopers* (1997).

With respect to these films (and numerous others belonging to the corpus), it is no exaggeration to say that there is barely a scene between them which, in one form or another, does not involve special effects techniques in its construction.[4] Whilst computer imaging techniques are assuming an ever increasing importance in these new spectacle films, they nevertheless still function as one element within an *integrated battery* of visual effects. Having said this, however, I want to stress that it is the digital element that is introducing an important *new register* of illusionist spectacle into such films. Indeed, the increasing centrality of digital imaging techniques within this kind of film (and increasingly also within live-action cinema generally) is symptomatic, in a further sense, of the current shift at the aesthetic level to formal preoccupations and excitations.

Assuming a certain familiarity with the films under discussion I shall tend to concentrate on specific scenes or extracts, indicating through examination of specific examples just how and what computer imaging is contributing to this novel current within mainstream cinema. In this regard, one of the key films is *Terminator 2: Judgment Day*, which, more than any before it, helped to consolidate the centrality of digital image processes within the mainstream feature film. It was not just the use of computer assisted effects that this film perfected and promoted, more significant still was its substantive use of computer generated imagery. *Terminator 2: Judgment Day* pointed the way to a new means of producing a distinctive mode of spectacle involving imagery originated by computer.

If *Terminator 2* finally convinced Hollywood that digital cinema was both aesthetically feasible and potentially highly lucrative, one of the films pointing the way to the sheer density of the digital imagery in this and subsequent films within the corpus was *The Abyss* – produced a year earlier. Particularly important here is the only scene in *The Abyss* to employ computer synthesised imagery. This is a sequence occurring about halfway through the unfolding drama, it involves a computer generated 'alien probe' – a so-called 'pseudopod' consisting of sea water – entering an underwater exploration rig and making contact with its human crew. The duration of the scene is a mere 5½ minutes of the film's overall running time (140 minutes), whilst the total duration of shots containing computer generated effects is barely 1 minute. Still, it provides one of the most engaging moments of spectacle in the whole film – no mean feat when one takes into account that the film itself is crammed from beginning to end with special visual effects, all of which are calculated for maximum visual excitation.

'Photographing' the impossible

It is worth dwelling for a moment on this example, looking both at what it does and how it does it, for it is the paradigm for much of what was to follow. What makes this scene so astonishing? It is the way in which the computer has been used to produce (and to assist in producing) an extraordinary example of what Metz describes as a 'perceptible but invisible *trucage*' (1977: 664). Specifically, the computer has been used to produce the effect of photo-realistic representation in a scene that is conceptually fantastic in character – a scene that could have no direct correlate in real life.

In this instance the computer was called upon to represent the image of a fantastic object, a sentient liquid tentacle, an alien probe. Given the serious dramatic tone and overall realism adopted, this thing had to convince: both in its visual aspect and behaviour and in the way in which it integrated and combined with traditional live action (high definition, high fidelity) cinematography of settings containing live actors. In order to do this the image was called upon to achieve a high degree of technical success on three levels of established cinematic transparency. Thus, despite its fantastic nature, the pseudopod itself had to look and behave in a convincing and credible manner. This involves surface or descriptive accuracy: naturalism. At the same time as distinguishing itself as other (alien) in relation to the human characters and the fictional world, the pseudopod must appear as *indistinguishable* at the level of representation, that is to say in its representational effect. It had to appear to occupy – to be ontologically coextensive with – the same profilmic space as the human actors. This involved the seamless combining of two differently realised sets of realistic imagery: of which one is properly analogical, i.e. photographic, the other seemingly photographic, i.e. digital simulation. Additionally however, it must also integrate, again in a perfectly seamless manner, into the *diegetic* dimension: the story space. In order for this to occur an exceptional amount of pre-planning had to enter into the carefully orchestrated decoupage that eventually stitches the shots together. Here, finally, surface accuracy is subordinated to the rather different codes of narrative illusionism.

The eventual goal of such carefully orchestrated editing, coupled with the high degree of mimetic accuracy of the imagery in the conceptually fantastic nature of the scene itself is the establishment of a powerful visual illusion: the visual resemblance of reality – an analogical effect – even in scenes of the utterly fantastic. It is precisely this effect of *impossible photography* that constitutes the dimension of spectacle in the scene. We begin to see very clearly in this early example one possibility for representational development that is released when 'photography' is cut loose, uncoupled from its physical ties to phenomenal reality. Of course, the potential for irresistible and astonishing visualisation *already* apparent in this scene from *The Abyss* has since been amply developed, initially in *Terminator 2: Judgment Day*, subsequently in films such as *Independence Day*, *The Lost World* (1997) and *Starship Troopers*.

Verisimilitude becomes spectacular

Beginning with *Terminator 2* subsequent films in the corpus have built upon the computer synthesised imagery first used so convincingly in *The Abyss*. This new modality of mainstream cinema is comprised of films that entail new levels of 'technological density'. Often this manifests itself on two levels: in the subject matter itself, and through means of image construction. Just as significant though is the new aesthetic that such films have engendered. Before looking a little more closely at what this involves I want briefly to say something about what has taken place in the decade or so since *The Abyss* was first released.

Whereas photo-realistic computer graphics are used in just the one scene in the late 1980s film, in *Terminator 2*, produced only one year later, there are over forty shots involving computer originated imagery dispersed in scenes throughout the film. This is because, for the most part, they are used to realise certain aspects of one of the central protagonists – the extraordinary T-1000 Terminator. At different points in the narrative, T-1000 – a 'cyborg' composed of liquid metal – is required to display transformation into and through different stages of its physical make-up (i.e. from amorphous blob of liquid metal to human replica) as well as further facets of its fantastic metamorphosing and shape-changing abilities. Needless to say, the scenes in which these things occur are visually rendered with the same photo-realistic accuracy as the scene in *The Abyss*, although in other respects this imagery differs in terms of the increased levels of complexity and sophistication involved.

We need only recall scenes involving this 'liquid man' in *Terminator 2* in order to indicate the extraordinary character of the imagery contrived for the film. About a quarter of the way in, in one of the many scenes involving direct confrontation between the two Terminator cyborgs – model T-800 (played Arnold Schwarzenegger) and the new improved model T-1000 (played by Robert Patrick) – a thrilling chase takes place inside the basin of a concrete flood canal. The scene culminates in a miraculous escape for the T-800 and the boy he is trying to protect, when the huge truck driven by the T-1000 speeds out of control, crashes into a bridge support and bursts into flame. The T-800 departs with his charge, safe from the single-minded determination of the T-1000 – the scene does not end here however. To crown the breathtaking spectacle, to which the viewer has already surrendered him/herself, computer generated imaging now comes to the fore. Out of the conflagration and striding towards the camera as it slowly pans left is a shining metallic figure. As it nears the camera the spectator sees it slowly metamorphosing from a featureless metal humanoid into the form and features of the actor playing the role of the T-1000 patrol cop.

At a point later in the film, the malevolent liquid-metal cyborg is at large in a mental hospital intent on pursuing its victim by capturing the latter's incarcerated mother. During yet another sustained action sequence in which the viewer watches with incredulous fascination this evil Terminator transforming itself into both objects and people in its dogged and terrifying attempt to complete its mission, an event occurs that is even more astonishing than anything that has occurred in the sequence thus far. Spotting its victim in a small group of people behind a locked, metal-barred gate at the end of a long hospital corridor, the Terminator – transformed once again into its cop disguise – strides purposefully down the corridor towards him. From the victim's point of view and in close-up we watch the cyborg approach the gate, pause momentarily then, still staring intently ahead at its victim, it moves forward. As it does so, the bars begin to pass through its face, head and shoulders (the only parts of its body that are in shot). As if composed of a heavy liquid such as mercury the T-1000's body allows the bars to pass through it, only to reform and reconstitute itself as its passage through them progresses. Needless to say, this event – digitally fabricated – is represented with an extraordinary degree of photo-realistic accuracy. The shots depicted in these scenes are in close-up and medium close-up, and they are graphically displayed within the shot, rather than disguised or merely suggested in some way by editing.

Terminator 2 exhibited unprecedented levels of verisimilitude in its avowed intent to marry convincingly digitally manufactured animated figures with live action (analogue) imagery – perfecting and elaborating techniques first realised in *The Abyss*. Other films since have used the techniques perfected in these films to create further examples of such impossible photography. In films such as *Jurassic Park*, *Independence Day* and *Starship Troopers*, for example, such techniques are used in scenarios which, though involving high (if varying) degrees of fantasy, similarly aim for a measure of classical realism in their overall affect. These films revolve around scenes of fantastic spectacle involving photographic mimesis, for example, a sequence in which a colossal alien spacecraft looms over the Empire State Building and then proceeds to totally obliterate it (*Independence Day*); scenes in which Tyrannosauri and other prehistoric animals run wild in both natural and human habitats (*Jurassic Park*); and shots of a sea of insect-like aliens swarming into attack or seen in ferocious and bloody individual combat with human soldiers (*Starship Troopers*).

Once again, these scenes are spectacular as much for their sheer transparency – the convincing way in which they render images of such fantastic events – as for the events themselves. They simulate photography of the fantastic, offering us the semblance of a moving photographic image of the impossible. In other words, these digitally rendered images seem real, they appear to have the same indexical qualities as the images of the live action characters and sets with which they are integrated. This is particularly pronounced in scenes that involve a certain intimacy in terms of point of view. Thus the increasing perfection of computer image synthesis *and* the ability – again via digital techniques – to seamlessly marry what would previously have been impossibly complex movements and actions, has enabled startling effects to enter the realm of the *close-up*.[5] I do not want to deny the other dimensions of these and like images, the way they represent and the questions of what they denote and connote.

However, I am concerned to emphasise as the dominant aesthetic feature this *game with spectacular illusion* that is taking place in the films of the new spectacle cinema.

The live action basis of such films has become more and more saturated in its artifice with computer image synthesis and with a host of other special visual effect techniques (many of which ultimately depend upon computer assistance for their success). In terms of the tonalities of spectacle involved, it is possible to make a broad distinction between the uses to which different kinds of effects techniques are put. Thus computer image synthesis can be grouped with animatronics, puppetry, make-ups and prosthetics, whilst the other group includes techniques involving models and miniatures, special sets and mock-ups, pyrotechnics and so forth. The former are utilised much of the time – either in conjunction or immediate juxtaposition – to produce photo-realistic imagery (usually of the most bizarre nature) that involves close-ups and medium close-ups, in scenes involving a relatively 'intimate' relation to live protagonists. The latter are more frequently used in scenes of epic or larger scale actions: that is, in sequences which also involve the use of long and panoramic shots.

Such scenes – at least by comparison to those involving the first group – are less bizarre, and may be viewed as attempts to produce highly exaggerated or rhetorical sequences which, all the same, are designed to display a kind of naturalism associated, ultimately, with documentary imagery (the Lumière tradition). The scenes associated with the first group on the other hand, whilst striving for analogical or mimetic accuracy, nevertheless represent characters, actions and phenomena that are thoroughly impossible (Méliès). Whatever the nature of the spectacle, however, and of course there are degrees and hybrid conjunctions of both (cf. *The Lost World, Independence Day* and *Starship Troopers*), then travelling mattes, motion control, blue or green screen and optical composites – the transparent cement of such seamless image combination – are definitively associated with the production of both.

A film such as *The Mask* on the other hand represents another strand of the corpus. It deploys techniques of computer image synthesis to rather different ends: humour and pastiche are central to this film. Ultimately, however, the digital techniques lead to a similar effect. Instead of using the computer to simulate live action cinematography, *The Mask* uses it to introduce techniques of graphic exaggeration such as 'squashing and stretching' – aesthetic techniques of the classical two-dimensional cartoon – into the 'three-dimensional photo-reality' of live action film. This produces extraordinary (and paradoxical) imagery whereby corporeality and verisimilitude gets injected into the graphic hyperbole of the cartoon aesthetic: impossible photography – yet of a different stamp. For here it is *as if*, inconceivably, the bizarre characters and worlds of Tex Avery cartoons and the comic strip hero have, in some kind of grotesque transmutation, come to life and been acted out before the camera lens.

111

Sutured excess: the paradoxical effect

With these examples in view let me return to my claim that films such as these represent something of a shift relative to traditional mainstream film aesthetics. This turns upon a kind of surfeit or *superfluity* that is directly related to the technological density of the imagery itself. The spectacle involved here does not just depend upon the extraordinary, outlandish, exotic and epic character of the events portrayed. In addition we must take into account the naturalism with which they are rendered, their indistinguishability from photo-reality: in terms of the way they look or appear and the undetectable way they are assimilated into shots and the narrative as a whole.

These films demonstrate that efforts to produce 'live action' cinema by means other than photographic recording are proceeding apace. At the moment, however, given the remaining limitations of the technology, this 'drive' has to be content with an increasingly complex, seamless *integration or blending* of computer and other visual effects within live-action based scenarios that are baroque and outlandish. And the possibility of their undetectable integration into an 'ordinary' *mise-en-scène* grows with the advances which follow each new production of the former kind. We need only recall here the portentous aerial shots in *Titanic* (1997) – shots that operate *as if* taken from a helicopter flying around the boat. For example, movement from an image of the boat speeding over the ocean towards the viewer then up and above the ship's prow, or sweeping over the whole length of the boat itself, revealing as it does so the ship's architecture and passenger life in astonishing detail.[6]

At the same time such films throw into relief a peculiar form of reception, encouraging an engagement with illusionistic image texts that operates no longer solely through traditional modes of interpellation, i.e. the 'willing suspension of disbelief', identification (with both camera and character), absorption in the fictional, though meaningful, world. Pleasure and gratification can now involve a different positioning: a knowing fascination with the play of intertextual reference and – at the same time as surrendering to the sensational delights of image and action – with the analogical perfection and spectacular application of such referentially uncoupled imagery itself. Imagery which, despite its seamlessness and its perfect illusionism, nevertheless offers itself for a kind of perceptual play with its own materiality and the artifice behind its fabrication. The *signifier* itself is here accorded as much weight as the signified.

One feels compelled to ask – and attempt to answer – what, more precisely, it is that constitutes such films as texts of realist or illusionist spectacle. In relation to cinema history, it would appear to be the so-called 'trick-film', first associated with director (and former conjurer/illusionist) George Méliès that introduced this tradition of visual 'magic' or illusion into the cinema. However, if there is a direct line leading back to Méliès and the trick film in the new digital effects spectaculars, there are echoes just as strong coming from other (opposing) directions. Ultimately, perhaps we have to view these new kinds of text as hybrids. Thus they evince both the potential for the 'marvellous' – which Méliès first saw and developed in special 'trick' effects – whilst, at the same time, displaying an overriding commitment to the dominant and 'naturalised' cinematic tradition which involves, to use Burch's expression, 'the Recreation of Reality' (1990: 6).

Indeed, it seems appropriate at this point to introduce the notion of *surfeit* or *excess*. Kristin Thompson (1981: 287–302) introduces a notion of cinematic excess, in her response to writing on the subject by Roland Barthes and Stephen Heath.[7] In this interpretation, excess is understood as a dimension of cinematic textuality that exists in all films. It revolves around both the physicality and the fabricated nature of films themselves: excess is comprised of all those diverse elements in a film that escape its unifying structures: unmotivated stylistic elements, indeed, everything which is *extra* to narrative function on the visual (and audio) plane. At the level of the image (though not only at this level, of course), classical narrative film has striven – for the most part – to deflect the spectator's attention away from such aspects as these, precisely through modes of address or reading that privilege concentration upon thoroughly motivated diageses. Those aspects of the cinematic text to which Barthes draws our attention relate to the superfluous, the chance, the incidental, that is, precisely to the *non-motivated* actions and appearances in various forms and combinations of actors, make-up, props, costumes, sets, locations and the like. Although these elements are present in classical Hollywood, they nevertheless tend to escape our attention – or, at best, only touch it, tantalisingly and fleetingly – because of the coercion of motivation that its particular form of narrative causality involves (see Barthes 1977). However, as Thompson says, 'the minute a viewer begins to notice style for its own sake or watch works that do not provide such thorough motivation, excess comes forward and must affect narrative meaning' (1981: 290).

Describing the operation of excess, Thompson says 'the material provides a perceptual play by inviting the spectator to linger over devices longer than their structural function would seem to warrant' (1981: 292). It seems that something not altogether dissimilar is occurring in the corpus of films under discussion here. By comparison with classical narrative, the sheer density, richness and dazzling character of the visual perceptual field in such films is far greater, the propensity for excessive detail correspondingly higher. As I have already indicated, such films represent a renovation and intensification of the potentially disruptive power of spectacle within narrative. The contradiction – ever present in special effects – between knowing that one is being tricked and still submitting to the illusory effect is operative here. Yet, particularly (though certainly not solely) in those scenes involving computer imaging discussed here, the more photographically perfect or convincing the images, the more – paradoxically – does their sutured and suturing aspect seem to recede and their fabricated character come to the fore. In these moments of heightened spectacle (within films that are already spectacular), the sheer perfection of the simulation encourages a curiosity or fascination with the materiality and mechanics (artifice) of the image itself, which tends to wrest it even further from narrative subordination. Indeed, because of the new imaging capabilities of the computer, increasingly this takes place in sequences that are more intimately integrated than ever before into the diagetic action itself. The tension between narrative and spectacle occurs, not only as segments of narrative redundancy, but also and increasingly in scenes that are part of the diagetic thrust. The 'pseudopod' scene in *The Abyss* is a case in point, though in recent examples such as *Starship Troopers* this occurs throughout – becoming relentless.

Trickery – the duplicitous character of the image – along with its status and operation as such, is no longer subordinated to narrative function. Fascination with the synthesis of visual illusions is one further symptom of the intense self-referentiality that now defines most forms of mediation. Now, the references of images are as likely to be other images (of other images) as first-order attempts at direct representation. However, the extraordinary lengths to which those involved in this kind of film production go in order to achieve illusionism or transparency in moving images is in inverse proportion to the spectator's incredulity. And the latter's curiosity as to how it was done is akin to that evoked by the spectacle involved in aspects of stage magic. This fascination involves a focus on details: elements of particular sequences, actions and images, which, even when they are part of the diagetic momentum, nevertheless vie with the latter for the perceptual attentions of the spectator.

Ultimately, of course, one has to wonder whether or not the intense forms of spectacle present within these 'technological thrillers' are strictly of a piece with the 'unmotivated', 'non-unifying' or strictly 'non-functional' elements that Thompson discusses as excess: concerned, as she is, primarily with a film that exists outside of the aesthetic conventions of the dominant film institution. My concern though, is the homologous way in which the spectacular scenes under discussion might be said to signal, in a manner similar to excess in Thompson's sense, the emergence and promotion of new developments in mass entertainment forms; that is to say, shifts at the level both of production and consumption that are displacing traditional concentration on narrative form and understanding. The growth of spectacle, and the fascination with image as image, in the sense both of visual excitation and technological density (artifice), is one indication that attention to *formal* facets – means and pure perceptual play – are finding a place within mass entertainment forms. One might then wonder – strange though this may seem – whether popular films such as the ones under discussion here, thereby share something in common with experimental or avant-gardist films that also downplay or even oppose narrative. The differences, however, revolve around the ways in which the excessive is foregrounded in each mode. For if it is the materiality of film (grain, focus, splices and so on), and/or the formal characteristics of the image (colour, tone, movement, etc.) that is concentrated upon in the one, in the other, it is spectacle – the image – itself enabled by techniques such as computer image synthesis which, paradoxically, attempt precisely the opposite, that is, the dissembling or covering up of those features foregrounded in the former. And this in order to produce a realism that is more transparent than ever before, a realism committed to the illusionistic representation of the impossible: a *super-realism* given over to rendering the fantastic with the surface accuracy associated with photography.

The mimetic accuracy and the seamless character of the computer synthesised imagery discussed above is in keeping with the illusionist aesthetic that predominates within New Hollywood generally. This illusionism, however – and this is particularly obvious with regard to scenes that involve computer image synthesis – is somewhat like the Eisensteinian artifice that Barthes describes: 'at once falsification of itself – pastiche and derisory fetish, since it shows its fissure and its suture ...' (Barthes 1977: 58). In the films in question here it is the bizarre nature of the imagery, rendered so faithfully, that similarly *denies and simultaneously points to* the highly sophisticated artifice involved in its production. It is *both* the bizarre and impossible nature of that which is represented *and* its thoroughly analogical character (simulation of the photographic), that fascinates, produces in the viewer a 'double-take' and makes him or her want to see it again, both to wonder at its portrayal and to wonder about 'just how it was done'.[8]

When the computer becomes capable of rendering imagery of 'the everyday world' with the same degree of mimesis and transparency to that it is presently achieving with respect to the 'wonderful, chimeric and monstrous', then we may well wonder what the resulting confusion between the indexical and non-indexical image will have on spectatorship and representation. For the moment though, the computer generated and assisted scenes of the new blockbuster cinema, are producing new registers of displayed virtuosity and formal engagement.

Music video: spectacle as style

Since the early 1980s music video has been firmly established as a significant cultural form: the latest addition to the pop music industry's perennial concern with 'the image' and images (see Goodwin 1987a). Music video brings together and combines music, music performance and, in various ways, a host of other audiovisual forms, styles, genres and devices associated with theatre, art, cinema, dance, fashion, television and advertising. Some of these have always been associated either directly or indirectly with pop, others have a more recent association. However, in music video these elements appear to combine with recorded music and musical performance in a new and *distinctive* way (see Wollen 1988). In this sense music videos are one of the most thoroughgoing forms of that dimension of contemporary visual culture that rests on an aesthetic of *displayed intertextuality* (see chapter 3). The definitive *hybrid* character of music video is manifest at the level of individual text through the

115

pervasive manner in which tapes appropriate and incorporate images, styles and conventions from other types of image and image form. Music video is implicated in a process of mutation involving the breaking down and redefinition of conventional boundaries (see, for example, Aufderheide 1986; Goodwin 1987b; Kaplan 1987; Wollen 1988).

One important enabling factor in this process is digital imaging. Indeed, the use of different computer imaging techniques has existed within music video production since the early 1980s and their use and significance has grown enormously within the form since then. They have been a central factor in the thrust towards the production of tapes that are constructed upon an intensification of modes of *combination or montage* of different kinds, styles and forms of imagery. This has resulted in an aesthetic that, whilst continuous with the cult of the image, surface and sensation characteristic of digital visual culture generally, has, nevertheless, produced its own distinctive miscellany of loose groupings, models and tokens. What, for the most part, these share in common is a propensity to frustrate attempts at categorisation along traditional lines. Thus asking whether a particular tape is illusionist or anti-illusionist, realist or anti-realist and so forth tends to be rendered meaningless, primarily because these texts are so thoroughly self-referential. That is to say, because their primary reference is already existing media models, image forms, circulating star discourses, and so forth, they largely escape a referential or representational logic.[9] Furthermore, music videos make little or no pretence at hiding their eclectic media saturated dependence on other forms. They are definitively and conspicuously *about* image: about creating an image for a sound, a performer or performers, and (as often as not) for a performance. The self-reflexivity of music videos stands in marked contrast to that of spectacle cinema. Narrative is even less important to their make-up, whilst 'laying bare the device' is no longer an indirect outcome of a fetishistic concern with the fabrication of surface accuracy, rather a (largely undeclared) principle of production.

I will concentrate in the following brief discussion on three 'classics' of the genre: Neneh Cherry's *Manchild* (1989) and Michael Jackson's *Black or White* (1992) and *Ghosts* (1996). With respect to digital imaging these tapes display something of the rapid technical developments that have taken place throughout the short period they cover. In aesthetic terms, each exemplifies – albeit in an exaggerated manner – some of the particular (and familiar) directions taken by the music video in its 'eclectic', 'combinatory' and 'intertextual' pursuits. Thus, *Manchild* is an early example of a peculiarly *decorative* mode of neo-spectacle that has become a constant of the music video genre or form. *Black and White* is a prominent instance of the conspicuous formal heterogeneity that music promos frequently display. Whilst *Ghosts* – which takes horror fiction film and associated special effects techniques as its object of formal play – manifests yet another aspect of such undisguised or knowing borrowing.

116

Style: the decorative image

The setting for the action/performance in the music video *Manchild* is highly contrived: a flat, sandy beach on which, in the middle ground, is a clothesline with a few items of washing. A film of water (a patently superimposed element) covers the surface of the beach reflecting the clothes and washing line. The sky is a saturated blue with wispy white clouds and tints of purple. The sea and sky – with the same breakers constantly rolling in and the same cloud pattern drifting across the screen – is on a cycle: it is the same piece of film repeated over and over again for the duration of the text. The sea itself is tinted an unnatural electric turquoise. This patently artificial set or 'stage' is itself a composite: the film of water covering the beach and the clothes line have been superimposed over the treated and cycled footage of the beach, sea and sky.

Against this backdrop we see the performing figure of Neneh Cherry who, most of the time, is on screen miming to the song. It is the way both Cherry's performance and the actions of the other figures – another woman, two children (a boy and a girl) and two male youths – are represented that makes the greatest contribution to the novelty of the visual aspect of the tape. There are several features to this: the sea-sawing motion of the whole setting within the fixed frame, such that the horizontal of the horizon (where sea meets sky) swings continuously and rhythmically approximately 40° with each up and down movement. The choreographed *layering* of the actions of characters over the initial composite set and over each other, such that on occasions one and the same character appears on the screen at the same time, performing the same or different actions on the same or different depth planes. The use of off-screen space and the frame edge to produce novelty and surprise in terms of when, where and how figures and their actions are introduced – in particular in terms of distance from the camera, that is, whether in extreme close-up, medium or long shot. Finally, one must mention the look of the figures themselves – their make-up, the mannered style and colour of their dress.

New techniques of image production and manipulation are here employed to effect innovative ways of visualising musicality. In other words, the velocity and rhythm of image combination, layered cycles and repetitions (reiterated and varied) is determined by the song's structure and by formal elements such as melody, beat and tempo. The complex patterning thus produced tends to engage not at the level of representation (and signification), but rather at the level of abstract, formal play. It is the *syntactic* and *ornamental* rather than the semantic and referential that predominate here. Indeed, this is reinforced by the fact that the instrumental musical accompaniment to the singing always takes place off screen (i.e. as 'non-diegetic' sound 'off'), never becoming part of Cherry's visual performance. This only serves to reinforce the concern with 'image', both in the sense of visual impressions and stimuli, and the representation of a public persona. If depth exists in this text, then it does so principally as a visual trope in its overall visual economy. The visual style, characterised by the artificiality of the setting and its unnatural pastel colours, the affectation and/or chic modishness of the costumes, and the posing of the figures, is ultimately decorative – flash and filigree.

Given this foregrounding of the visual and the demotion of representational meaning as traditionally conceived (i.e. realism, narrative), it would appear that extra-textual factors come into play to a significant degree here. The visual dimension is opened up not so much to representation, more to identification with the *feelings* (mood, affect) produced by a certain sound – 'Neneh Cherry' – and the style and aura attached to her circulating star persona (see Figure 5.1).

There is more, however, for *Manchild* belongs to a particular corpus of (loosely) related music tapes in which certain features are preponderant at the level of the image.[10] The defining characteristic of this trend turns upon the use of multiple image overlays and repetitions. Frequently this involves utilisation of the same imagery at different depth planes: the repeated and 'depth-cued' recycling of the action of figures and objects within the scene. It is not the signified, in terms of a representational or narrative logic, but the *disport* of signifiers that forms the dominant and perhaps defining aesthetic feature of this 'sub-genre'. What this particular playful manipulation of the image depends upon, of course, is the greater ease afforded to the production of such effects by the integration

Figure 5.1   Stills sequence from the music video *Manchild* by Neneh Cherry (1989)
Source: Courtesy of Virgin Records Ltd.

of the digital computer into video production and post-production technologies. As commentators have already pointed out, the result is an aesthetic based upon dense and complex forms of spectacular, playful and *rococoesque* image effects.[11] Such texts are designed to encourage multiple viewing on the part of the spectator, the formal tropes and devices, and the *mise-en-scène* produced being just too elaborate to apprehend in a single screening (see, for example, Hayward 1991a).

It is important to note here how far this aesthetic – though enabled and encouraged by many of the same fundamental digital imaging techniques – nevertheless deviates sharply from the kind of 'astonishing of the senses' involved in the attempted synthesis of what I have called 'the impossible photograph'. Although there is undoubtedly a sense in which a video such as *Manchild* might also be said to display a certain newness at the level of visual aesthetics, it does so in a very different way to, say, the eagle trope in the advert *Reflections* (see chapter 4), the dinosaurs in *The Lost World: Jurassic Park*, or the *Titanic* in *Titanic*.

Utilisation of (many of) the same techniques could not have resulted in forms that are more diverse. For here we have texts that foreground technique *not* through the fabrication of impossible illusion, but through perfected forms of *conspicuous* image juxtaposition and re-cycling. Of interest here is the way in which the computer provides for the complex choreography of multiple image overlaying, re-cycling and mixing, thereby enabling the emergence of an aesthetic that involves a kind of *intra-textuality*. Indeed, it seems that a central element of the 'sub-genre' or cycle of which *Manchild* is but one example, is the way in which the technique involved produces a kind of involution. Thus, from a limited number of original images, stylistic features and actions, a text is constructed or organised through their continual and varied recombination (layering and cyclic repetition). The slightly varied and potentially endless or recursive play of reiterated and repeated actions and motifs within the visual channel is itself reminiscent of the kind of regulated musical variation that typifies pop music generally.

The trend or cycle represented by *Manchild* is *not* by any means the only way in which the computer is enabling novel developments within the music video form. I end this chapter with a short discussion of two further examples, both of which are similar to *Manchild* in terms of their visual compulsion, yet each in its own way is very different in its aesthetic character. *Black or White* and *Ghosts* both contain strong extra-textual references to media myths about their featured performer, Michael Jackson – myths that were prominent in subsidiary modes of circulation at the time each of the tapes was released. It is not this aspect of these videos, fascinating and significant though it may be, that is of primary interest here, however. Rather, I am concerned to look at the aesthetic form of these tapes with an eye primarily on their potent visual efficacy.

119

Formal heterogeneity: 'montage of attractions'

Like myriad other music videos, only more so, the image track of *Black or White* is formally heterogeneous: made up of a variety of forms and approaches involving different kinds of live action, animation, video and digital technique. Narrative fiction, documentary (archive footage) and various forms of staged performance, coexist with cartoon animation, three-dimensional animation, as well as new digital techniques that blur established categorical and conventional distinctions. This use of different techniques and forms produces a text involving a veritable profusion not only of kinds of image but also of kinds of image combination.

Thus, taking the latter first, there are seamless, digitally engineered dissolves such as that which freezes dancing live action figures, and, without a cut, fixes them as dolls inside a toy ornament. There is a long, spectacular travelling take which opens the tape – again produced by digital means: a seemingly unbroken first-person point of view zoom from flight high above the clouds to entry into a suburban home. In the scenario inside the home itself, narrative editing of a classical kind is used. Yet, at the same time, in-frame compositing is a distinctive feature, for example, in the Statue of Liberty sequence, where both the background and the dancing Jackson are matted in, or in the scene of the singing/performing Jackson superimposed over archival footage of burning crosses and similar imagery. Whilst, as a final example – and at the time the most striking kind of image combination of all – there is the digitally engineered transformation scenes, where extreme head and shoulder close-ups of singing faces metamorphose into different people and Jackson changes into a panther. Add to the above the fact that the shifts between the major scenes or segments of the tape itself produce similarly conflicting or conspicuous juxtapositions, and the overall sense is one of fragmentation and diversity at the level of the image channel. The tape as a whole is distinctly non-narrative in its decoupage, and, if anything, is more akin to the editing style associated with the more radical tendencies of avant-garde cinema. There is a continual displacement of time and space that contrasts markedly with the verisimilitude and continuity of classical audiovisual forms.

The main scenes are only partially unified by the music track with its intended themes of children, multicultural and multi-racial globalism and the performing presence of Jackson himself, for there is much that exceeds this. The inordinate formal density of the tape and the hybridisation of (previously) incongruent styles and conventions involved, is produced by an allusive intertextual play arising from a mélange of different techniques and their attendant forms and visual styles. Thus, the suburban street we fly down at the beginning is reminiscent of the then recent film, *Edward Scissorhands* (1991), and the family drama that precedes the song alludes to both the TV sitcom and the soap opera. Throughout, the tape incorporates different forms, genres and styles, and there are references and allusions to other kinds of text. These range from the nature and anthropological documentary, through advertising and the musical, to – in the dance performance scene at the end – *film noir,* horror (indirectly – *Nightmare on Elm Street*) and cartoons (directly – *The Simpsons*).

Of course, all of the above entails, as well, a complex diversity of visual styles: a rich and clashing weave of pattern, shape, texture, of setting, costume, action and colour. All of which adds to the impression of contrast and conflict at the formal level. Indeed, the tape calls to mind the idea of the *extravaganza* and a notion coined by Eisenstein to describe his first experiments in the theatre, a kind of 'montage of attractions'. The senses are assaulted with a profusion of incongruent images, styles and conventions, meanings partially emerge and are cancelled or replaced by different ones, or are overtaken by the distractions and fascination offered up by the simultaneously complex and fleeting character of the imagery itself.

And yet, despite all this, there is a definite thread of unity here. It is carried by Jackson's performance, the song itself, and the attempt to tie the whole together via return at the end to the family context: a direct mirroring of the introductory scene, only this time it is a cartoon father (Homer Simpson) who is attempting to impose his distaste for Michael Jackson's music upon his son. In terms of form, therefore, it would be incorrect to attempt to associate *Black or White* too closely with either modernist avant-gardism or popular realism. It is, rather, a complex hybrid, displaying formal and stylistic features that are characteristic of both, but ultimately producing an overall impression which is very different to either.

Perhaps the most engaging facet of this visual extravaganza – indeed, at the time it was its newest attraction – are image sequences produced by what was then a recently perfected technique of digital imaging called 'morphing'. This is a technique that enables the on-screen metamorphosis of one live action figure into another. *Black or White* used this to striking effect, producing further distinctive examples of what I have referred to as 'impossible photography'. Thus we witness a 'simulated recording' – a 'live action photograph' – of someone changing into a panther, and an extraordinary sequence in which live action head and shoulder shots of people of different races and sexes metamorphose in real time one into the other whilst miming to the title song. If the novelty of this image effect already calls attention to itself as such, then the context in which it appears sanctions its use as a further instance of visual enticement.

Spectacle of a third order

By the time of the later promo – *Ghosts* – special effects are no longer just a means to spectacle. This visually arresting video is *about* special effects: trick effects are now essential to the 'self-reflexive', mannered character of the work itself. Using the horror genre as an entry point, the tape revolves around a kind of playful exposition of the fabrication of spectacle which then becomes a self-conscious or second-order form of spectacle in its own right. *Ghosts* implements and promotes the fabrication and operation of spectacle, whilst simultaneously disclosing it.

Ghosts is a veritable compendium of the history of cinematic trick effects. Indeed, for the most part the allusions are so direct that one can pinpoint the individual films in which they first occurred. Thus, the scene in which the ghosts walk up walls and dance on the ceiling is a latter-day elaboration of a trick that was first seen in films such as *The Ingenious Soubrette* (1902) (see Burch 1990: 228). Méliès' pioneering film *The Indiarubber Head* (1901) – the *Terminator 2* of its era – is clearly apparent in a scene where the unsuspecting and relieved mayor opens the door to leave and is confronted by a giant head filling the whole of the doorframe. In another sequence, one of the latest modes of computer animation, so-called 'motion-capture', is used to simulate a *skeleton* performing in the particular dancing style of Michael Jackson. Once again, there is an inescapable comparison to be made here with the Fleischer Brothers' cartoon *Snow White* (1933), which itself includes an arresting dance sequence involving their character, Ko-Ko the clown, metamorphosing into a long-legged 'strutting' spook.[12] The dance movement in this sequence is that of the jazz singer Cab Calloway and it was produced using the rotoscope technique, itself a direct forerunner of motion-capture.[13] Of course, the illusionism in the *Ghosts* sequence is far more convincing – following the drive to photographic perfection, it involves live action, three-dimensionality and the camera moving freely around the dancing figure. Nevertheless, there is a sense in which ultimately the effect is the same: a highly individual dancing style is transposed to a most unlikely recipient. More recent allusions include the sequences depicting the creation of the ghosts from 'ectoplasm', which are directly rendered using the techniques of computer image generation first developed in *The Abyss* (see pp. 106–7). New, so-called morphing techniques, used to such great effect in *Black or White*, and later in such films as *The Mask* and *Terminator 2*, figure prominently, alongside and in conjunction with the stunning use of prosthetic techniques, themselves so important to the history of the horror genre.

So convincing is the use of prosthetics here that one is completely confounded when one of the central characters – the mayor – a 'straight' middle-aged, large-built man, wearing a grey suit and spectacles is 'possessed' and begins to dance in Jackson's inimitable style. Only in the remarkable credit sequence that ends the tape does the viewer discover that the mayor was played all along by Michael Jackson himself. Indeed, this final sequence is absolutely indispensable to the aesthetic import of the tape as a whole. For, as the title song is replayed the credits role over scenes that systematically expose the ways in which the illusions and tricks seen in the tape itself were fabricated and achieved. Thus we are given direct access to the production process itself: alongside shots displaying the use of the blue screen stage, and the use of motion-capture, are sequences showing the laborious work involved in building the various prosthetics for the characters Jackson plays. Intercut with each of these is a repeated sequence from the scene in the tape in which they are employed.

In the true tradition of 'distantiation' and 'laying bare the device', *Ghosts* not only plays parodically with a currently dominant mode of representation – in this instance, spectacle cinema – it also exposes the fabricated character both of its own fabulous effects and, by implication, those of others in the genres to which it refers. However, the peculiarity here is that this work is primarily about nothing other than signifiers: a 'star image', image as image and the means of fabrication. Reference to anything beyond image – 'representation' in an earlier sense – has definitively disappeared. In this respect, *Ghosts* is more than just an exemplary instance of neo-spectacle and surface play within music video: it seems somehow emblematic of the whole aesthetic ordering discussed both in this chapter and the one that precedes it – the perfect ensign for the so-called 'age of the signifier'.

6

THE DIGITAL IMAGE IN 'THE AGE OF THE SIGNIFIER'

The last two chapters took a closer look at the aesthetic make-up and operation of several of the constitutive expressions of digital visual culture. They describe in more detail how computer animation, certain TV advertisements, music videos and 'blockbuster' films exemplify a kind of 'neo-spectacle'. I was concerned to draw attention to the specific ways in which the digital image is taking its place within and is constitutive of aesthetic forms that are markedly distinctive from their counterparts of thirty years ago (where they existed). Here, whether consciously or otherwise, images *excite* and/or draw attention to themselves as images, whilst concomitantly skewing representation – in the traditional sense of that word – being, in the first instance, more *about* (prior and coexisting) styles, forms and genres.

Of course, and as we have begun to see, this is not straightforwardly so. Nor do I want to be misunderstood as arguing that mass visual culture is now completely a spectacle or sensational culture. Clearly this would be incorrect. Yet I do want to support the observation that a significant aesthetic space or preserve has now opened up within mainstream visual culture that is largely given over to surface play and the production of imagery that lacks traditional depth cues. Imagery that at the aesthetic level at least is only as deep as its quotations, star images and dazzling or thrilling effects.

The tendency to what I call 'surface play' manifests itself in different ways: it exists as a dimension within mass visual culture generally, but – and thinking specifically here of digital integration – it also has more localised or specific expressions. I began to probe some of these in the preceding pages, seeking to show within the forms at issue some of the specific – and now extensive – ways in which digital image making is both enabling and stimulating this aesthetic preoccupation with signifiers and their formal arrangement. Indeed, I shall continue this close aesthetic exploration in the next section, particularly when looking at computer games and new forms of simulation experience – only there, the discussion will be framed more directly through the lens of spectatorship.

Here, I step back slightly from the rather close interrogation of chapters 4 and 5, to consider more generally how all the forms of visual digital culture

124

under consideration relate to this new aesthetic space: the 'culture of the copy' or – to borrow a phrase from Jameson – 'the age of the signifier' (Jameson 1992: 162). If the forms of visual digital culture are themselves exemplars of this distinctive space, then how might they be further distinguished – in terms of aesthetic understanding – from preceding moments and their cultural-aesthetic regimes? Referring at different moments to examples from our constellation – digital cinema, TV advertising, music videos, computer games and special venues – I shall introduce and explore debates revolving around the notions of *repetition*, *montage*, *authorship* and *genre*, looking at the way in which these concepts, so central to the aesthetics of the technological media forms of the twentieth century, figure in understanding the aesthetic dimension of contemporary visual culture that interests us here.

Repetition as the measure of visual digital culture

For the most part, the new features of contemporary culture that revolve around repetition and its allied concepts have been discussed in relation to established forms such as film and television (see, for example, Baudrillard 1983a, 1990: 63–97; Eco 1985; Calabrese 1992: 27–46; Jameson 1992: 9–34). The following is a brief rehearsal of the discussion, paying more attention to digital cultural forms. I revisit the notion here, because I want to underline its relevance *as a framing or structural concept* that is inextricably tied to the aesthetic character of the genres and expressions at the centre of this discussion.

Repetition is a notion that carries enormous import for grasping what it is that makes the visual culture of the late twentieth century so distinctive. Tied to the consolidation and phenomenal evolution of technological reproducibility within visual cultural production, repetition – together with the string of inter-related concepts that it helps to generate and sustain – is an inescapable fact of mass cultural practice. However, the kinds and levels of repetition existing within contemporary culture are in certain respects markedly different to those that existed in earlier cultures and periods.[1]

Technological reproducibility (first mechanical and then electronic) involves repetition as replication. The ability to produce sets of identical copies of works by technological processes brings with it far reaching implications, first cogently explored by the critical theorist Walter Benjamin (1973). Mechanical repro-ducibility, in the sense in which Benjamin was concerned with it, implies a sense of repetition as (potentially indefinite) copying or replication. As he is concerned to point out, it tends thereby, to confound notions of art founded on ideas of the unique, the original, the individual work. Thus the fact that we can make many identical copies (prints) of a particular film, means not only that more people get to see it but also that as a work it is thereby made less precious. Indeed, Benjamin looked forward to what he thought were the democratising potentialities inherent in these developments.[2]

Repetition in terms of the copy or replication has grown phenomenally since

Benjamin first drew attention to it in the 1930s. Indeed, the serial production of identical objects based upon machine power carries the important, if rather obvious implication, that it enables the production of *more* of the replicated object than ever before. A crucial factor in the growing self-referential character of culture has been the accelerating growth and proliferation in the twentieth century of the development of new means of cultural production and in the reproductive capacity of those means. The ever increasing proliferation of signs, the rapidly evolving *seriality* that this entails is, I want to argue, a vital consideration in the increasing dominion that form and surface has assumed in many mass cultural aesthetic practices. What appears to be happening is that this phenomenal *quantitative* development of mass reproducibility is beginning to produce mutations with significant *qualitative* effects. New and increasingly convoluted kinds and levels of repetition are one symptom of this.

Serial forms

Thus, one effect of mechanical reproducibility involving repetition concerns the development of forms of seriality within the cultural domain in the twentieth century (see Baudrillard 1990; Calabrese 1992). Seriality is akin to genre (see pp. 138–140), and yet it is subtly different from it. The serial mode appears to operate and organise – in the first instance at any rate – at a more general or inclusive level than does genre, whilst at the same time being more precise or prescriptive in terms of the processes it defines. Lacking the more open (and involved) character of genre, it appears to be tied as much to the demarcation and regulation of *forms and modes* within material production processes as to the distinguishing of types or kinds (along with their delineation) in *aesthetic* ones. It seems thereby, to be more intimately bound to the standardisation involved in commodification itself. It may be that seriality is, in some sense, coming to replace or subsume genre in the more recent manifestations of mass visual culture, this, however, is something to which I shall return. For the moment I am more concerned to consider the functioning of seriality as a manifestation of the *repetitive impulse* released by mechanical reproduction.

It is with forms of cultural production that are actually referred to as 'series' and 'serials' ('the episodic serial'), that a more specific sense of seriality enters into practices of contemporary cultural production. This kind of seriality first begins to manifest itself in practices such as the publication of novels in regular periodic instalments in the nineteenth century; in the emergence of the comic-strip and related forms; and in certain instances of serialisation in photography and early cinema. Clearly, such types of seriality developed and multiplied on a massive scale during the twentieth century – a direct function of the continued development and growth of new means and forms of cultural reproduction. They involve a kind of repetitiveness which in certain respects is akin to that which Bruno Latour analyses in his short study of pre-scientific religious paintings (see Latour 1985). That is, although specific instances of a given series or

126

episodes of a particular serial are different from one another, they nevertheless rest upon a kind of repetitiveness that involves an inordinate degree of *iteration* and *similitude.*[3] Yet, unlike the pre-Renaissance regime of representation described by Latour, within which religious painting functioned, the suggestion is that today it is not *what* is repeated between given tokens of a series that counts for spectators, so much as the increasingly minimal differences in the *way* this is achieved (see Eco 1985; Calabrese 1992). Burgeoning 'replication', the repetition at the heart of commodity culture, forestalls the threat of saturation and exhaustion by nurturing a *homeopathic*-like principle of formal variation (i.e. based on infinitesimal modifications and changes).

Omar Calabrese sketches the close structural affinity between the serial forms of mass culture and the production of material commodities, by referring to the motor car. As he says:

> We have only to think of new methods of automobile production: a small number of structural invariables, known as 'basic models', a large number of figurative invariables, a very large number of regulated variables, and, finally, an extremely large number of so-called optionals, those small details that personalise the vehicle.
>
> (1992: 45)

Of course, the systemic manifestation of the serial within the forms of contemporary cultural production is an integral part of developments that are occurring at a more general socio-economic level. 'Modulation', 'stylisation', 'versions' of 'the latest model', these are marks of regulation and control within ever more intensified and systematised modes of commodity production, and they have come to dominate every sphere – culture included.

Representation dissembled

In addition to the recognition that something like a new 'poetics' of repetition might now govern the production and consumption of mass culture, others argue that the expansion and multiplication of seriality has now effectively made the idea of 'the original' a volatile one. As we saw in chapter 3, Baudrillard subscribes to such a view (see, particularly, Baudrillard 1996). From what he now takes to be a generalised condition involving the reproduction of 'copies' or equivalent tokens that lack any original, Baudrillard constructs the notion of the culture of simulation and the hyperreal. This – our present culture – exists and grows entirely through self-reference, definitively uncoupled from traditional notions of representation (which entailed such concepts as 'the referent', 'innovation', 'authenticity' and 'the new') (see also Jameson 1992: 17–21).

We have already begun to see in the preceding two chapters something of the significance that the mechanisation of repetition has for the character of contemporary cultural forms. Animation, Hollywood cinema, advertisements and music videos – all forms we explored in previous pages – are indeed, exemplary in this regard. Music video is particularly interesting here, not just because it is a relatively recent form but also because it seems to take repetition to it limits, both *within* its individual tapes and in terms of its overall or outward form. More than just an endless and regular stream of tokens, music video is repetitive through and through. To a certain extent this is reinforced (one is tempted to say amplified) by the musical basis of the form – particularly its insistent rhythmic character.[4] This, in its turn, has a tendency to determine the image track itself: the tempo of editing, regulation of the play (occurrence and recurrence) of iconographic, performative and other visual figures or tropes, colour and tone, and so forth. Whilst as a token of the form, expectations revolve precisely around music, length, performer/performance, images and, beyond this, perhaps, a certain affect or mood. Vitally though, and however we choose to describe it – 'marginal difference' (Baudrillard), an 'aesthetic of variables' (Calabrese), 'stylistic variation' (Jameson) – a principle of differential regulation operates here, as in all forms of mass seriality.

Consideration of the principle of differentiation within repetition (the 'selfsame') in music video must, however, take into account the 'uncoupled' and self-referential nature of the form. In common with the other genres of contemporary visual culture at issue here, music video exists as a form that refers primarily to other texts – something which, in this case, I have already characterised as an extreme eclecticism. Music video is part of an accelerating tendency to take already (re)produced signs themselves as the subject of reference or as material for 'new' or further instances of (audio) visual textuality. As a form constituted through repetition, music video lacks any concept of originality in the traditional sense. In Jameson's words, 'repetition effectively volatizes [sic] the original object – the "text", the "work of art" – so that the student of mass culture has no primary object of study' (Jameson 1992: 20). In which case we are left – in music video at any rate – with the concept of novelty understood as mere variation: a kind of formal play centred upon relativity. Hence, the constant 'raids on the image bank', the game of perpetual *recombination* and, wherever possible, the employment of techniques to turn such activity into virtuoso display.

When such variation is elevated to a mode of primary aesthetic regulation, it becomes easier to understand the place of digital imaging technologies within such processes. They serve as a further and vital component of modes of cultural production that are primarily preoccupied with formal concerns, functioning much of the time as restorative aids to further bolster the aesthetics of marginal difference that now comprise much of visual mass culture. The new techniques become tied to the preoccupations of variation and accentuation inherent within ways of remaking, repeating, imitating, recombining and suchlike; providing (at least for the time being) highly impressive and sophisticated ways of combining and recombining, of animating, copying and manipulating. At the same time, these new techniques draw attention to the artifice involved in the visual image itself, further helping to displace reflection upon the substance or significance (such as it is) of that which is being depicted. In this way, technique itself becomes a crucial element in the armoury of superficial formal variation located at the heart of many mass visual forms.

The genres and expressions of visual digital culture under discussion do not escape the shaping pressure of the repetitive and serial aspects of contemporary culture. This is not to say, of course, that they manifest this subordination in exactly the same ways: the overall effect may be similar but there are – as we have already begun to see – variations in the manner in which this is realised. Even fields such as computer games and simulation rides, which are the most recent and appear to depend more on the novelty of the technology itself, are – as we shall see in coming pages – just as much subject to this aesthetic of repetition. They may involve new formal elements – the much vaunted 'interactivity' and 'immersion', for example – and these may well affect their individual aesthetics. However, just as much as the more established forms, they also seem destined to operate within the logic of self-referentiality and the preponderance of the 'depthless image'. All are manifestations of an altogether new dimension of formal concerns that established itself within the mass cultural domain of the late twentieth century, helping to constitute both cultural forms and practices of production and aesthetic sensibilities.

Montage and the digital image

The digital techniques entering contemporary fields of image production are furthering the expansion and refinement of an elliptical culture of image and form: a culture of surface play. One important way in which this is occurring is through the computer's prodigious potential for copying and simulation. We need only think of examples already explored in this respect – in contemporary cinema, animation and advertising – to remind ourselves of this. Just as crucial however, indeed, perhaps even more so, since it is both part of the copying ethos and also operates separately from it, is the role digital technology is playing in the area of *image combination*. So central is this to current aesthetic practices within the forms at the centre of this investigation that I shall take a few pages here to explore it further.

I want to examine the relevance of the new imaging techniques associated with the computer to the dichotomy – prevalent for much of this century – between modes of aesthetic realism on the one hand and an aesthetics of anti-realism on the other. Broadly speaking, the former is associated in the first instance with the industrial, commercial development of (mass) cultural forms, and the latter, with the practices and forms of modernist art. The suggestion is that in many ways the computer functions to consolidate (and further develop) contemporary forms that, in a manner of speaking, constitute an 'accommodation' or 'reconciliation' of this dichotomy. At the centre of this process – if, indeed, it can be called such – lies the notion of *montage*.

Continuity versus discontinuity

The emergence of new techniques for the mediation and reproduction of images (i.e. recording systems such as photography and film) introduces a hitherto unprecedented potential for aesthetic developments along the lines of heightened forms of *mimeticism*. At the same time it also leads to hitherto unprecedented developments in modes of image *juxtaposition* (forms of sequential combination and forms of direct combination). Montage – the aesthetic idea and practice to which the great mid-twentieth-century proponent of realist cinema André Bazin takes such great exception – together with collage, photomontage and assemblage, are aesthetic techniques or devices which were first introduced and theorised within the discursive practices of modernist art (see Bazin 1967: 9–16, 23–40). All have, in the historical modernist view at any rate, a connection with the techniques of industrial production practices (see, for example, Wollen 1969: 32). However, as a modernist artistic technique, montage differs quite radically from industrial montage. In industrial usage, the term refers to a particular process of combining different parts to form a complete and fully integrated 'organic' product or commodity (an automobile, for example). Crucially, such products are assembled always the same way, out of similarly identical components, and in identical series after a model or prototype. Within modernist art practices however, montage is associated far more with the combination, re-combination or juxtaposition of diverse or disjunctive elements within a work to form new, surprising, disturbing or shocking images and ideas.

Indeed, the elements of disunity and 'provocative shock', are what most distinguishes modernist montage from its use in other mechanically produced cultural forms: most importantly, from the point of view of this discussion, from the commercial and, already by the 1920s, the industrially organised production of films. Indeed, the latter was always much closer to notions of montage associated with mechanised industry. For its mode of assembling pieces of film (shots) into a whole, had quickly solidified into a tight and unvarying system, soon to be called 'continuity editing', utilised for the production of mimetic, illusionist narrative films.

There arise, therefore, with the new stage of technological mediation based upon photography and film, two fundamentally different conceptions of montage: one theorised and challenging, the other viewed as intrinsic and natural. One links montage with highly specific modernist aesthetic techniques and the other connects it to industrial and mainstream (traditional) cultural and aesthetic development. The latter is, perhaps, most apparent in the conventional make-up of classical Hollywood film. It appears to be inherent or at one with the medium in which it occurs, remaining unobtrusive, functioning as a transparent glue or catalyst for the organic whole that constitutes the work – subservient to forms of mimetic or illusionistic realism. The modernist version, however, is conceived and used to create precisely the opposite effect: fragmentation, dissonance, disunity and an impression of incoherence and disorganisation. Thus it tends much more to foreground itself as a technique within the work itself – thereby linking itself to anti- or counter-realist/illusionistic forms.[5]

Both of these modes of montage practice have survived to this day. Yet, this has not been without a constant (and continuing) subjection to changing circumstances and pressures, which, needless to say, have had considerable bearing both on their character and functioning. Living in cultures in which we are surrounded on all sides by moving images, we are now particularly accustomed to the kind of montage that strives to hide its artifice. Such inherent forms of montage, those that somehow seem to be an essential (natural) part of the medium, continue of course to operate as a fundamental principle in both the cinema and television (though even here, as we shall see presently, things cannot be taken for granted). At the same time, also operative in contemporary culture are forms of montage, and associated concepts such as intertextual reference, which first found their expression in modernist art practices (see, for example, Huyssen 1980: 151–64; Wollen 1993: 35–71). However, through their subsequent repetition, incorporation and assimilation into mainstream forms, and the consequent familiarity that has ensued, such techniques have been stripped of much of their power to estrange and/or shock today. Thoroughly domesticated in forms such as TV advertising and music video, such montage functions rather – as we have already begun to see – more as a means to playful exhilaration and ephemeral visual fascination.

Rapprochement

It is the 1960s which sees the onset proper of 'a whole new culture of the image' (Jameson 1984: 58): a new preoccupation with already existing images and image forms – the beginnings of an elevation of intertextual reference to a more central position within many visual cultural practices. It is also no coincidence that the same period inaugurates a certain '*rapprochement*' between mass culture and modernist art.

In the first place, there occurs within the modernist visual tradition a return to representation, after the hegemonic rise of high modernist abstraction in the two decades or so following the Second World War. A key part of this involves the re-emergence and renovation – after a period of comparative stagnation – of devices such as allusion, parody, pastiche, citation and quotation: devices that were in widespread use in the practices of the historical avant-gardes. Devices, moreover, that had a special connection to montage: one need only think, for example, of the Dadaist 'ready-made', the Cubist collage, early photomontage, the films of Esfir Shub or Vertov, or accounts of Brechtian theatrical productions in the late 1920s and 1930s. It is mass culture and its media – greatly expanded and evolved through the post-war intensification of commodity production – which forms the immediate object of new modernist interest in the 1960s. Various attempts to *display* and/or *critique* this new phenomenon, mass mediated culture, quickly ensue. These involve practices ('self-referentiality' in its broadest sense) which return to copying, repeating, recombining, re-situating, quoting, referring to pre-existing texts – that is to say, to the forms, idioms, styles and images of this greatly expanded cultural horizon.

Indeed, this happened irrespective of whether or not those concerned directly associated themselves with the radical tradition of the pre-war artistic avant-gardes. Thus, Warhol – a graphic designer by training – found the subject for his ironic practice, his 'ready-mades' or 'found objects', in already existing advertising, packaging and news images. He copied and mechanically reproduced such images in the form of repetitive series and juxtapositions, frankly displaying them in new and antithetical contexts. Another development that in many ways similarly prefigures current aesthetic developments in the mass cultural domain is evident in the work of film-maker Jean-Luc Godard. The primary reference of Godard's anti-illusionist counter-cinema is Hollywood itself – a mode of representation that he attempts to 'deconstruct' by stylistically displaying and countering its specific codes and conventionality: the device most central to this project being *montage*.

As far as cross-cultural reference is concerned, a distinct loosening between mass culture and modernist art has been increasingly apparent since the 1960s on both sides of the (slowly dissolving) boundary. Indeed, as Peter Wollen was one of the first to point out, this whole aspect of intertextual reference – embryonically linked to the modernist concept of montage and collage, and radically rejuvenated in the 1960s when those working out of a modernist tradition *return to representation taking representation itself as their subject matter* – has entered a whole new stage today with the introduction of new digital technologies (see Wollen 1993: 35–71). That currently such development is more apparent within modes of *mass* culture such as those under review here is hardly surprising given its long-standing ascendancy. As the continued influence of Pop Art and counter-cinema (though not only these, of course) within such forms clearly demonstrates, such traffic – though it *isn't* only one-way – is flourishing.

In a peculiar way the grand opposition between the naïve realism of mass visual culture and the anti-narrative montage tradition of modernism – which has prevailed for much of this century – is now beginning to break down. It is leading instead to hybrid forms that display elements both of a heightened inter-texuality and a heightened realistic-ness or illusionism. Thus at one extreme there is the eclectic and mannered 'montage as spectacle' phenomenon of music video, at the other, the heightened illusionistic spectacle born of new techniques of image combination and manipulation, and evident in spectacle cinema and special venue extravaganzas. The new technology of the computer and computer imaging is providing ways of enhancing both intertextual forms *and* mimetic forms, and increasingly begins to combine both in the same text. Though it is not the emergence of digital imaging that has caused the emergence of this new image-centred culture, there can be no doubt that its techniques and emerging forms are proactive in expanding and shaping important aspects of its development.

Thus, in terms of techniques, the computer not only adds new capabilities with regard to the established means of image production, it also introduces completely new possibilities. Through integration into established forms, already existing techniques such as editing are made easier, cheaper and faster. At the same time, digital imaging introduces distinctive modes of image combination and recombination: this may involve combining imagery specifically produced for the purpose, imagery from the archive, or a mixture of both. Thus, the montage or collage of moving images derived from a multitude of different sources is readily achieved, and, what is more, not only – if it is so desired – with near perfect precision, but also with hitherto unseen levels of convoluted sophistication. We have already seen how in different ways such techniques are operating to startling effect in TV commercials and music video. In particular, it becomes possible to combine in a perfectly *seamless* manner – through the absolute precision of computerised motion-controlled cameras – many different sources or types of imagery to simulate a shot or a sequence. Examples of the latter are films such as *Who Framed Roger Rabbit?* (1988) and *Space Jam* (1996), both of which combine traditional live action with animation to spectacular effect. Films such as *Terminator 2* and *Starship Troopers*, variously combine archive footage or computer generated moving imagery with staged live action. The effects – as we have seen – are scenes involving 'impossible photography', perfectly mimetic images of outlandish actions and occurrences.

Moreover, image manipulation assumes a new importance with the arrival of the computer. Once again, the new technique of digitisation enables the distortion and modification of images in ways which foreground such interference, yet it is just as easy to produce undetectable changes and alterations in existing photographic, video and film images. Add to this the computer's capacity to originate and synthesise both still and moving images – ranging from simulated drawings to the fully 'photographic' – and it becomes clear that a formidable and novel technology of image fabrication has emerged. Of particular import, perhaps, is what effectively amounts to the uncoupling of photography from any dependence on recording processes. Realism (mimesis) not only plays a part here, but it may well be mutating into an altogether different phenomenon; one involving both the undetectable manipulation (superimposition, combination, alteration) of already existing imagery, and the origination (and reproduction) of synthetic 'photographic' images. These are significant examples of simulation in the sense of copying by other means and of the (re)production of copies without originals.[6]

Even computer games and simulation rides, which of all the forms under discussion might appear to be the least affected by the developments just alluded to, do not escape the montage-enhancing possibilities of the computer. Clearly, both are caught up in the culture of the image: they involve serialising, remaking, sequelisation, and reference back to prior texts, which (for the most part) themselves lack any reference other than modulated renditions, distant versions of versions. Nevertheless, despite the often extraordinary character of their imagery – games, for example, frequently operate in cartoon modes; both games and rides involve the most outlandish scenarios, characters and events – these forms appear to be situated squarely within the continuity system when it comes to editing. And yet, even here things are not quite so simple, for, in their own ways, both games and rides involve pronounced augmentations of certain aspects of continuity editing. Indeed, these are so marked as to become a dominant and defining characteristic. Thus, most rides (and a good portion of games too) consist in a kind of intensification of first-person point of view: promoting and perfecting it to such an extent that it becomes a distinctive feature. Rides may offer the spectator/participant little by way of interactive input into this vicarious experience of immobile – though far from motionless – travel, but they do constitute an extraordinary physical exaggeration of the point of view trope. Games, on the other hand do, of course, permit the player/spectator a degree of control as to what s/he sees, explores (and shoots at) and when. In the more elaborate games – such as the first-person shoot-'em-up *Quake* – the addition of this element of controlled choice introduces a distinctive dimension of real-time involvement to spectator positioning in the classical mode (see chapter 7).

Thus, new possibilities inherent within still developing techniques of digital imaging conform to, but also enlarge and intensify already established modes of self-referential or intertextual cultural production. As Wollen indicates, the computer not only enlarges the storage capacity of the 'image bank'; at the same time it makes access to it easier and it multiplies in hitherto unimaginable ways the different possibilities of image combination (1993: 65, 66). It further expands the horizons and dimensions of montage precisely along lines that Bazin found so disconcerting: privileging meaning as a function of image combination as opposed to reference. Today, however, meaning has become far more rarefied, at least within many of the expressions and genres of mass visual culture. Within this new order of image re-cycling and heightened intertextuality (with its more or less sophisticated forms and variations) a concern with technique and form takes precedence over substantive content and the image becomes increasingly autonomous from 'any extrinsic purpose'.

Genre and authorship in visual digital forms

'Genre' used to be a term reserved only for the literary forms of 'high culture'. Yet, with the advent of new technological forms centred upon mass reproducibility and the industrialisation of cultural production, generic classification became commonplace within the sphere of 'popular' or mass culture. A culture governed by commodification and the imperatives of commercialism, along with the necessary limits this is seen to place upon production, goes hand in hand with the idea of a system within which differentiation occurs only within high degrees of regulation, repetition, customisation and standardisation. Here, 'genre' enters as a term of description: mass culture is generic, its forms may be systematic and routine but they are differentiated by distinctive types, particular instances of which – whilst clearly recognisable as such – are also different one from the other. As such, genres are said to have acted as cues and precepts of aesthetic expectation for producers, distributors, reviewers and consumers alike. They contained a high degree of conventional stability whilst still leaving room for a certain variability at the level of individual instances (see, for example, Neale 1980a; Schatz 1981; Altman 1989) all of whom take the cinema as their chief object of study).

If 'genre' has been associated with mass culture more or less from its beginnings, the same cannot be said of the idea of 'authorship'. Precisely because mass culture was a commercially driven, *mass-produced* culture – thought of as operating within formulaic and tightly defined categories – it was not considered conducive to individual 'creative' expression. In the first decades of the twentieth century, rather, the 'true' space of creative autonomy and originality – the space of the artist or authorship – lay primarily with modernist forms and practices. Only here, or so it was believed, did there exist that traditional freedom which allowed for the sort of individual expression that led to 'genuine art'. The idea that there may also be artists operating within the constraints of industrially based cultural production comes later. The decades immediately following the Second World War see not only the beginning of the canonisation of pulp fiction writers but also, and perhaps more importantly, the idea of authorship entering the critical appraisal of mainstream cinema. In the search to validate the products of the film industry, the status of *auteur* or artist is attributed to (some) Hollywood film directors (by implication, of course, certain films thereby achieve the status of 'art' in this the traditional sense).[7] Since that time, such ideas have also entered the field of popular reception and appraisal, primarily through their mediation in popular or journalistic criticism. Nowadays spectators have their favourite directors. It may not be 'art' that they seek to affirm thereby, still, certain expectations as to what one will see when attending a screening of a film directed by a certain director seems a key factor in explaining preferences.

Of course, mainstream cinema has been one of the main sites of the enormous amount of critical work undertaken into both genre and authorship in mass visual culture in the second half of the twentieth century. Indeed, from the point of view of the history of film criticism, genre – always a given (in some sense at least) for producers, distributors and audiences alike – becomes an object of concern for theorists only *after* earlier *auteur*-centred approaches are found wanting. It is not my intention to rehearse these histories and the complex debates they entail. Instead, I shall ask in what ways might the concepts of genre and authorship apply to an aesthetic apprehension of the forms of visual digital culture that concern us here? In this way we shall undoubtedly run across issues and debates that have previously been assigned to the cinema. However, relative to visual digital forms the main claim will be that, appearances to the contrary, ultimately neither of these concepts is able to provide the work of aesthetic explanation they once did for classical cinema and forms like it. The forms of visual digital culture at issue here only serve to expose even further some of the inadequacies and doubts already associated with these notions. Exploring why this might be so does, however, help us to become clearer about the particular character of our emergent digital forms.

Genre and authorship are notions that continue to enjoy extensive use both in popular and critical appreciation of mass cultural forms and within the ranks of the producers themselves ('the culture industry'). Let us begin by quickly surveying the forms at issue in terms of genre and authorship. Starting with authorship we might ask how it manifests itself within industrial and promotional discourses (journalistic) surrounding visual digital forms. In this way we may also begin to grasp audience conceptions and uses of authorship.

Authors de-centred

To begin with, authorship does not figure in the same way or to the same extent across or within the examples at issue. One can detect a certain more or less public discourse of authorship both in the spectacle cinema discussed in the last chapter and with respect to computer animation and special venues (see chapter 7). Yet, the same can hardly be said of TV advertising, music video and computer games. There are distinctions to be drawn in this respect not only between the forms in the first group, but also between those in the latter. For one thing, the forms in the first group still fall within the Hollywood tradition of Academy standards, whereby directors are recognised and promoted – both at award ceremonies and within subsidiary forms of journalism. Furthermore, the impact of *auteur* criticism in the 1950s and 1960s – associated first with the critics of the journal *Cahiers du Cinéma* and then with influential American critics such as Andrew Sarris – is still evident as a bolstering influence on already established industry notions of a director's worth. This is a legacy which, regardless of sustained and damaging subsequent criticism, continues its work both in journalistic and academic criticism. Thus, in the sphere of digitally enabled spectacle cinema and the popular discourses that inform it, the names of certain directors have begun to appear more frequently than others do.[8] Whilst in the domain of computer animation and special venues the focus of authorial concern – at least so far as the journalistic critics are concerned – has lighted, more or less exclusively, on two directors only.[9] Hailed, to a great extent, as creative pioneers, these names function as signs of a new creative mastery in a new technological horizon. Significantly, however, in all three areas other names have consistently appeared alongside those of creative individuals: those of special digital effects *companies*. 'Industrial Light and Magic', 'Digital Productions', 'Pixar', 'Digital Domain' and so forth: the new techniques and technicians such names represent receive considerable exposure in the popular reviews and exegeses of subsidiary forms of mediation. As such, whilst not exactly displacing director names, it could be argued that they have tended to vie with them as a way of accounting for or measuring creative worth within the popular aesthetic imagination.

In the other group of forms things are rather different. For, in at least two of them – advertising and music video – names associated with individual creative origination, where, indeed, they exist, are confined by and large to the realm of production itself. That is to say, in the main they are restricted to the pages of trade journals and the associated institutions they represent, only occasionally leaking out into more public discourses. Certainly, with respect to the notion of authorship, advertising and music videos operate for the ordinary viewer through relative *anonymity* – though they do so in different ways. Thus, TV advertisements are received with a minimal amount of extra-textual information having been supplied with respect to their production. To most of us they just appear. They may engage a considerable amount of our time, they may even divert, surprise and entertain, but there exists no corresponding popularising critical journalism in the way there is with the cinema. Music tapes (like advertisements) sometimes employ directors from the realm of cinema. However, the name that one associates with a particular tape is rarely, if ever, the tape's director. Of course, the additional prestige derived by association (of a given pop star or band with a 'name' director) may be a factor, in which case subsidiary forms of publicity would draw attention to this collaboration.[10] Ultimately, however, it is the music and the music performer that is being promoted (their 'art', their 'creativity', their 'image'), and the presence of additional creative 'names' is for this very reason, usually consigned to production credits on the packaging.[11] Typically, however, and as I have already begun to suggest, it is not the search for or, indeed, the presence of, a creative artist that matters here so much as image itself (for reasons already mentioned, see chapter 5).

Nor are things very different when it comes to computer games. Since the rapid and rather short-lived rise to fame of a number of young game hackers during the early years of the form, author names – though still maintaining a regular residual presence – have receded somewhat in succeeding years. Taking their place in the burgeoning popular journalism surrounding the field (much of which, incidentally, is now 'on-line'), are the names of game developers and publishers. Tellingly, much of the time, reviewers of the latest games tend to write in the plural when referring to game development and production. Discussion is about 'the makers' of games and these have names such as 'Activision', '3DO', 'Sega', 'LucasArts', 'Sierra On-Line' and 'Westwood Studios'. Preponderant here, despite the occasional focus on a game 'inventor' or 'designer', is the idea that game production is a team effort; moreover, it is one that takes place in a highly commercial context involving intensive industrial research and development practices. Beyond this though, rather than creative origins, the focus of this work of popular criticism and exposure – the circulation and promotion of a game image (adapting Ellis 1982) – is upon what *kind* of game it is and, accordingly, what it involves, how it plays and what it looks like. The focus, in other words, has more to do with generic appreciation than it does authorship.

The rarefaction of genre

So, how does the idea of genre figure in our new digital forms? We can begin by considering video games, for in many respects they appear the most clear-cut in this respect. One of the most recent of the forms under consideration, video games summon up parallels with the earlier rise of the mainstream cinema, if only because once established it too settled down relatively quickly around a core of finite and relatively stable genres (see chapter 1). Clearly, this occurred for the same reasons it did in the cinema. Establishing a relatively stable number of classes within a form, each with its sub-set of aesthetic expectations around which the regular production and distribution of new instances of 'difference within repetition' can take place, is clearly advantageous – if not downright necessary – for commercial success. Computer games operate within such a system. Importantly, however, and not unlike the cinema itself – although in the case of games this has happened with far greater rapidity – the genres concerned have changed, been added to, cross-bred and so forth. No form escapes the shaping influences of historical development, which includes forces of an aesthetic, technical, commercial and political character. I shall return to this idea of change presently when I turn to consider the forms in terms of their contemporary cultural context.

With regard to the other forms, genre figures in something of the same chequered fashion as authorship. It seems to make little sense to attempt to classify TV advertisements generically. There is not much to be gained from such an endeavour, it hardly serves commercial or marketing interests, for adverts are '*given*' rather than sold to us, at least that is how it appears, for we only purchase them indirectly. Of course, the principle of 'difference within repetition' applies here as elsewhere, yet, possibly because of their 'incidental' status, there is nothing pressing for further aesthetic regulation other than that they be distinctive in their self-sameness.

Certainly, music video shares certain characteristics with TV advertising; promoting a product being one of the most central. Whilst pop promos are sold as cultural commodities in their own right, they also function like commercials, appearing 'as if for free' on TV music shows and MTV. For study purposes, of course – indeed, as I myself am doing here – critics have attempted to isolate and construct groups or classes within the form (see, for example, Kaplan 1987). There does not, however, appear to be any corresponding 'natural' or institutional classification arising out of music video production. Like advertisements, music videos are at one pole of the generic spectrum insofar as they appear to dissolve any need for the term, other than as an alternative to the notion of a 'form' itself. One could make similar observations about special venue attractions and simulation rides: the difference being that to a certain extent the basic formal unity that characterises each of the other forms breaks down here. Special venue attractions – in particular those which exist in major theme parks – may involve spectacular mixed media events involving cinema and theatre or may themselves be grandiose simulation rides (for example, and respectively, *Honey, I Shrunk the Audience* and *Back to the Future: The Ride*). Beyond this though, given the newness of these forms, it may be some time before we can say for certain whether or not some kind of generic system will come to characterise them.

This said, it seems clear that conceptions of genre (and authorship) are anyway being radically affected – outstripped, even – by the prevailing trends in contemporary visual culture. As defining examples of the culture of the 'depth-less image', the expressions of visual digital culture under consideration here are prime examples of what this might mean for aesthetic reception. We can begin discussion of what this involves and how it affects the forms of visual digital culture by looking initially at digital cinema. I have already pointed to the way in which the technologically dense spectacle films of the late twentieth century are symptomatic of a new aesthetic: manifestations of a particular space within mass visual culture that is now even further removed than ever before from traditional ideas of representation. In many of the visual cultural practices of present day mass culture – long since saturated with (visual) mediation – inter-textuality has become institutionalised as an aesthetic norm. Invariably, reference is first and foremost to prior or already existing forms, texts, styles and images. This can take many forms, it can be ironic, parodic, decorative, ludic, spectacular and so on – yet, hardly ever, if at all, does it escape the vicious circle of its own entrapment in self-reference. At their most extreme such practices of 'doubled', second- or even third-degree renovation turn into a fascination with form and imagery – and its technological reproduction – in and for itself.

One important dimension of this whole process involves intertextuality as the straddling of forms. For some time now texts in one form – and this has been particularly apparent with regard to blockbuster movies – have been specifically designed with an eye to translation into other 'branches of the culture industry'. As Thomas Schatz says, such films – produced and distributed by ' "multi-media" conglomerates, for global markets ... ', are 'multi-purpose entertainment machines that breed music videos and soundtrack albums, TV series and video cassettes, video games and theme park rides, novelizations and comic books' (1993: 9–10). Of course, when we look at the larger picture such 'trade' is even more widespread, systemic and not at all one way (that is, not emanating solely from new Hollywood cinema). Thus, comics breed films, games and animation, and games breed films, comics and TV series. Meanwhile – in a broader sense – details, fragments, styles and techniques are constantly migrating between each of these and the other forms at play (i.e. TV series, advertising, music videos and so forth).

We have here another manifestation of the increasing structural importance of the growth and refinement of the repetitive and the serial within mass cultural production: a further dimension of the increase in self-referentiality. To reiterate: the various kinds of remaking, sequelisation and serialising implicit in the above, all encourage and exemplify reference back to prior texts, whether it be that which was immediately preceding (sequel, serial, series), or one of the same or another kind in processes of formal cross-over. However, when such texts are *already* – in the first instance – themselves thoroughly intertextual in character, then one begins to grasp something of the extent and structural reach of this new condition. A *familiarity* on the part of the spectator with previous texts, their styles, generic features, character tropes, and so forth, becomes a central feature of spectator involvement in current ones. Extra-textual reference recedes as such convolution and the complex circularity it involves takes over spheres of mediation.

The phenomenal proliferation of repetitively regulated signs is the key to this view of today's media-dominated world. Increasingly *intertextual*, increasingly '*simulacral*', it is formal difference, rather than representational reference – the preponderance of relativity over correspondence – that increasingly appears to hold sway in many spheres. Certainly, the advent of the computer has speeded this process of evolving fascination with the formal material support (generic, stylistic and visual) of mass mediation. The visual digital genres at issue here look hardly at all to the world itself, rather more to already existing techniques of mediation and to the further stylisation and exaggeration of the different kinds of wrapping they have accrued. Above all, the computer's enhanced techniques of image combination and manipulation and its powerful simulation capabilities have pushed this aesthetic further and further towards emphasising the fabric of representation itself. Not only are the images so produced sharper, they are both more outlandish and yet more realistic by the same turn – impossible yet photographic (spectacle cinema, computer animation). With digital techniques image combination and modification becomes increasingly, flagrantly, more elaborate as it becomes more artificial – and this along opposing trajectories involving verisimilitude on the one hand and decoration on the other (spectacle cinema, TV advertisements, music videos). On another level, our enhanced sense both of presence in and manipulation of the image appears to lead us ever closer to absorption within the material substance of mediation. Rides and games respectively collapse the space of reception into an experience of pure stimulation or involve a kind of programmed symbiosis with the artificiality of representation.

The advent of aesthetic management

Within this context two phenomena in particular come to bear upon considerations of authorship and genre: the so-called 'loss of originality' and the impetus of what might be termed 'de-differentiation'. I shall set aside the argument that 'authors' have always been more a product of the re-creative work of reading itself, and not the one true point of 'genuine' ideas and expression in a text. We must consider the thought that within the major part of today's mass visual culture aesthetic independence – always a relative concept anyway – is becoming severely curtailed. In many ways this involves a return to a perspective that pre-dates the emergence of *auteur* criticism. For the suggestion is that even in its contemporary qualified or 'de-centred' guise, the idea of authorial freedom has become so attenuated by the workings of the system itself, that quite simply it is no longer an issue.

At least this is the case, by and large, within the expressions under discussion here: authorship is being displaced by different aesthetic concerns, those centred upon the ephemeral playing with and working-over of visual forms, styles and tropes. This culture of the perpetual and regimented discharge of the fleeting or transitory would seem to demand not so much the author as the modifier, not the originator, but rather the adjuster or the renovator. Indeed, the disciplinary operation of the present-day 'culture of the copy' appears far more constricting in this sense than its immediate predecessor – i.e. the era of classic cinema (thinking here primarily of the visual) – ever was.[12] At any rate, contemporary visual culture is quite clearly very different to the slower tempo and relative simplicity of the earlier period. A period where, as Jameson point-edly remarks, it was possible for a Hitchcock to pass 'from a craftsman of grade-B thrillers to "the greatest director in the world" … ', or, to 'enlarge the older generic framework so powerfully, in a film like *Vertigo* (1958), as to approximate an "expressive" masterpiece of another kind' (Jameson 1992: 84). The space for such an eventuality has not entirely disappeared, though it is severely curtailed in the aesthetic regime under consideration.

Moreover, I would suggest that there is a clear sense in which this holds true as much for practices such as spectacle cinema – where it might, perhaps, seem to be less obvious – as it does for advertising, computer games and music video. Subject to the imperatives to repeat and remake afresh our examples – and this, I believe bears just as heavily on the idea of authorship – are forms in which the imperatives of a new technology are beginning to predominate. In fields where it is important to forever make one's copies distinctive and where a technology has emerged with so many imitative and manipulative possibilities, then so called 'state of the art' leads the way. Technique, technicians and technology itself take command: cultural production becomes first and foremost a technical problem. To a certain extent this always existed as a dimension of mass cultural practices. Indeed, Martin Jay has argued that it is with the 'discovery, redis-covery, or invention' of perspective itself that a preoccupation with technique at the expense of content first begins to assert itself. Jay claims that, 'as abstract, quantitatively conceptualised space became more interesting to the artist than the qualitatively differentiated subjects painted within it, the rendering of the scene became an end in itself' (1988: 8). He views this as culminating in twentieth-century modernism five centuries later. Yet might not it also apply with equal justification to current trends in the field of digital imaging practices? Certainly, the intensely formulaic and habitual character of contemporary culture sits very comfortably with the idea of practices that are highly procedural at a technical level. A profoundly regulated aesthetic that seems predominantly preoccupied with recombination and the manipulation of image itself entails a considerably different idea of what constitutes artistic practice. Traditional notions – stemming from romanticism – are today displaced even further by the prevalence of a certain technical instrumentalism.[13] The producer as expressive 'artist' and 'stylist' gives way to the producer as 'programmer': the manager-manipulator of formal play in the '*perpetuum mobile*' that is contemporary visual culture.

The '*heterogeneous palimpsest*'[14]

As for genre, it would appear to be undergoing a similar transformation under the pressure of current conditions – and for roughly related reasons. No one would deny that one of the key characteristics of genre in its recent aesthetic functioning has been to mark distinctions both within and between forms of mass mediation. Just as obvious however, has been the increasing difficulty associated with attempts to define and characterise such distinctions in the present. Old categories and boundaries are breaking down, blurring in the face of self-referential impulses that are being spurred by new technological development

I have already drawn attention to the way in which the blockbuster films of digital cinema defy attempts at description in terms of traditional 'genre film' categories. They are not alone, of course. Since the 1980s mainstream cinema has demonstrated an increasing tendency to produce films that cut across established genres in an eclectic and hybrid manner, or, alternatively re-work – in ways that Jameson describes as 'metageneric' – prior genres (Jameson 1992). In both instances it is the *palimpsestic* character of these texts that seems most vital: the fact that one has to read *through* and across them for references which themselves, ultimately, rest in prior signs, styles and genres. Importantly, it must also be recognised that these prior genres, styles and so forth are less and less confined solely to the history of the form itself. New Hollywood cinema is just as prone to quoting from, alluding to, copying from music video, advertising, animation and video games as it is from itself – just as each of these latter forms are from it (and each other).

As I have already indicated even video games, which, of all the forms at issue here, operate with perhaps the clearest sense of a generic classification, are still subject to the rarefying strictures of the encompassing culture. Not only are their genres – platform, beat-'em-up, shoot-'em-up, simulation, adventure, role-play, puzzle and so on – somewhat crudely drawn relative to those in earlier/other popular cultural fields, but, already, description is becoming confused and problematic because of the rapidity with which earlier distinctions are blurring through hybridisation. Furthermore, the crossover element whereby feature films are turned into games and vice versa has operated widely for some time now. Indeed, computer games are now spawning TV animated series – exporting characters and scenarios and invariably taking their 3-D computer imagery with them (trade in the other direction, that is, from TV cartoon series to game, has existed considerably longer). A certain 'metageneric' element has entered even here, in one of the youngest forms of mass culture. Moreover, never has the flattening of meaning or depth in the traditional aesthetic sense of these words been so pronounced as in the action-simulation genres of the computer game: here, aesthetic experience is tied directly to the purely sensational and allied to tests of physical dexterity.

Plainly, it would be wrong to assert categorically that the (young) player of games does not use the established generic classifications when deciding what to play or what to purchase. However, one might still argue – and with some justification – that what counts more is *how* the game plays (action simulation) and, allied to this, what it looks like (crudely, does the imagery reinforce the illusion of control and participation – see chapter 7). If this is so, then genre works in a less specific manner than it did, say, in classical Hollywood. Indeed, this seems even more likely when one considers the fact that, by and large, the differences between games of a particular genre involve fewer variables than did those of the earlier form. Would retrospective critical work on this question produce a more rigorous aesthetic appraisal of game genres and their characteristics to replace the makeshift and market-oriented groupings that currently operate within the institution? Perhaps, though I am not at all sure that this would necessarily add up to anything like the genre criticism of earlier popular forms. For here we are talking about differences and distinctions that are a matter of detail rather than substance. Generic variables no longer operate on the plane of signification with the complexity they once used to (say, in classical cinema or pulp fiction). The idea of genre that exists here is one that is highly abstract and nominal: it is 'genre' that is of a piece with the culture of the image in general and its repetitive and serial character. Genre may be a factor in game marketing, but at the aesthetic level it has to compete with the newer cult of 'taking part'.

The 'variable' or 'differential' element within the 'difference within repetition' which is characteristic of the forms of twentieth-century mass culture is even more vital today, precisely because of the apparent de-differentiation that is under way. Indeed, the marker of difference would seem to be increasing in importance at the same time as it becomes smaller in scale and simpler in its operation: a mechanism for minuscule formal or surface distinctions. Thus we have the endless variations of the same contexts depicted for (essentially) the same simulated shoot-'em-up; minute adjustments to the way a game plays; tiny variations in the behaviour of protagonists; tiny variations in the look of protagonists; the endless nuances of the same advertising trope; variations in the production of photo-realistic scenes of the fantastic; variations on ways of rewriting or reworking prior styles; variations in the way recombination is achieved; variations in the manner of recombination; and so forth. In this

143

context authorship and genre do not entirely disappear, but they have a far more limited structural role to play. As internal distinction becomes more confused both within and across forms, genre no longer reliably refers to anything other than the general level of a form itself – narrative cinema, music video, computer game. If anything, genres themselves have been turned into historical signifiers, and as such they become – in various ways – additions to the storehouse of styles and figures, or objects of pastiche and allusion: further elements for the surface play that constitutes contemporary visual culture.

What are the implications of all of the above for spectator experience and consumption? The final part of this book will consider this question. First, however, I shall look in more depth at the most recent – and, for many, the most representative – forms or genres of visual digital culture: computer games and special venue attractions. If these really are as distinctive as some are claiming then what does this involve and what might it mean? How are we to situate these forms with regard to their digital relatives? Only after a more searching exploration of the aesthetic character of these modes, shall I move on to consider more broadly spectatorship and consumption in contemporary mass visual culture. Indeed, in many ways the next chapter will serve as a kind of bridge to such concerns, focusing – as it inevitably has to – much more centrally on issues of spectatorship anyway.

Part III

SPECTATORS

7

GAMES AND RIDES

Surfing the image

The computer game and special venue attraction – particularly the so-called 'ride film' or 'motion simulator' – are certainly among the most recent of the visual forms under consideration in this book. Indeed, it is only the computer or video game that issues *directly* from or with the new technology itself. Still, it would be highly misleading to attribute the character of the genre itself solely to digital techniques: it owes much to prior and adjacent cultural forms (traditional games, animated film, cinema, certain modes of literary fiction and so forth). Indeed, this fact seems all the more apparent in this case given the remarkable facility of the computer itself to modes of imitation and simulation; indeed, it is tempting to see this as the computer's destiny or apotheosis. Imitation and simulation are vital to any understanding of computer games. Though, even here – as we shall see – the upshot of such efforts in the sphere of games involves more than a mere procrustean aesthetics of uniform substitution.

As the discussion has shown, it is frequently difficult when considering aesthetic form to determine where the boundaries between aesthetics and spectator experience begin and end. Despite the clear sense that in many respects different things *are* involved, the conventional and coded character of cultural practices implies that a good deal of discursive sharing (both tacit and otherwise) must take place between both producers and consumers of culture in the sense we are discussing it here. From this perspective an understanding of the aesthetic or formal character of a visual genre also conveys important information about *how* viewers are invited or encouraged to engage with or to receive that genre. Of course, spectators may fail to engage in the way a particular work (or genre) solicits them to, but whether they do or not the character of the aesthetic form involved remains crucial to any understanding of what is (or is not) taking place in the sphere of reception.

This, however, is not why computer games and special venue attractions are being discussed in the section dealing with spectatorship. It is rather, that they seem to warrant – even to press for – such inclusion. For it is difficult to escape the impression – so insistent has been the clamour in support of the idea – that they are kinds of audiovisual culture that significantly reconfigure the role and character of aesthetic engagement as it has traditionally been understood. At least, this is what is widely proclaimed both in the journalistic and (much of) the emergent critical commentary surrounding them. Computer games in particular have been singled out as one of the most visible of the new modes of representation to involve what is known as 'interactivity' – one of the most widely used terms of media commentary in the last decade of the twentieth century. It is this notion or defining attribute – at least in the first instance – which is seen as signalling what is different (or special) about games (see, for example, Myers 1990; Cameron 1995). This focus on the way in which one relates to or engages with the genre immediately elevates the *spectating* experience itself to a position of central importance. In the popular discourse of the motion-simulation genre a similar centring on spectator experience takes place: under terms such as 'immersion' and 'virtual reality' arise intimations that something distinctive – relative to other media forms – lies at the heart of engagement with this one (see Huhatamo 1996).

To begin properly to determine what is at issue here, it becomes important to stress that our concern is with the ideas of interaction, participation, immersion and so on insofar as they bear upon screened images in two emergent expressions of mass visual culture: computer games and special venue attractions. To date the latter have received relatively little serious attention from the point of view of aesthetic style or formal make-up.[1] Among the more culturally oriented work to emerge on computer games it is broader semantic issues – connected to ideas such as gender, militarism, instrumentalisation and consumerism – that predominate (see, for example, Skirrow 1986; Kinder 1991; Provenzo 1991; Stallabrass 1993). A concern with form and style is not the primary motivation of such approaches: the former figure, rather, more or less as means or props to interpretations involving wider social/symbolic exegesis. Though, having said this, the stylistic analysis that does occur in such work is often highly suggestive (see Kinder 1991; Stallabrass 1993). Indeed, it is often more interesting than a good deal of the more considered commentary in the area of 'computers and art', which to date has concerned itself with speculating upon the future potentialities and prospects for ideas of 'interactivity' viewed as a general notion (see, for example, Youngblood 1989). Alternatively, such approaches have tended to think about computers and 'interactivity' in relation to other, purportedly 'more serious' spheres such as theatre (see Laurel 1991; Murray 1997). It is not that this work has nothing to say about computer games or rides – or that what it has to say is not illuminating – rather, its real agenda lies elsewhere. It is interested in speculating on and attempting to influence what *might be* rather than on understanding *what is*. Because of this, what is said about our subject is usually said in passing.

Not all of this speculative writing is the same, nor am I suggesting that a speculative approach is by definition necessarily problematic or unproductive. However, I want to align what is being attempted in this book more closely with an approach that seeks to explore 'particular technologies in specific

148

contexts' rather than viewing '[t]echnology as a monolithic demonic or liberating historical force' (Woodward 1994: 49). I propose an exploration of these 'new' forms that turns more upon comparisons centred on their conventional make-up: in terms of conventional operation how are they similar and how are they different to their digital cousins? How do the norms of the computer game encourage specific kinds of engagement on the part of the player? What are they? Clearly, attempting to ascertain just what 'interactivity', 'immersiveness' and suchlike involves in this sense will be a crucial aspect of such an exploration. If these terms are adding something that is distinctive to the forms in question, then what does this consist of and what conclusions might we draw from it with respect to spectatorship and visual digital expressions generally?

My aim is to contribute a precursory formal examination. It is one that is intended to reinforce the work already begun by others eliciting and delineating what one might describe as key distinguishing characteristics, whilst at the same time elucidating what are clearly marks of continuity. Indeed, I shall suggest that it is precisely the distinguishing elements in these genres (such as they are) that qualifies them for inclusion in the new mode of visual formalism under discussion. Computer games are part of a cultural space of surface play and neo-spectacle. However they are also – like the other forms discussed here – distinctive in the way in which they manifest or qualify for membership of this particular aesthetic dimension of contemporary visual culture.

Computer games: 'into the image'?[2]

The main focus of this examination is on those computer or video games that are primarily action oriented. It is these games – the so-called 'shoot-'em-ups', 'beat-'em-ups' and 'sports simulations' – which have historically been most popular both in the arcade and the home: they are the dominant expression within the genre. However, I also want to look across the genre as whole to attempt to take some account of slower or more leisurely games, as well as games that are supposed to typify current moves in some quarters of the computer games field towards the notion of the 'interactive movie'. In each case I shall concentrate on one game in particular, referring to others when it becomes necessary. The games in question are principally *Quake* (1996) and *Blade Runner* (1997), and to some extent, *Myst* (1995). Not only are these quite recent examples of their kind, but each carries the distinction of being among the most popular produced to date: they are typical examples of the late twentieth-century computer games genre.

I shall explore these particular games in relation to the interconnected concepts of *narrative, interaction* and *image*. These ideas are not listed in any order of precedence, though it does seem to me that as an initial starting point they offer a way into exploring and testing the stylistic formations of the games in question against their correlates in other domains. More often than not, discussion of one of these ideas will be seen to entail discussion of another – so intimate is their relationship to each other in the context of computer games. Moreover, they also give rise to other, more specific terms – among the most prominent being 'control', 'mastery', 'game-play', 'real-time', 'simulation' and 'spectacle' – all of which help us to get more of a handle on the aesthetic character and experience of the computer game.

In the popular criticism surrounding the area computer games are frequently referred to as 'clones'. *Quake* is a clone because it is a version of an earlier game – *Doom* (1993) – only with minimal 'improvements' or changes. *Doom* – the most popular (and lucrative) of the first batch of subjective or first-person viewpoint shoot-'em-up computer games – casts players as marines who must single-handedly shoot their way through a hostile and labyrinth-like environment. This is not only a location full of obstacles and hazards, but the enemy are 'demons from hell' whose only aim is to kill the player – unless, of course, the player kills them first. Essentially *Quake* is the same game with slightly different detailing such as location, weaponry, opponents, levels of difficulty and so forth. A little more attention has been paid to the production of graphic detail within the 3-D illusionistic world – either that, or the increased number and diversity of scenarios depicted adds to the impression of greater visual complexity. Certainly, the impression of first-person movement within these diverse environments involves a greater degree of mimeticism: the number of actions are more or less the same (walking, running, jumping, swimming, shooting and picking up things) but control and responsiveness is improved.

The stated goals of *Quake* are very much a standard of the type: 'First, stay alive. Second, get out of the place you're in.' There are several levels of difficulty to select from (ranging from 'easy' to 'nightmare'). The player is the principal protagonist and what s/he sees on the screen is viewed as if through a subjective or first-person viewpoint. The initial visual impression that one is located in a three-dimensional setting is reinforced when one begins to move around, thus activating elements of spatial and temporal coordination. One of the distinctive (and pleasurable) features of games such as *Quake* is the impression of realistic mobility and presence within (occupancy of) a fictional parallel world.

Narrative: recounting, repeating

Before we consider questions of interaction and simulation, let us first look at the idea of narrative. How does narrative operate in *Quake*? The so-called 'back story' of *Quake*, presented in the instruction booklet that accompanies the game disc, is short and basic in the extreme.[3] Invariably in these background scenarios, the reader/player who forms the first-person fulcrum of what takes place in the game itself, is addressed directly. Thus: '*You* get the phone call at 4 a.m.', *your* formidable reputation has led to a summons to a secret military installation experimenting with an instantaneous transportation device. The noxious army of an alien enemy, code-named 'Quake', which is from another dimension, is infil-

150

trating this installation. *You* are put in charge of finding and stopping it. However, whilst *you* are out making a reconnaissance the whole of *your* own force is wiped out by Quake's death squads. Now it is just *you* against them.

Formally, this is about as close to traditional modes of story telling as games such as *Quake* get. Clearly, the background story is offered as justification for the material of the game itself: it is a scene-setting rationale and the overarching motivation for the iconography and events encountered in the game. Moreover, the 'story' is supplemented with further preliminary information which, given the amount of space allocated to it, appears – at the very least – to be of equal importance. Thus, explaining the basics of play, control functions, weaponry, enemies, hazards and suchlike of the game extends over many pages, whereas the 'story' is related in one. In the literature that accompanies games whatever is being related or explained is kept to the absolute minimum and expression is as simple as possible. The aim is to relate essential points about how to play the game and about the 'environment' one will find oneself in.

Relative word count is not necessarily a measure of genuine significance. Nevertheless, I would suggest that the background story is a relatively minor part of the game genre – any significance that it pretends to have evaporates once the game is under way. What counts far more is the actual playing, and this involves a certain kind of *kinaesthetic performance* that becomes almost an end in itself. In the action-oriented game certainly, though I would suggest this is true for most computer games, fictional narrative as it is traditionally understood is *de-centred* – relegated to a subordinate position within the overall formal hierarchy that constitutes the game aesthetic.

The expectations of the computer game player have relatively little to do with the identification and voyeurism attached to the curious and privileged spectator of classical cinema.[4] The latter, as John Ellis has explained, is situated in a position of 'separation and of mastery', given 'the power to understand events rather than change them' (Ellis 1982: 81). By comparison with the *narrative* fiction of popular literature and film, playing a computer game comprises something that is rather distinctive. In the case of *Quake*, for example, players must initiate the events that ensue by involving themselves in a kind of vicarious performance within a fictional representational world which is – within certain limits – responsive to their presence and actions. The players of *Quake* have to be physically engaged with controls (joystick, or whatever) in order that intended actions be translated and reproduced within the world represented on the screen: in order, that is, *for something to happen*. In a film by contrast, the events and actions unfold in a plot structure of storytelling that, much like the spectator's solicitation itself, is predetermined and fixed. Whilst the spectator's response – be it active or passive – consists, nevertheless, of sedentary perceptual and mental activity. Such a viewer cannot alter the course of the action – hence the story itself – whereas the player of a game can. Does this mean that video game players create their own narrative? In a manner of speaking, perhaps. However, this requires a good deal of qualification.

To begin with, if we are to allow that some form of narration exists in games such as *Quake*, then we must, it seems, operate with a far more rarefied notion of narrative than any discussed thus far. The simulation of movement and action within a realistic three-dimensional 'virtual' environment with *a set* of more or less predetermined possibilities of where to go, what to do and – again, within limits – ways of doing things, certainly allows for connected events to occur within some kind of time period. True, the events are produced 'as we go along' and depend on which choices within the built-in limits and opportunities of the game the player makes as s/he proceeds, nevertheless, change (movement) occurs. At the end of a period of play, no matter how long it has lasted or how it has been terminated – whether the player has been killed by a 'Grunt', whether s/he decides to 'save' or 'quit' – it is possible to recount what occurred to that point: a kind of story is possible. In this sense a game such as *Quake* – indeed, this is true of most games – is capable of generating many such stories, retrospective accounts – many of them similar, some of them different – of what happened each time one played afresh.[5] Should the players eventually work their way through all four episodes then it would seem they are in a position to recount a story of near-epic proportions. One hastens to add, however, that this is only likely after considerable practice and frequent repetition. It would certainly entail acquiring ability with controls, spatial knowledge, discovery of 'secrets', many 'saved games', innumerable 'deaths' and restarts down the same corridors (killing the same enemies) and – ultimately, perhaps – the aid of a Strategy Guide.

The problem however, is twofold: first, the *fragmented* character of this story passage – symptomatic of the game experience generally; second, the extraordinary *poverty* of such an 'epic' relative to other forms of narrative. Thus, the numerous partial and oft-repeated forays into the world of the game itself, the fact that one could *at best* only hope to complete it over a considerable number of playing sessions stretching over many hours, suggests that something other than the pleasure of story telling, at least as it is traditionally understood, is operative here.[6] Indeed, this impression is further strengthened when one considers the highly 'schematized and purposely reductive vision of the world' that games offer in their scenarios (Murray 1997: 140). In *Quake* for instance, almost everything in its formal make-up is geared to simple action and spectacle: weapons, ammunition, artefacts, the various types of enemy – all are mere tokens or emblems. They function for the most part in instrumental terms either as means (and/or obstacles) to an end – i.e. the player's passage through and out of a space – and/or as a means of titillating the eye (see, Stallabrass 1993: 88).

In particular, there are no discernible characters here – psychological depth does not enter into it – the motives both of players and their enemies are basic in the extreme.[7] Enemies – though varied in kind and appearance – are mostly significant insofar as they employ different ways of attempting to 'slay' the player (thereby ending/winning the game). Enemies do, however, 'die' in a multitude of spectacular ways. One of the primary norms of classical narrative fiction – the primary site of narrative causality and an important source of its richness and depth – is located in the psychological traits and motives of character portrayal. Variously watching – and identifying with – characters as they strive in their fictional world to 'overcome obstacles and achieve goals' that are intensely personal or psychological, and usually highly involved or complex, stands in marked contrast to the direct physical involvement of the game player. For in the computer game it is the spectators/players themselves who are the locus of the action, it is they who are trying to achieve certain objectives and surmount difficulties (see Skirrow 1986: 129–33, for a thought-provoking interpretation of the computer game performer). Characterisation and psychological motivation recedes and is replaced by player-centred problems which – in the case of the action game – concern survival and one's successful passage through a difficult-to-negotiate and obstacle-littered setting. Of course, this introduces new difficulties to do with skill acquisition, dexterity and recall.

If psychological causality is at a premium within such game scenarios, then so too are other dimensions of traditional narrative. Indeed, as other commentators have pointed out, several other codes that are central to narrative – codes that produce a certain plenitude, a depth and richness of meaning – are largely absent in computer games (see Cameron 1995: 37–8). Thinking particularly of cinema, the key conventions of enigma resolution and of narrative closure so central to classical Hollywood representation do not have the same significance in the formal make-up of the computer game. In the game the enigma is always the same – how to find a way through, how to finish? An *agon*istic process involving struggle with on-screen adversaries and the underlying program itself is operative here (see also, Skirrow 1986: 126–9). Problems and puzzles are largely *technical* in character, often repetitively similar, and are dispersed throughout the playing experience. Like closure itself, solving these problems rests with the player. Ideally, closure means completing a game – that is, successfully playing one's way through all the levels, overcoming all the obstacles and defeating all the enemies. However, as I have already indicated this rarely happens. Far more likely are countless attempts – some aborted, some saved – to progress further and further towards a win. In this sense 'closure' is frequent and variable – at times satisfying, at times frustrating. The satisfaction of completion is more that of technical mastery or achievement than of 'knowledge'. Certainly, the knowledge gained is of a different order to that of traditional fiction, the answers being to different questions. They are not about complex character relations in a highly 'realistic' fictional world, rather, game knowledge involves answers to questions of a more practical kind. In the main these entail finding solutions to formal puzzles and learning how to become proficient with controls.[8]

Of particular interest with respect to narrative is a related issue concerning the different ways in which *time* is represented in games and traditional narrative forms (Cameron 1995). If the representation of space is – certainly in the games addressed here – to a certain extent continuous with classical narrative cinema (see pp. 158–60), the same can hardly be said of time. We return here to a contrast mooted earlier: that of a pre-constructed, closed and unalterable narrative form (such as those we experience in the cinema), as against a form where events – despite being determined by a pre-designed 'framework of conditions and possibilities' – are nonetheless, constructed in *real time* as the player proceeds. In the former, time is conventionally represented: the duration of the film is not the duration of the narrative.[9] In the latter – *Quake* or *Myst*, for example – fictional time is more or less coextensive with the time of playing, because the player is both active within and activator of the game: s/he is the central protagonist. This does not mean that the player has total control over the pace and timing of events, for there are moments, particularly in action-oriented games, when once something has been set in train the option to do nothing is hardly possible: one is forced to act or to 'die'. Nor would I want to suggest (as Cameron seems to) that the apparently more open character of the computer game experience – the space for a certain (albeit prescribed) agency on the part of the player – is ultimately any less regulating or controlling of its assumed spectators than classical narrative texts are of theirs. All the same, the relative control that the player has over time in a game, the *de facto* sense of present-tense involvement – the impression of being there, responding and being responded to – is central to the genre.[10] Of course, this leads us directly to considerations of interactivity. First though, let me round off the present discussion of narrative.

In terms of traditional narrative meaning, games such as *Quake* are even more shallow than the blockbuster movie or the music video. What takes the place of narrative here is the experience of vicarious movement and fighting itself: precisely the illusion of control and agency in real time and in a realistic looking (and behaving) environment where things get more complicated and frenetic the more players progress towards their goal.

However, it is not only action-oriented games in which story telling as traditionally understood is drastically reduced: stripped of its complex linearity, 'narrated time' and significatory plenitude. As I have already noted, the puzzle-based adventure *Myst* displays a similar tendency. But what about other games that are striving to make more direct inroads into the production of interactive story telling – games that are often described as 'interactive films'? Based on the feature film *Blade Runner* (1982), the late 1990s game of the same title places the player in the same setting as the film itself, a visually ravishing futuristic Los Angeles. Here – as with other 'interactive movie' games and in a similar way to *Myst* – there *are* distinguishable characters with names, roles, traits and motives. The player controls the movements, actions and conversation of an on-screen surrogate – a Blade Runner detective. The game is an exploratory adventure in which players direct their surrogate character around and within the diverse locations of the futuristic city, interrogating witnesses and suspects, searching for clues, analysing evidence, hunting for (and being hunted by) rogue replicants.

Unlike *Quake* and *Myst*, the player's viewpoint in *Blade Runner* is not – at least for the most part – through identification with a first-person or subjective camera set-up. Instead, the player views the scene with the surrogate within it – usually in medium long shot – and controls his movements and actions (including exiting to another location).[11] Once again, however, despite there being close ties to a particular feature film and despite the increased emphasis on character motivation, ultimately, 'the plot' that the player reveals or 'produces' as s/he progresses in the game is a pretext for something else. Only marginally is the game more about characters than say *Myst* (or even *Quake*). True, the characters in *Blade Runner* are far more rounded, individuated and complex than the one-dimensional 'tokens' encountered in games such as *Quake*. They have things to say: they respond to the player's questions. Nevertheless, they are still mere ciphers by comparison to the characters in the film itself. In a sense the characters in *Blade Runner* the computer game are far more continuous with the visual style and the architecture of the fictional world they inhabit. Like the character depiction itself, motives remain simplistic and shallow, not susceptible to further development. They are a vital part of the exotic world of which the player is an 'inhabitant', but they do not invite identification or the desire to want to get to know them better. They serve the function – along with the clues one has to discover and the images they supply for examination (play) on the 'image analyser' – of enabling the disclosure of different locations, new spaces and new characters to explore and gaze upon. It is the mechanics and pleasures involved in this peculiar pretended residency or *vicarious sense of presence* in a fictional world which is uppermost: the ability to talk with people, move between and within spectacular locations, to find things, analyse things and so forth. Once again, narrative is subordinated to the more obvious fascination of being able to take an active part or role in a fictional world, to mingle with the exotic denizens of this future megalopolis exploring their spectacular environment.[12]

Interaction: vicarious kinaesthesia

Although there are vestiges of traditional story telling in computer games, narrative in the classical sense is not their most dominant formal feature. One can certainly see in more or less distinct ways traces of narrative conventionality, particularly those of the film, in games (I shall discuss one such presently). All the same, it would appear to be a set of quite different expectations that under-pins the notion of the computer game. At the centre of these expectations lies not the idea of story telling rather that of *interaction*.

I have already begun to allude to this notion when considering games and narrative, suggesting that it is this rather new-fashioned element, along with the features that are attendant upon it, that constitutes the principal and defining idea of the computer game genre. Still, we need to ask what, more precisely, is 'interactivity' in the context of computer games? How are we to define it, in what way is a computer game interactive? And what does this entail with respect to questions of aesthetic form and spectator experience within the genre?

The past decade has witnessed the emergence of several different uses of the concept of 'interactivity' to describe processes and systems associated with new digital technology. One such use refers to the rise of integrated and mutually affecting information or multi-media systems (e.g. the personal computer which integrates telephone, CD, Internet, electronic mail and other desktop facilities). Clearly, however, it is neither this sense, nor those associated with the growth of commercial interactive information services that is being used to describe the video game. Here, the term 'interactive' refers, as we have already begun to see, to a distinctive mode of *relating* to audiovisual representations or fictions. The player is provided with a way of directly taking a leading role in what occurs, given the means to control – at least in part – what will unfold within the scene on the screen.

Of course, one of the things this entails is that the player – the person trying to control the game – must become familiar and proficient with the game controls. S/he must learn which buttons and/or keys to press in order to achieve a sense of 'agency' within the game. Depending on the kind of game played and the system it is played on, becoming skilful in the use of controls may involve a considerable amount of application and dedicated practice. The sophisticated 'interfaces' of the arcade and game-specific home consoles on which the majority of games are played are fast paced and action laden, and can be extremely complex and difficult to master. This is an important factor in the game playing experience (for differing interpretations of this aspect of games see, for example, Kinder 1991: 112–20; Stallabrass 1993: 93–4). Indeed, for many, acquiring the near-automatic responses necessary to play such games successfully is what provides much of the pleasure. In these so-called 'twitch' games puzzle solving and the time or necessity for deliberation is minimal – once the game is under way the player is compelled continually and immediately to respond.

The degree of difficulty may vary from game to game and system to system, however, acquiring familiarity and competence with controls is something that is required by all games: control aptitude is a convention of computer game playing. Such competence allows the player to carry out various kinaesthetic actions – vicarious though they are – such as running, jumping and shooting *within* an on-screen scene. This is certainly distinctive. In some ways it is analogous to another common mode of interactivity – driving a car. When driving a car one is involved in an activity that involves a similar familiarity with controls. These controls also produce certain kinaesthetic responses, the difference being, of course, that the car occupies actual three-dimensional space and time rather than a simulation of it. Despite its vicarious character the real-time element of gaming – the sense that things are occurring in the present – is analogous to driving. Certainly, the sensation of control experienced in each activity is not at all dissimilar. Indeed, this correspondence is particularly striking in those instances where the player controls the game from a personal perceptual perspective, i.e. from a subjective camera point of view: here, the parallel between the screen and the windscreen is difficult to resist (see Stallabrass 1993: 84).

This dimension of direct physical involvement or 'hands-on control', which the computer game grants to the spectator/player, is perhaps the central and defining characteristic of the genre. The player expects to be able to make things happen, s/he expects to be able to change and affect the course of the action. However, this capability is not unlimited. On the contrary, there are strict limits placed on what is possible in this sense. For example, in *Blade Runner*, although players are allowed certain latitude in terms of what they can do with (and through) their on-screen avatar, control and choice are, ultimately – as in all games – strictly bounded. After only a short time playing the game one realises that the questions one can ask of other characters are limited in number, that there are many places within the setting that are inaccessible and denied one's closer scrutiny. Even more disconcerting is the discovery that one's ability to progress through a game depends not just on finding all the clues (the only things in the set that one can 'pick up'), visiting all the relevant locations and asking all the questions, but doing this in the right order. Not doing so can entail a frustrating stasis: one gets trapped, endlessly running between all-too-familiar locations, revisiting the same characters and scouring the same settings, imprisoned and unable to progress further because a certain vital move is now denied one.[13] Not only are the conventional limits of the game itself revealed at such moments, but so is its pre-programmed character: the element of control and choice it seems to offer is revealed as illusory – just as predetermined as the most formulaic narrative.

It is precisely difficulties such as these that help to make the action-oriented games – the shoot-'em-ups, racing simulations and so forth – the most popular, whilst at the same time also revealing something of why such games typify what is most distinctive about computer games *per se*. With their radical demotion of narrative, it is precisely the heightening of sensation, evinced through the necessity for skill with controls, and the resulting impression of kinaesthesia induced by illusory participation in acts of spectacular risk and speed that lies at the heart of such games. In the vernacular of computer gaming the term for this is 'gameplay'.[14] It is this that most clearly encapsulates what is both novel and desired in computer games. Of course, action games carry frustrations too: the player has to make frequent replays in order to advance a little further. The sheer *sense of presence*, however, conveyed in the best of them – and here *Quake* is a key example – compensates for such defeats.[15] In other words, it is the experience of *vicarious kinaesthesia* itself that counts here: the impression of controlling events that are taking place in the present. Although this is at its strongest in games such as *Quake*, it is nevertheless a crucial component of all games.

157

Image: sumptuous sight

Interactivity in the sense we are discussing it here appears to give the traditional spectator entry into the fictional world: no longer merely a viewer, the player also becomes a doer. In similar ways, each of the games mentioned above gives to those who play them a more or less pronounced illusion of dynamic presence within an alternative world. A game only begins when the player initiates it, and, in order for it to continue, s/he is forced to intervene continually in both a proactive and a reactive manner. Among the various pleasures associated with this, the so-called 'gameplay' aspect of computer games, is precisely this illusion of presence, whereby the player has the impression of agency inside the world of the game. Cameron (1995: 39) discusses this in terms of representation and time. Citing the work of Comrie (1976) he argues that interactive representation involves a mode of representing that is 'inside the time of the situation being described'. That is to say, time is represented as viewed from a first-person perspective – literally *as if* one were really there, thereby, producing the impression that things are continually open to any possibility. Clearly, something similar can be argued with respect to the representation of *space* in many video games. Indeed, it becomes difficult to untangle space from time in this respect so intimate is their relation. We might say that the illusion of experiencing events as if they are taking place in present time in computer games is largely dependent upon visual simulation. This is most apparent in those games which involve subjective viewpoints – though not only these, of course.

In this sense, I want to suggest that computer games – particularly in their more recent development – *have* continued to develop and intensify a central aesthetic attribute of classical narrative cinema: namely, the realistic – which is to say illusionistic – representation of space. In his exploration of the 'formative phase' of the 'language' of the cinema, Noël Burch considers the evolution of the spectator positioning that is peculiar to the cinema. He describes a certain '*centring* of the spectator by making him or her the reference point "around which" was constituted the *oneness and continuity* of a spectacle destined to become more and more fragmented' (1990: 209). Burch demonstrates that part of the constitution of what he pointedly describes as the 'motionless voyage' of the cinema spectator involves the production of the effect of a 'haptic' space; that is to say, a countering of visual 'flatness' and the 'conquest of space' through the development of camera set-ups and movement and editing (shot juxtaposition) to produce the impression or feeling of three-dimensionality and depth. Intimately coupled (among other things) with an editing system that takes the fabrication of a 'single unique point – the spectator-subject' as its guiding principle, this impression helps to produce the sense of being taken or transported into a world that is distinct from the spectator's real bodily location.

Of course, in the sophisticated system of spatio-temporal representation that is classical narrative cinema, the spectator is given the status of a ubiquitous

voyeur: a seer with a guarantee of invisibility. Truly subjective camera shots –
which is to say, first-person spectator/character viewpoints – only occur in
contexts where there is no danger of the look being returned (i.e. of being
looked back at and directly acknowledged). This is to prevent exposure of the
identification between spectator and camera that is so vital to the illusionist
aesthetic that comprises this type of cinema. The first-person perspective in a
computer game such as *Quake* clearly differs in this respect, and yet only
marginally: there is a definite sense in which it constitutes an extension of the
sense of presence that is already a key part of the aesthetic make-up of classical
cinema.[16] In games such as *Quake* and *Myst*, for example, 'the motionless
voyager' of classical narrative cinema – privileged passenger/voyeur – gives way
to the (almost) motionless explorer: the spectator is given the scope for a kind
of vicarious independent visual exploration. In present time and from a first-
person viewpoint the player is enabled to explore the space s/he inhabits. The
semblance of realistic spatial orientation is maintained from the cinema
aesthetic, but at the same time it is heightened both by the capacity of the
computer to model three-dimensional space and by the control one is given to
determine where one goes and what one does. The representational spaces of
the diorama and the cinema fuse – it is *as if* one has been assigned the role of
camera-person in this virtual world. Despite the fact that ultimately this
control/presence is limited and illusory – one can't go just anywhere nor do
and look at just anything one wants to – this partial freedom does, nevertheless,
augment the impression of kinaesthetic presence or involvement in the image.
Indeed, it may be precisely at this point that – looked at from another perspective – the cinematic is surpassed.

This component of the game experience has become an important consideration in the design and development of the whole computer game aesthetic.
Indeed, the whole aspect of kinaesthetic presence converges with issues of
image simulation. Once again, and not unsurprisingly, we find that 'realism' in
the sense of surface accuracy is central to the discursive practices of games (and
simulation rides). An increased sense of presence or reality in the sense under
discussion here is seen to depend upon a constant refining of visual representation in particular. However, we must be careful not to overstate what is
occurring here. There is indeed a real sense in which the player's relation to the
image has been significantly altered by the interactive aspect of computer
games. Yet, as we have already begun to see, this shift is not without its para-
doxes. For the increased sense of presence in a three-dimensional world that the
best games offer to the spectator/player is achieved largely at the expense of
depth of meaning. Extension of entry into the spatio-temporal world of the
image in computer games entails *not* a semantic intensification so much as a
heightening of sensational and spectacular encounters with imagery.

The 'motionless voyager' of the classical cinema gets to see images that are
extremely diverse, and that have high definition and detail. Partly as a consequence of this and partly as a function of their place in a complexly coded

narrative schema, the spectator is *led* through and into a relatively high degree of discursive involvement with the images displayed. The images of games are of a lower definition and the fascination they hold is of a different order. One may well feel more of a participant existing inside the world imaged, however, the imagery itself elicits different exchanges. Thus, in the case of action-oriented games such as *Quake*, the player relates to the image in ways that have to do with architectural exploration and topographic orientation, and – crucially – as indicators of things to respond to (i.e. shoot at, pick up, avoid and so forth). This is not to say that the imagery in such games is not distinctive. On the contrary, more often than not it involves the portrayal of fantastic locations and characters that range in style from gothic to the graphics of the science fiction paperback cover. Clearly, such imagery signifies in itself. It also exists to be looked at – to titillate the eyes of young (male) players who appear to relish such iconography. However, given the player's overriding goal of finding a way through a maze-like environment populated by bloodthirsty enemies, the space for involved aesthetic meaning is placed at a premium.[17] The sensation of appearing to have mobility and agency in such a hostile environment is what is central: imagery is an integral component of a rather direct and visceral stimulation.[18]

Even in a game like *Myst* where threats are few and far between and careful exploration involving puzzle solving is the key to one's progress, there exists an intrinsic lack of significatory depth. Traditional pleasures of plot and character involvement are not what concerns the player here, rather delight and fascination in being able to discover and uncover new things (images) to prospect. *Myst* is about solving visually based conundrums in order to see more of its fantasy world (and its different 'ages'). Puzzle solving is primarily a means to further spectacle, rather than to narrative knowledge of the traditional kind. Again, the impression of being enabled to act within and upon the world one gazes upon is central to the kind of aesthetic pleasure derived here.

Simulation rides: the almost motionless voyage

Before summing up this discussion of computer games and drawing some key distinctions in relation to computer game interactivity and traditional modes of spectator solicitation, I want briefly to look at a related phenomenon, the so-called 'simulation ride'. Simulation rides provide clear aesthetic parallels with games and yet in crucial respects they are quite distinctive. These leisure attractions are designed to simulate motion and the experience of travelling or voyaging (chapter 1). In this respect they share something of the conventionality of the cinema of the past and the computer game of the present. In the simulation ride the 'motionless voyage' involved in the narrative cinema is sharpened and concentrated. Indeed, it is the intensification of *one* particular variant of the subjective point of view shot – that assuming the perspective of a travelling projectile – which has come to define the locus of such experiences.

With the advent of digital technologies the simulated rides of early cinema are reinvented and rejuvenated (see Fielding 1970).

Even at its most modest the physical scale of the simulation ride is grander than the computer game. The apparatus of the motion simulator comprises a theatre incorporating a screen, an imaginary vehicle and often sets, props and actors: spectacle and visceral thrill are what these attractions deal in – as in the computer game, narrative is subjugated to more instantaneous pleasures. Similarly, they also involve a heightening of kinaesthetic affect; in this case *actual* physical movement helps to produce and augment the sense of riding within a fictional space. Yet, the spectators/passengers do not physically travel anywhere – they are seated in an auditorium the whole time. The extraordinary impression of being physically transported is achieved, rather, through hydraulically controlled seats that have been programmed to move 'on the spot' in perfect synchronisation with the movement imaged on the screen itself. This added dimension of real movement, carefully choreographed to mimic the positional shifts and variances of the forward motion represented on the screen, intensifies the spectator/passenger's sense of haptic presence.

The idea most frequently used to describe this spectator experience is 'immersion' (see Huhatamo 1996). This term refers to the more or less convincing impression of presence in a fictional world, for example, the sensation of travelling in the fictional world of *Back to the Future* – even though one is not. In this sense, 'immersion' does not refer to anything new. It is about the production of the 'suspension of disbelief', an aesthetics of realistic illusion. Of course, as we have already begun to see, the ways in which such a sensation is achieved vary, and 'new' or distinctive dimensions are being added to it, notably in the computer game and the simulation ride. However, as Huhatamo points out, there is a distinction to be drawn with respect to immersion, between games on the one hand and rides on the other (1996: 173). Simulation rides lack the dimension of control and response ('interaction') that is so important to the sense of 'immersion' in computer games. The ride is an experience that one gives oneself over to. The spectator is solicited with the promise of visceral thrills, the pleasure of experiencing sheer spectacular illusion and a sense of speed. S/he does not expect to resolve any enigmas, to gain answers to questions, nor to be able to intervene in what is taking place. Surrendering oneself for the duration to the convincing illusion that one is being taken on a fantastic (and giddy) ride – a ride produced by the machinery of representation and its conventional system – is where the simulation ride begins and ends.

Of course, what makes such extraordinarily convincing simulated rides different to actual journeys in cars or trains (which is to say, more than just banal counterfeits) are the excessive details. As with the mechanical thrill rides of the early amusement parks – undoubted relatives of the current simulation ride – there is a conspicuous exaggeration of certain aspects of everyday modes of transportation. Thus, 'speeds' are faster and 'manoeuvres' are astonishing in their seeming impossibility. Likewise, the scenarios, events and characters represented in these mock journeys are more often than not outlandish and bizarre.

Closer to the roller-coaster than any of the other forms of visual digital culture, the simulation ride is perhaps the genre that is the most keenly playful and depthless.[19] Of course, the form is not just about corporeal sensation, for integral to its overall effect are imagery and sounds. However, these tend to function largely as means of extending direct sensory stimulation: in addition to motion the sensational assault takes on visual and auditory dimensions. This is not to say that the simulation ride produces a totally abstract experience. In many respects it is highly figurative in its representational character and thus – despite its greatly inflated aspect – is recognisable and familiar. It is just that, at the core of such expressions of visual digital culture, what is being represented or reproduced – so directly and hyperbolically – is a kinaesthetic sensation. Visual and auditory elements are subordinated to this overriding aim: the simulated experience of a stupefying and dramatic caper. Once again, what we experience takes place in real time, it directly involves several of the senses and it is *about* itself: the (almost) motionless voyage in which narrative is de-centred by more immediate intensities.

Interactivity and immersion as mass entertainment

Relative to the other expressions of visual digital culture under review here, the ways in which the spectator engages with games and rides are – in the first instance and in certain key respects – distinctive, not least because they introduce certain direct registers of physicality to the experience. We must be careful however. As I have indicated, submitting to the illusion-inducing experience of the simulation ride is not altogether new, neither is it completely distinct from modes of solicitation already operative in mechanical amusement park rides and the classical cinema. If anything, the differences are ones of degree: I have stressed qualitative advances in the way in which the motion simulation experience has become more convincing or 'immersive' (see Huhatamo 1996: 166). Certainly, the re-emergence of this early form of technologically based entertainment, 'digitally improved' so as to be enticing to contemporary audiences familiar with modes of high speed travel and saturated with realistic representation, marks a difference concerning *level* of intensity as much as kind. The submission to physical movement as a crucial part of the audiovisual representational experience *is* (relative to the other forms under discussion) distinctive. The spectator's expectations of the sensational and the ludic – which are attendant upon the ride genre – are, however, very much of a piece with the other expressions of visual digital culture under review here.[20]

The 'interactivity' of computer games on the other hand, is something resembling rather more of a break. The ability and expectation that the spectator physically intervene to change or affect what is occurring on the screen does seem to mark a shift which has more significance. Here the simulation experience is not of travelling or of being taken on a ride, but rather that of actively participating in something: of flying an aircraft or racing a car, of exploration and discovery, of combat and survival. One is offered the semblance of control. Although, ultimately, constrained by the game program, nevertheless, up to a point one *has* control over what is occurring and what will occur – one adopts the mantle of prime mover in a surrogate world. Within the numerous parameters established by the game itself the player has the commensurate 'freedom' to select options and is permitted, thereby, a certain degree of agency within the world of the fiction. As we have seen, given the increasing surface realism of the moving imagery, the sophistication of real-time graphic representation and the use of first-person perspective, the impression of actual occupancy and agency within the space of the game's fictional world can be extremely convincing.

In both the game and the ride – in different though related ways – there is a sense in which it might be argued that the spectator is allowed a contact with the image that is more intimate than any previously enjoyed. In the case of the simulation ride we might describe this as involving a particular intensification of the *suturing* mechanism already familiar with respect to the formal workings of the classical cinema. Insofar as the spectator in such attractions experiences a powerful and persuasive illusion of vicarious travel, it could be said that we have thereby, and in a sense, entered further 'into the image' than at any time previously. Using similar reasoning the same could be said for our relationship to computer games. For here, at least in their most sophisticated expressions, an even more inclusive mode of getting 'into the image' might be said to occur: not only does there exist the sense of presence within the image but additionally the sense of agency too. Of course, things are not quite this simple, and to begin to see why it is vital to allow the phrase 'into the image' its full complement of senses (see Robins 1996). Doing this enables to us to open up and get a clearer understanding of the aesthetic character of both games and rides; it also allows us to define another sense of 'into the image' that is most appropriate here.

We might begin by highlighting a disparity. Computer games allow a degree of entry into the image (interaction/agency/control) that previously was unheard of. Yet, looked at from another perspective this 'entry' or 'participation' remains far more *superficial* than classical forms – even of narrative – where the spectator remains in this sense comparatively 'outside' the image. Vicarious embodiment within the scene and the ability to act within it does not necessarily entail increased aesthetic depth. Of course, there is no reason why it should, for we are talking here of different kinds of entry 'into the image'. Problems only arise when concepts such as 'active' and 'passive' are conflated with the different character of spectator solicitation and practice involved in games on the one hand and forms involving traditional modes of engagement on the other. Players are often perceived as being more active than viewers are, yet, this is only true – at least with respect to the computer game – in a vicariously 'physical' sense.[21] As we have already seen, interactivity in the computer game involves a kind of relative or regulated agency: the constraints of the game allow the player to choose between a limited number of options. However, such 'active participation' should not be confused with increased semantic engagement. On the contrary, the kinds of mental processes that games solicit are largely instrumental and/or reactive in character. As I suggest above, the space for reading or meaning-making in the traditional sense is radically reduced in computer games and simulation rides. In this sense the much maligned 'passive' spectators of conventional cinema might be said to be far more active than their counterparts in the newer forms. For here another sense of entry 'into the image' is apparent, one that does not simply turn upon the pleasures of vicarious agency, the sensations of presence and spectacle, but involves, rather, at the poetic level (form and style) itself, a more profound dimension of semiotic resonance and semantic depth.

A de-centring of narrative alongside ways of refining the representation of haptic space, both these things occur in the computer game and the simulation ride genres. Interactivity itself – so-called 'gameplay' and the control and skill acquisition this involves – together with simulation and image display are fore-gounded in games. The player as protagonist is involved in goal-oriented activity within a 'micro-world' which, despite its realistic tangibility, is nevertheless constructed (hence 'inhabitable') along lines that are highly procedural and rule governed. Computer games are machine-like: they solicit intense concentration from the player who is caught up in their mechanisms, trying to fathom and master their workings. Leaving little room for reflection other than an instrumental type of thinking that is more or less commensurate with their own workings, they offer little scope for independent initiative or deviation. Yet, out of such a system an aesthetic emerges: agonistic in character it is clothed in the pleasures of vicarious agency and intense visual stimulation.

Likewise for the simulation ride, for it too has far more to do with visual spectacle and the simulation of sensation for its own sake than with traditional modes of representation. Once again, despite the quasi-motionless state of the spectator, the motion simulator manufactures the sensations of occupancy and movement within and through another space. It is the sheer illusion of pretended travel – which still manages to persuade and convince despite its hyperbolic character – that comprises the aesthetic measure of the simulation ride. The spectators who submit themselves to the experience of the simulation ride become, for the duration, part of an extraordinarily sophisticated machine of the visible. This machine is built solely to 'centre them' in its manufacture of fabulous and visceral visual illusions: as before, new technologies of the visible converge – the cinema turns into stage magic and vice versa – often to quite dizzying effect.

Finally, though, we might invoke yet another sense of the phrase 'into the image' to capture what is involved here. This links computer games and rides more intimately with the cultural-aesthetic regime dominant within the forms of visual digital culture that I am describing. For the use of 'into' in the phrase in question might also be taken as referring to a currently popular way of expressing the idea of being engrossed or enthralled by something. To be 'into the image' in this sense describes a general attitude of being 'taken up with' or 'wrapped up in' the image. As I have suggested, the forms of digital visual culture under exploration here manifest a distinctive preoccupation with the image as image: images are the material or ground for new modes of combination, new levels of illusion, new kinds of surprise and delight. In this sense I am suggesting that such a preoccupation with the image entails a mode of reception that is fascinated not so much by what images signify as with their power to induce direct stimulation, visceral thrill and formal and spectacular excitations. Computer game players and those who embark upon simulated rides do not expect to be told deep stories, let alone to be intellectually taxed or challenged. They are 'into the image' at a more corporeal and tactile level. In the first instance, the image touches them not so much in an affective, symbolic or meaningful manner, but rather more directly as a crucial element in a playful simulation that excites the senses.

In other words, these two expressions of digital visual culture are manifestations of the aesthetic of surface play outlined in recent chapters. Though both introduce distinguishing elements and considerations to this aesthetic (interactivity and simulation), it is precisely these elements which contribute most to its production. That both of these forms are caught up in and shaped by the broad framing culture of the copy and serial repetition discussed in previous chapters goes without saying. Indeed, it may be precisely in the field of video games that the impulse 'continually to reinvent and update the same idea' is most clearly demonstrated (see Hayes and Dinsey with Parker 1995: 7). Be this as it may, it is undoubtedly the case that both are deeply imbued with the marks of intertextuality – just as both are vital components of the 'multi-purpose entertainment' conglomerates cited in the previous chapter. [22]

Claims of increased participation, responsiveness and dialogue have accompanied discussions of interactivity. But when 'interactivity' is viewed in the grounded and specific context of computer games, it becomes difficult to sustain such claims. The ability to choose to do something to change or alter the scene, to intervene in the action *does* constitute an increase in participation relative to the quiescent state of the usually sedentary viewer. However, as we have seen, increased participation along the axis of simulated participation does not necessarily make for less passive reception, especially in the semantically denuded or 'thinned down' fictional worlds of computer games. For once engagement is measured in terms of significatory depth or substance, then, appearances to the contrary, computer games players must be viewed as being far less active than they might at first seem. Increased involvement is not in doubt, but for the most part this has to do with extrinsically defined relations and exchanges. Computer games are surface play. The pleasures they promise entail distracting contests of skill together with simplistic and make-believe role-play within increasingly convincing simulations. They *are* games, though, peculiarly, as such they exist 'at one remove', and it is this, their simulacral or so-called 'virtual' aspect – this dimension of incorporation in fabrication, through image, motion and sound – which provides most of the fascination and fun.

8

SURFACE PLAY AND SPACES OF CONSUMPTION

In this book I have advanced an aesthetic description of some of the major expressions of contemporary visual digital culture. I have suggested and argued for an understanding that posits visual digital culture – in the bounded sense I am defining it – as instituting a new modality of formality within contemporary mass culture. This chapter is concerned with questions of how we might begin to characterise spectator experience within this distinctive aesthetic.

Whether spectator experience is viewed as being determined wholly by the text (film, programme, advertisement and so forth), only partially, or hardly at all, the assumption has been that in various ways the spectator is part of an activity or process that is fundamentally and profoundly one involving signification. However, given the aesthetic trends described in Part II and in the last chapter we might wonder whether the latest genres in question here invite a different understanding. I shall suggest that, although the notions of reading and meaning are hardly – of course – redundant here, nevertheless, they do not figure as prominently as in many prior or adjacent forms. Indeed, the visual digital aesthetic forces us to consider other ways of characterising and thinking about the spectator.

Reading de-centred

Certainly, it is not too difficult to begin to discern what these new digital expressions entail with regard to spectator experience, for the aesthetic explorations undertaken above are highly suggestive in this regard. I do want to caution against over-simplification, however, for if one thing emerges from these analyses, it is that we are not dealing with an aesthetic that is wholly homogeneous or uniform in character. And it follows that neither should we expect the mode of spectator solicitation in the several genres of visual digital culture explored here to be the same in each case. Like the expressions themselves which, despite the significance of their shared characteristics and tendencies, are, nevertheless, more or less distinctive in their aesthetic make-up, recipients of these latest genres are not engaged in exactly the same way by each of them. Thus the way in which a music video solicits its spectator is different from the way a video game does so, just as the kind of TV advertisements we discussed differ in this respect from, say, simulation rides. Having said this, however, I do want to suggest that – relative to other genres or forms – there *are* features of commonality operating here with respect to spectator expectations and, further, that this warrants a specific and clear grouping or association. In other words, there exists a common core within the expressions in question in this regard that allows us to talk about the arrival of a broader, distinctive mode of spectator experience – at least within this aesthetic space of mass visual culture. It is precisely the *shared* characteristics that I shall be concerned with in the discussion that follows.

Sensual and formal intensities

What is it that spectators (for want of a better word) of each of the diverse genres under discussion here share with one another? Borrowing and adapting an expression from art historian E.H. Gombrich we might say that they share a broad 'horizon of expectations' (1996: 52–4). The key feature of this horizon, which cuts across the genres in question, is that recipients expect certain *intensities* of direct sensual stimulation (see also Jameson's different use of this term, 1984: 58). The anticipated 'intensities' themselves are not always the same, but they are part of the same continuum existing within the same genus: defined by formal excitation, spectacle and physical stimulus. In their distinctive ways, the various expressions of visual digital culture all position their spectators as seekers after modes of direct visual and corporeal stimulation.

As I have already suggested, in their very make-up and by contrast with other comparable forms, the genres and expressions in question display little by way of significatory depth: they are shallow modes of representation. The emphasis (following Sontag in a different context) – though this varies both across and within the genres themselves – is 'less on what they are saying than on the manner of saying it' (Sontag 1967: 19). Little space is allowed in these ephemeral and semantically exhausted forms for meaning-making on the spectator's part. They do not propose spectators who are bent on interpretation, or who are looking for semantic resonance. The activity mobilised in this instance is not primarily intellectual, not reflective or interpretative in character, but rather sensual and diverting in various ways.

Here is a dimension of contemporary visual culture that is conspicuous insofar as it cannot easily be reduced to a process of interpretative activity – to a process of 'meaning-making' (see Bordwell 1991). Indeed, it may well be that the distinctive aesthetic of visual digital culture is a prime candidate for the fresh approaches to critical appraisal and understanding that Bordwell has urged in his recent writing (1991: 249–74). For – at least in their aesthetic aspect – these particular cultural expressions force us, precisely, to take much more account of 'phenomenal qualities', to pay more attention to their surface appearance.[1] As

Sontag has argued, 'sensations, feelings, the abstract forms and styles of sensibility *count* [my emphasis]' (Sontag 1967: 300).

I should not want to be seen as uncritically adopting an argument against hermeneutic approaches (broadly conceived) to understanding cultural practices and products. In this instance, however, it does seem that the cultural expressions at issue push both spectator and critic precisely to attend more to form and style: their semantically rarefied character, their obvious foregrounding of surface and sensation make such a line of approach compelling. For, as we have seen, 'sensations, feelings, the abstract forms and styles of sensibility count' enormously in visual digital genres.

Of course, traditional meaning is not suppressed here in the radical way that it is in, say, high modernist painting – a most uncompromising mode of visual formalism. And yet, engaged by such things as the language of style, artifice and image for their own sake, and a certain sensuous immediacy – the spectator of our contemporary mass forms might be described as sharing in processes and activities that are, indeed, similar to those of abstract art. Similar, though not – as we have seen – the same. The formality within visual digital culture is not an art of pure or unadulterated signifiers: there is still figuration, still narrative (and traces of narrative) still traces of constructed meaning in the forms in question. Forged from resurrected forms of popular spectacle which arise from within the crucible of a maturing culture of mass reproduction – the aesthetic at issue here is one in which the exaggerated emphasis on form and image still retains vestiges of traditional representation.

This said, I still want to suggest – again in a manner that is not entirely dissimilar from the spectator of abstract art – that the spectator of the forms under consideration is more of a sensualist than a 'reader' or interpreter. The spectator of visual digital culture is positioned first and foremost as a seeker after unbridled visual delight and corporeal excitation. The centre of sensual assault s/he is someone who – depending on the genre – is in pursuit of the ornamental and the decorative, modes of embellishment, the amazing and the breathtaking, the nuances of the staged effect and the virtuoso moment, the thrill of vertigo or the *agôn* of competition.

The 'programming of sensations' that Sontag discusses in relation to art practices of the 1960s, now appears more appropriate than ever – a near perfect description of the process involved in the digitally produced aesthetic discussed in these pages (1967: 302). Of course, no longer part of the 'painful challenging and stretching of the sensorium', which Sontag propounded for the experimental art of the time, our expressions of digital culture have little to do with the earnest and rather serious tenor of modernist art. Their aesthetic involves a sensuousness of a lighter stamp – seemingly far more playful and spontaneous in character than the intellectual pretensions involved in reception of the latter.

Spectators as players

If the recipient of digital genres is positioned primarily as a sensualist – someone who, in a variety of different ways, is mainly embroiled in phenomenal form – how do we begin to characterise their side of the experience? To put it another way, if interpretation is not the main activity of such spectators what else might they be doing when they engage with such work? I shall tentatively suggest that concepts of *play* give us a more precise description of what the spectator of visual digital culture is doing when engaging with such forms. It is play (or something very much like it) that brings us closer to describing what is experienced in these cases. But what does this entail? For does not all cultural consumption (and production for that matter) involves an element of play (see Huizinga 1955)?

The element of playfulness that operates in the genres under discussion is not of one kind. Indeed, it operates within and across all four of the main 'principles' that, according to Roger Caillois, rule various types of play or game: they are '*mimicry*' (or simulation), '*agôn*' (or competition), '*alea*' (or chance) and '*ilinx*' (or vertigo) (see Caillois 1962: 11–36). Within these broad classes and relative to their positioning between the two governing poles of '*paidia*' (uncontrolled, anarchic play) and '*ludus*' (regulated, conventionalised play) (1962: 13), certain of these principles are preponderant with respect to spectator activity in the digital genres at issue. All of the cultural expressions under discussion here can be located at that end of the continuum that Caillois designates with the term *ludus*. As we have seen, they are highly regulated, intensely repetitive, institutionalised and governed by established aesthetic rules and norms. Although the spectator appears to have considerable leeway or freedom – particularly in computer games – we must be careful not to overstate this. The operation of the ludic principle in Caillois' sense also works its disciplining effect on the playful aspect of spectating in the genres of visual digital culture. For, quite clearly – and in this regard they are no different from other 'institutional modes of representation' – the latter do not involve the 'free improvisation', 'carefree gaiety' and 'uncontrolled fantasy' that Caillois attributes to *paidia* as a kind of unconstrained pure mode of play.

Still, certain notions of play have clear descriptive relevance when applied to spectator activity in the expressions under consideration here. This is most apparent perhaps in the competition, skill and perseverance (*agôn*) that form part of the experience of playing many computer games. It is present in the intoxication – the thrill, speed, dizziness, panic and so forth – that accompany the vertiginous experiences (*ilinix*) of rides and other special attractions. And it clearly occurs in the various kinds of 'play with appearances' (*mimicry*) – involving different kinds of visual and fictional illusion, artifice, decoration and so forth – that we have associated with the simulation, visual effects and montage-based expressions of spectacle cinema, TV ads and music videos. Moreover, it would be wrong to think that only one kind of play principle can be associated with each of the forms in question. Clearly, elements of simulation and spectacle (*mimicry*) enter into appreciation of the computer game, just as they do in the special venue attraction. And equally, elements of vertigo – disorientation, shock and astonishment – operate in reception of expressions such as the TV advertisement and the action film.

Certain principles of play are particularly pronounced in (the reception of) the genres of visual digital culture. Somewhat 'naïve' in character (in a certain sense, perhaps, also somewhat distorted – see pp. 172–3), these principles denote a particular register of experience: one that is associated more precisely with pleasures that are ephemeral, sensuous and physical. It is this rather elementary and uncomplicated playfulness that I want to highlight. Distantly related to games of the mask and pretence, to racing, to doodling and to swinging – the pleasures of reception in visual digital culture are direct, sensual and quasi-ritualistic, considerably removed from the interpretative dimension of meaning and significance (compare, for example, Huizinga 1955: 168 and Gombrich 1984: 12–16).

If anything the stimulus–response couplet operates here in a way that is less constrained or regulated than it is in other forms. The spectator of visual digital culture in our sense of this term seeks after and expects certain intensities of visual/sensual experience. As we have seen, one of the main pleasures of such reception revolves around a particular mode of looking in which the image itself is foregrounded. Blown up, ornamented, overstated, stylised – in these and other ways – the image, even when it is figurative, takes on an imposing and arresting presence of its own. It becomes excessive, and its accentuation of illusion, of form or of style captures and entrances the eye. There are, of course, stronger and weaker manifestations of this subjugation in which the reflective or interpretative faculties are overpowered by immediate sensuous impressions – though I am suggesting that it is a pronounced feature of the aesthetic of digital visual genres.[2] And I need hardly point out that such formal or phenomenal manipulation does not stop with the visible. Its extension occurs in the direct stimulation *and* simulation of bodily sensation in the rides of the special venue and the computer game (see chapter 7).

Such spectator engagements entail various degrees of heightened physical activity and sensual stimulation. Looked at from a different perspective, however, the spectator activity I am describing appears as rather passive, particularly so given that I am attributing strong play elements to its functioning. For we tend to view play as active by definition. The problem is that the measure of activity in cultural reception (even that of mass culture) tends – and with considerable justification – to centre on signification and reading. Looked at from this perspective the play-related and sensuous activity of the spectators of digital culture appears rather superficial. Of course, as I am trying to suggest (not least in some of the description of aesthetic make-up in preceding chapters) such play-related reception itself entails spectator activity. This may not involve activities of reading and interpretation – not at any rate, to anything like the usual extent. Nevertheless, acts of perceptual recognition centred on various modes of illusion and simulation, identification of artifice, recognition of pattern, variation and order, the memorising of moves and the acquisition of skills implies that such reception is not entirely passive. Indeed, this might be seen to be even less the case when one crucially adds that such activity is all in the cause of a deliberate search for engagement in certain direct forms of sensual pleasure. And yet the fact remains – and this is perhaps particularly clear in the operation of spectacle – that this activity and the play principles that help contain it seems to be one in which the spectator is both worked over and more rigidly positioned than ever. It is extremely difficult – despite its seemingly trivial or superficial nature – to counteract the spectacular at the moment of reception, even averting the eyes is an option that is hard to achieve. There seems to be nothing that corresponds to the (highly relative) freedom to produce counter-readings in the kinds of text that concern us here. As Fiske argues: 'Spectacle liberates from subjectivity. Its emphasis on excessive materiality foregrounds the body, not as a signifier of something else, but in its *presence*' (1994: 243). Operating primarily on the plane of the sensual and in a context of 'thinned down' signification, our texts are only really *working* when they produce sensory distraction. The semantic dimension has become so attenuated that whilst interpellation may not entirely disappear, it would, all the same, seem to be reduced or simplified. Here, it is the senses that are directly hailed – thereby making it more appropriate to speak of physical pleasure that is more immediate and unalloyed in character.

Of course, even if, as I am claiming, certain kinds of rudimentary play principle are in operation in the genres of visual digital culture, it still must be acknowledged that these are highly mediated. That is to say, they do not operate in quite the same ways they do in earlier or 'ideal' manifestations of playing. Not only are they further removed from the direct (imaginative and physical) control of the player, but they are also to an increasing extent mechanised (made more mechanistic) by their inscription in the expressions and genres in question. The element of creative control and imaginative spontaneity that is attached to true play – 'child's play' – is diluted (see, for example, Provenzo 1991: 72–98; Wollen 1993: 144–5). Another way of putting this might be to say that the play principles in the forms of visual digital culture have been subjected to further processes of instrumentalisation (see Stallabrass 1996). Perhaps this latest disciplining of the play principle constitutes an extension of the operation of Caillois' notion of 'ludus'?[3] What is clear is that the playfulness involved here is not without its contradictions. It is not a matter of spectators playing *with* these texts (insofar as the expressions at issue *are* texts) more that play principles are inscribed *already* within their different modes of address. Spectators are playing to the extent that they decide to engage with a particular text within a particular genre, however this play – even in the computer game – is largely taken out of their hands, it is contained and regulated. A certain logic is evident, a logic that certainly contains elements of play (and games) and yet it is one that always cedes ultimate control to the genre or text itself. Indeed, to a great extent it is not incorrect to say that it is the spectator who is 'played with'. And yet, for all this it is precisely the discrete, bounded and conventionalised character of these forms, their marked independence of the real world and their *design for sensual stimulation* that still – no matter how tenuously – connects them to play.

I am marking out a mode of spectatorship that is relatively distinctive though by no means unprecedented. The viewer of the firework display, the tightrope walker, the trick effect, the kaleidoscope, the diorama, the 'Shoot the Chutes' and so forth was engaging with cultural products in very similar ways to the spectators we are discussing here. Like spectacle itself, such spectatorship – diverse, yet related in kind – manifests itself in different ways at different times. It also is more or less prominent at certain moments in history. Presently, after a period of relative quiescence, a new space involving the kind of sensation-based aesthetics that I am exploring here has opened up within mass visual culture.

I have characterised the spectators of this cultural-aesthetic space as playful seekers after style, spectacle and visceral thrills, prepared in the main to be perceptually (and physically), rather than intellectually, active. On the whole, such spectators are receivers and sorters of immediate sensuous impressions. How are we to assess or evaluate this mode of spectator engagement: sensuously rich and dynamic in terms of perceptual activity, yet semantically compromised and relatively quiescent in terms of interpretative activity?

This constitutes an implicit injunction to begin the work of attempting to understand the place and function of such an aesthetic in terms of the broader context. Of course, the overall aim of this book sets itself more limited goals: situating and starting to describe the emergence of a new or distinctive aesthetic trend within the mass visual culture of the late twentieth century. When – as inevitably we must – one begins to ask these further and broader questions then it quickly becomes apparent that a whole host of complex and fraught debates, issues and problems arise. I shall limit this discussion by highlighting two questions only. The first revolves around *representation* and associated debates about its role and function within mass media culture. The second looks at how the consumption sites of visual digital culture and the aesthetic experiences they contain and engender relate to certain conceptions of experience that are far more encompassing in character – held as constitutive categories of late or postmodernity.

Active spectators?

Given that the mode of spectatorship I describe above does now exist as an element within contemporary mass visual culture, how might we begin to understand the significance of the emergence of genres that position and mobilise spectators less and less as 'readers' and more and more as 'sensualists'? This depends upon where one locates or positions oneself within cultural thought and critique – particularly with respect to debates about the operation of cultural consumption: a huge and contested area of contemporary social and cultural criticism (see, for example, Featherstone 1991; Qualtier 1991; Morley 1993; Fiske 1994). Narrowing the focus to the field of media and cultural studies it becomes possible to isolate two important approaches to under-standing audience and spectator activity within contemporary consumer culture. The first and predominant perspective is what might be termed the 'productive audience' approach. This stands at the end of a line of criticism that has increas-ingly countered ideas both of authorial centrality and/or textual fixity *and* ideas of the media as a mere mode of manipulation or legitimation. Against these it proposes texts that are polysemantic (i.e. only relatively 'closed'), spectators who are themselves active producers of textual meaning and audiences who, rather than mere dupes are viewed as deliberate and discriminating users: media literate consumers in search of meaning and pleasure (for example, Fiske 1994).

The other perspective is not as prominent and it is more recent. It emerges from a cautious reappraisal of the 'productive audience' perspective, arguing – among other things – that the latter's empowered and creative cultural consumers may not be quite as 'free' nor as 'assured' as they think they are (for example, Morley 1993). This approach – and, once again, I caricature some-what here – believes that an important element has receded from the active audience idea. Ultimately, this might be described as involving the loss of any way of accounting for those social and political processes that affect and shape human relations and that operate at the 'macro' level, beyond (though in addi-tion to) questions centred on the desire, identity and agency of the individual consumer. This perspective does not view spectators or viewers as mere passive receptacles totally at the mercy of what they are fed by the media. But neither does it accept that considerations of power and ideology that are more global in their effect have all but disappeared from the processes of reception.

Intoxication

Cultural geographer Kevin Robins avowedly adopts such an approach in his discussion of contemporary television's representation of war, death and violence (see Robins 1996: 107–26). Robins argues that the relation of contem-porary audiences to such television – be it in the form of news reportage, documentary or fictionalised images – may well be active, but that this activity is of a kind that involves complex mechanisms of 'screening out' or self-shielding: a process in which 'reality is simultaneously acknowledged and evaded'(1996: 125). Robins takes this argument further, however, when considering new image technologies – the central preoccupation of his book. Drawing upon critiques of modernity associated with Benjamin, Simmel and Freud (and repre-sented in the recent work of Susan Buck-Morss 1989), he argues that the 'phantasmagoric' and spectacle culture that emerged as part of nineteenth-century modernity can be understood as a kind of 'compensatory reality'. The pleasurable and diversionary shocks and sensations that issued from the new forms of technological entertainment, the arcades, the amusement parks, cinemas and so forth, functioned to block out 'competing stimuli of a more threatening kind'. The new media forms constituted 'responses to the shock of modern existence, not in terms of the numbing or deadening of sensation, but rather through the management and control of stimuli' (1996: 120).

Robins argues that a similar thing is occurring with the current 'phantas-magoria' that issues from 'television and post-television technologies'. A kind of 'anaesthesia' through 'intoxication' – through a flooding of the senses – is effected. Robins focuses specifically on what he calls television's 'reality shows' – its supposed 'representation and documentation of the real world'. And he suggests that we 'must take account of the nature of audience engagement ... . [w]hat are being mobilised by reality shows are feelings and sensations, at the expense of reason, analysis, reflection. Engagement is about flooding the senses and shocking the emotions' (1996: 121). Moreover, he goes on to suggest that 'virtual reality' – at least in its current idealisations – constitutes the desire for further extensions of this shielding from the real by media that are supposed, in part at least, to be representing it. As he says:

> Generally we may see image technologies as still being 'in touch' with reality. But they may also be mobilised as intoxicating and narcotic distractions or defences against the vicissitudes of reality. And, at their most extreme, they may be used to construct alternative and compen-satory realities.
>
> (1996: 123)

Much of what I attribute to spectator experience in the expressions of visual digital culture explored in this book, Robins ascribes to television viewing at its most typical – i.e. in its (mythical) function as a 'window on the world'. This is particularly true of the way in which we both believe we can discern an emphasis on 'immediacy of involvement and participation' and the solicitation of the senses and feelings rather than reflection and interpretation (Robins' 'reason and analysis') in our respective objects of study. Were I to follow Robins, then it would seem that the digital expressions under aesthetic scrutiny in these pages have to be considered as clear instances of the 'intoxication of phantasmagoria' that he proposes for today's media culture. For, on the whole, they would appear to be far more obviously and directly about pleasure and 'intoxication of the senses' than are television documentaries, news reports and fictional programmes that represent 'violence, suffering and death'.[4] Clearly, however, the expressions or genres that I explore are semantically more shallow, rarely about the real world – at least not in the direct sense that many of Robins' examples are. They are not primarily about a 'drive to know', but rather about a drive to play or distraction.

Despite a certain tendency to homogenisation, not all mass mediated representation is the same. Robins argues that viewers are actively involved in (unspecified but clearly complex) psychic processes of 'blocking out' and 'screening' whenever they engage with the 'material of pain and death'. However, even accepting that this is so, it is still not clear that all such representations are the same or that they operate on the same level. On the face if it, certain expressions appear to require far more by way of mechanisms of disavowal than do others. Is graphic television 'news footage' of starving and dying children in war-ravaged Somalia equivalent in this sense to the graphic and realistic scenes of carnage between humans and aliens in a science fiction film such as *Starship Troopers*, or to the 'deaths' the viewers/players themselves inflict in computer games such as *Quake*? Could it not be that audiences themselves are far more sensitive to the context and to the mode or kind of representation they are watching than Robins allows? Might not certain processes or mechanisms relating to a now widely internalised spectrum of ontological kinds and genres of visual representation enter here to complicate the issue further?

These are questions that are beyond the purview of this book. In certain respects the aesthetic and spectator experience I describe above is consonant with that which Robins outlines. It is spectacular, repetitive, concerned with 'form and rhythm' and may even be considered 'phantasmagoric' – at least in terms of its aesthetic make-up. Certainly, this aesthetic is a product of its time – despite the persistence, the resurgence even, of older modes of visuality in its genres and practices. In this respect – particularly in its increasing dependence upon intertextual reference and its fixation with surface play – it certainly shares something of the uncoupling from 'the real world', the simulational aspect that Robins describes. Taken overall it certainly constitutes a thickening of preoccupations with the sensuous and the sensational. Questions remain however. For example, just how typical is it of mass visual culture in general? Whilst the visual digital aesthetic I outline may be symptomatic of broader shifts it may well manifest this in a particular way, a way which should not or simply cannot be glibly generalised. Perhaps its apparent dilution of meaning is rather untypical, or, just a particular manifestation of a general shift in the way the sense of meaning is changing – asking to be understood afresh in the light of the emergence of 'new systems of imagery' (see Wollen 1993: 35–71). Likewise, are its playful and diversionary characteristics – no matter how distorted they may appear – to be condemned out of hand? Along with their 'narcotic' and 'compensatory' function (Robins) might they not also contain elements which offer something that is more positive to the spectator?

Playful resistance

What I am calling the 'productive audience' approach would certainly find something more positive with respect to spectator experiences in visual digital genres. Cultural theorist John Fiske is keen to demonstrate that certain television viewers not only 'resist the dominant ideology' and 'generate their own meanings' but that they do so as active seekers after pleasure (see Fiske 1994: 224–64). Fiske appropriates Roland Barthes' two senses of pleasure in reading – *plaisir* and *jouissance* (see Barthes 1975). Barthes elaborates his distinction between the pleasures of the so-called 'readerly' mainstream literary text that 'contents, fills, grants euphoria', and the 'ecstasy' or 'orgasm' that he associates with the pleasures of reading a 'writerly' text – the kind of text he identifies with modernist literature. Fiske reworks these notions applying them to late twentieth-century television. He produces an understanding of active television viewing that – at least for certain 'subcultures or groups' – involves different kinds of pleasurable 'resistance' to dominant encoded meanings or ideas.

Fiske develops the idea – again adapted from Barthes – that 'the pleasure of creating a text out of a work involves playing with the text'. The television viewer is involved in a game-like experience, 's/he voluntarily accepts the rules of the text in order to participate in the practice that those rules make possible and pleasurable; the practice is, of course, the production of meanings and identities' (1994: 230). Indeed, he wants to suggest that television is the medium that in its very form – i.e. the 'foregrounding of its discursive repertoire, its demystification of its mode of representation' – introduces or enables the possibility of such 'empowering' pleasures as meaning-making and 'playing with the semiotic process' (1994: 239). Unlike the more closed realism of the classical cinema and its association with 'voyeuristic' and suspect pleasures, television provides a perfect parallel in the popular domain for the kinds of pleasurable work that Barthes locates in relation both to mainstream *and* to modernist literature. For, if the making of meaning (whether it conforms to or opposes the rules) is most closely associated with *plaisir*, it is through importing notions to do with carnival that Fiske believes he can discern television viewing experiences that begin to approach the physical bliss of Barthes' *jouissance*.

Here Fiske introduces notions of spectacle, surface and style to his discussion – notions that are central to the subject of this book. According to Fiske, 'carnival is an exaggeration of play' it is a space where the normal rules of playing, with their tendency 'to replicate the social', are freely flaunted, turned on their head and ruthlessly and ritually transgressed through acts 'of grotesquerie, of degradation and spectacle' (1994: 242–3). He discusses wrestling on television detailing the ways in which it operates as the genre, which, perhaps, most clearly manifests these carnivalesque elements. Similarly, the style involved in the videos of music television constitutes a continuation of the 'liberation of carnival', undermining ideology by 'fragmenting sense into the senses'. For Fiske, style involves a 'carnivalesque concentration on the materiality of the signifiers and the consequent evasion of the subjectivity constructed by the more ideologically determined signifieds' (1994: 250).

Once again, I find myself sharing much of what Fiske has to say about the workings of viewing experience in contemporary visual culture, particularly with respect to music video. His emphasis on the way in which, much of the time, a sensual swamping of meaning occurs in such texts, his identification of a play element in contemporary modes of reception and his conception of spectacle accords with my own understanding. Robins would cast such developments into an understanding that interprets them as part of a mechanism of defence on the part of audiences, part of an escape from the difficulties, complexities and threats of the real world. Fiske views such developments as, on the whole, encouraging positive and empowering pleasures. Television, he argues, is 'semiotically democratic' it delegates the 'production of meanings and pleasures to its viewers'. Furthermore, the productive viewer of television is often involved in activity that resists dominant ideology and social control. One of the principle ways in which this occurs, according to Fiske, is precisely through engaging with the surface pleasures of postmodernist spectacle and style. By doing so, the spectator 'refuses sense, refuses the notion of subjectivity as a site where sense is made' (1994: 254).

Fiske advances this argument whilst discussing music video and programmes such as *Miami Vice*. Undoubtedly, he would make similar claims for each of the other expressions of digital culture explored in this book. I also have argued that contemporary visual culture – *at least on the evidence of the forms at issue* – tends (at times quite drastically) to demote the semantic, signifying dimension of representation. Indeed, it does so in ways that are not wholly dissimilar to those that Fiske outlines. All the same, I am reluctant to take the extra step and make the kind of positive attributions for spectatorship that he does. Do the distinctive shifts in the modes of reception I am associating with visual digital culture and its various expressions constitute a mode of resistance? I am not so sure. For one thing, I am not as willing to accept that there is such a neat analogy between traditional modes of playing (games) and the consumption of television programmes or any other contemporary mode of mass cultural representation for that matter. It seems to me that there are, indeed, differences here and that upon further investigation these may prove to be significant. For instance, I have already expressed doubts about the degree to which the spectator of the expressions I am investigating *has* the freedom to 'play with the semiotic process' or to participate in the mode of representation in the productive way that Fiske describes. For the sense remains – though I realise that this is also to overstate the case from the other side – that given the sensuous and physical character of the aesthetic in question, there is as much happening from the opposite direction by way of producing or 'playing with' the recipient. The feeling, I suppose, is that often the 'productive audience' approach claims too much: a retreat, therefore, to a prior and less adventurous position? Perhaps, until, at least, certain counter-intuitions concerning the power that these texts also seem to exert over spectators and their ability to play are dispelled or more clearly understood.

Exhibiting spectacle (and style)

Cinemas, special venues, amusement arcades, television, video players, game consoles and personal computers: the exhibition modes of the genres that lie at the centre of this discussion are easily named and all would seem to be more or less familiar. This ease of recognition, however, might also be said to mask peculiarities and complexities that are extremely significant. The consumption spaces of visual digital genres warrant more description, indeed, their closer exploration is an apt starting point to furthering our understanding of spectator experience within visual digital culture: it adds another vital dimension to the picture.

Panoramas to special venues

It is both intriguing and illuminating to explore the genealogy of visual digital culture (discussed in chapter 2) from the perspective of its presentation or exhibition. Initially one is struck by the strong sense of symmetry and continuity between those earlier sites for exhibiting spectacle and the current ones at issue here. As we have seen, the new visual media of the nineteenth century – the panorama, the diorama, the 'optical theatre', the film – all, in various ways, can be looked upon as prefiguring the aesthetic trends of the forms that lie at the centre of this book. In many respects they similarly also presage the apparatuses of exhibition of these forms.

Thus it is possible to draw distinct continuities between those peculiar sites and apparatuses of exhibition that emerged during the 'frenzy of the visible' that characterises late nineteenth-century culture and the new space of spectacle instanced by visual digital culture (see Charney and Schwartz 1995).[5] The emergent entertainment forms of the nineteenth century discussed earlier begin to constitute distinctive exhibition modes. In more or less radical ways they diverge from the typical spatial arrangement of the live theatre. One tendency is for the new technologies of visual production to press for a darker more concentrated viewing situation. There is a distinct sense in which the image exhibited takes on a more precise definition as image. *It* becomes the clear and indisputable visual dominant diminishing the 'festive character of the theatre' and the 'social desire to see and be seen' (Schivelbusch 1995: 209). Although they remain public these consumption spaces begin to solicit the audience more as individuated and attentive spectators.

Just as important, however, is the new technological character and novelty of the forms. Here the distinctive physical spaces in which they come to be consumed *themselves* stand for and embody changing forms of aesthetic experience. For, though it was perhaps only dimly registered in the minds of spectators at the time, an ontological distinction was coming to be recognised between the newer technologically fabricated imagery and the 'live' nature of traditional theatrical forms. Schivelbusch touches on this issue in his discussion

179

of the industrialisation of light, observing that, 'the picture world of the new media [the diorama, magic lantern and film] offered endless opportunities for creating illusions, belonging as it did to *a different existential sphere* from the reality in which the audience was sitting (my emphasis)' (1994: 213–14). It was not only pictorial illusionism that was heightened by the new technologies, the visceral and directly sensational must also be included. Yet also significant is the sense in which the aesthetic experiences associated with the new exhibition sites are perceived precisely as different and exciting – in part, at least, because they appear to emanate from an elsewhere that is technological in nature.

Here, of course, actual physical space becomes entangled with symbolic resonance. Intrinsic to this experience and the dawning awareness of a categorical shift in aesthetic representation are both the outer lineaments and internal topographies of the exhibition spaces themselves. Whether specifically constructed or adapted spaces, whether the technical apparatus they house is visible, hidden or integral, the physical sites of presentation are themselves vital to this distinctive aesthetic change. New kinds of buildings, rooms and contraptions with evocative names – 'diorama', 'magic lantern', 'optical theatre', 'cinema', 'switchback' and 'phantom ride' – emerge to give tangible expression to the new media forms. These containers, or so we might surmise, are variously perceived as *machines* for the production of new kinds of spectacle and illusion (the diorama, Théâtre Optique) or as *engines* for novel modes of direct visceral thrill or simulated sensation (Ferris wheel, Hale's Tours). Symbols of new visual and kinaesthetic experiences, they not only extend the popular appreciation of technology as spectacle, but simultaneously stand for technology's production of a radically distinctive visual cultural sphere (see Kasson 1978: 73–4). Technologically mediated culture is predominant and commonplace today, yet not entirely dissimilar observations apply to the exhibition spaces of the digital visual aesthetic we are exploring. For many, digital technologies are endowed with the same mystery, and inspire the same awe, as the new machines of industrialisation. The houses and locations of visual digital forms are as redolent as ever both of technology as spectacle and with intimations of categorically distinctive sorts of mediation.

Public and private

There is however at least one major difference between then and now: the subsequent emergence and widespread development of *private* modes of delivery and aesthetic consumption. Indeed, there is no clearer example of how complicated is the notion of any direct and uniform lineage in certain modes and sites of consumption between the two *fin de siècle* cultural spaces at issue here.

The arrival of broadcasting as a new mode of *mass* cultural distribution is the twentieth-century marker of a definitive shift towards more privatised kinds of cultural consumption. Radio, television, outgrowths of televisual technologies such as video and – even more recently – the advent of home computers, all have been instrumental in helping to rebalance the relation of public to home consumption of cultural products. So much so, in fact, that the latter now predominates. Of course, domestic consumption of cultural products has always existed. Certainly it is possible to discern such consumption in relation to the spectacle forms of the late nineteenth century. Thus, the kaleidoscope, the thaumatrope, the stroboscope and suchlike – all arising out of the flowering contemporary interest in optics – were marketed in the form of so-called 'parlour toys': popular amusements for the more affluent middle-class household. The magic lantern itself existed increasingly in a domestic form and, as the century wore on, photography began to enter the bourgeois domestic space. One of the earliest ways in which photography entered into privatised consumption was through the marketisation of the stereoscope. Here was an instrument that in many respects anticipated later forms of armchair viewing: once the stereoscope had been purchased there was no lack of new material (stereo cards) to feed the viewers' appetite for new images (see Huhatamo 1995).

Yet, despite a certain encroachment into the private sphere, most of the new optical forms of late nineteenth-century modernisation maintained the tradition long since established for spectacle and assumed exhibition modes that were public in character. The privatisation of spectacle – by which I mean *not* the propensity already noted towards more individuated modes of address (though clearly this *is* a crucial connection) but the physical move out of the public domain and into the home – is a more recent phenomenon. At the end of the twentieth century there existed a complex and multifaceted 'mixed economy' of public and private consumption. If, for the majority of nineteenth-century patrons, the new visual forms were enjoyed via novel modes of public exhibition, the same can hardly be said of today's audiences of digital spectacle forms.

The implications of the rise of an economy of mixed private/public modes of consumption carries significant implications in terms of the changing character of spectator experience. In their public manifestations the exhibition spaces of visual digital genres maintain and even refine perhaps, the functions of their nineteenth-century forebears. Special venues, video game complexes and first release cinemas are spaces arranged specifically to mobilise and intensify sensual experience – particularly, though not solely, that which is visual. Containers and regulators of new media and their forms, they also function – largely through their internal and external architectural characteristics and styles – as symbolical spaces: sheltered playgrounds, more or less spectacular in themselves, and redolent of the latest techniques and newest kinds of image. The experience of consumption itself may well be more individuated, more privatised and self-centred in these spaces than it was in those of the nineteenth century, nevertheless, it remains essentially *public*. Although the *domestic spectator* may be involved in activities that in certain respects are similar to those on offer in the domain of public exhibition, at the same time the differences are crucial.

Thoroughly interrelated, these differences range from questions of physical scale to notions of personal space. Consider, for instance, the aspect of scale and the simple difference between viewing a film such as, say, *Terminator 2: Judgment Day* on the large, high definition screen (with digital sound) of a first-run theatre and seeing it on video on the small TV screen in one's bedroom. A host of issues arise here: the diminution, for example, of sheer sensual impact – the reduced character of the spectacle involved in the case of private consumption. But then, in part perhaps to counteract this, are considerations surrounding the idea of increased control that the video player allows the domestic viewer (pause, rewind, repeat and slow motion). Then there are issues attendant on the different character of the apparatuses themselves – cinema projection versus video playback, theatrical architecture versus the arrangement of furniture. And, related to this though at another level still, are the qualitative aspects of intimate versus public, familiar versus collective, and informal versus regulated spaces of consumption. Among other things the incomparably larger scale of public exhibition spaces involve higher degrees of sheer technological complexity and/or power. Home delivery – tailored to the scale of private life, to the measure of furniture and the various appliances of domestic reproduction – offers forms of play and spectacle 'on tap' as it were. Game consoles, video players and television sets are small objects that, with the flick of a switch, literally *replace* 'going out' for amusement, presenting us instead with miniature – and in certain respects degraded – versions of their public relatives, turning living rooms into secluded and increasingly solitary playgrounds.

Nowadays, enjoying the forms of visual digital culture both publicly and privately – the exception being those attached to special venue attractions – is not difficult. However, it is not just differences of a technical/formal character – power and format – that renders what is, for instance, ostensibly the same computer game considerably *altered* between arcade and home versions. The place of consumption also counts of course, for the act of consuming is more or less subtly shaped – the experience of spectating is more or less subtly affected – by the context in which it takes place. It is clear, for instance, that one's awareness of and behaviour towards others will vary greatly and in more or less complex ways between the arcade and one's bedroom. Playing a video game in public one puts oneself on display – whether one likes it or not. Indeed, the social dimension of such public playgrounds – administered and policed and with their spoken and unspoken rules of conduct – inevitably and variously encroaches upon the central activity itself. Some may be driven to play computer games in private precisely because of such visibility and the feelings of vulnerability that this induces. For others it is precisely this visibility that draws them, whilst still others go to arcades not to play and/or be seen playing computer games, but primarily and variously to watch, for it is not only the sanctioned games themselves that are pleasurable or spectacular.

In a similar way to the amusement parks at the turn of the last century, the amusements, the games themselves *and* their public setting are exotic (Kasson 1978: 8). And it is not difficult to see, thinking beyond immediate contexts of exhibition – beyond architecture and the housing of apparatuses – to the topography and geography of locations that this dual exoticism carries over into several of the other public manifestations of visual digital culture. We might cite, for example, the location of many special venue attractions in theme parks such as Futuroscope, the Universal Film Lot and Disneyland (to name but a few). Such sites – born of the amusement park, the World's Fair and, increasingly it would seem, designed as spectacular beacons to the technology/future couplet – are idealised places contrived to produce excitement, wonderment and fascination in those who visit them even *before* the specific attractions, rides and so forth are experienced.[6]

But what of the spectacle machines of private consumption, the video, television and computer – can we say the same of them? The living room, bedroom and kitchen are hardly exotic in the grand manner of the theme park, the mall or the arcade. They seem far more banal and everyday. Home furnishings, domestic décor and the occasional company of family intimates is rather different to the physical topographies and kinds of social intercourse encountered in Disneyland or the amusement arcade. Digital visual culture consumed at home is spectacle of a peculiar hue: the television, video and home computer are precisely machines that defy social location, the rooms they exist in cut across such categories as urban, suburban and rural. In keeping with this character of crossing social space they offer up forms of spectacle which – as we have already seen – are not only highly regulated and repetitive, but also further removed or distanced from 'social reality' in their stylisation and second-order character. Smaller in scale, sheltered and secure, such private reception tends towards solitary engagement. The relative amount of control the domestic spectator has over the image may provide some compensation for lack of magnificence and magnitude. But then so too does the all-important element of making the same always strikingly different: the domestic appliances for visual pleasure are designed precisely to cope with a far greater rapidity of turnover of new tokens of spectacle than are many of their public counterparts. The apparatuses of domestic delivery appropriately accommodate the ephemeral, the fleeting and the minimal character of these forms.

Domestic consumption of visual digital culture must be sharply contrasted to the metaphor of 'the window on the world'. Despite misgivings and objections to this characterisation of *television* as a form of domesticated visual culture it remains, nevertheless, an idea that is not altogether misplaced. Ellis, for example, talks convincingly about a 'complicity' between broadcast images and the television viewer, 'that tends to produce the events represented as an "outside world", beyond the broadcast TV institution and the viewer's home alike' (1982: 112). I shall suggest that, in the case of the highly artificial, depthless and self-recursive imagery of visual digital genres, the idea of an 'outside world' makes little sense. Whether broadcast or not – and many of them aren't – these image forms (i.e. advertisements, music videos, spectacle films, video games) are more about themselves, they are not attempts to represent the world. There is little reference outside or beyond their own stylistic, decorative, dazzling, fascinating and manipulable circularity. Indeed, this applies just as much to the public manifestations of such forms. Whereas the latter carry with them that ineffable dimension of wonderment and pleasure that accompanies collective (shared) engagement with spectacle in the grand manner, domestic reception of such forms increasingly seems to involve playing on one's own (as Baudrillard 1987 and Bauman 1993 have pointed out). It involves another kind of pleasure: a kind of auto-sensualism of repetitive and superficial play in which the room and the image coextend into a cocooned space of solitary diversion and enjoyment. In this space one's encounters with 'others' are, for the most part at least, solely through images: that is to say always at one or more remove. *If*, eventually, the surprise and delight one experiences in this sensual bubble is shared, then, usually this occurs after the fact and perhaps in another space altogether: the classroom, supermarket or street.

Postmodern experience

Let me stress the specificity of the observations and suggestions made above. I speak only with respect to the visual digital forms discussed in preceding chapters. Contemporary genres such as television documentary and news, kinds of serialised television drama, neo-classical cinema and animation, modes of marginal or independent video, cinema or digital art and so forth, figure only peripherally or in qualified ways in what I am claiming.[7]

However, if as I am suggesting, it is inappropriate to generalise the already diverse aesthetic space of visual digital forms to the rest of contemporary visual culture, how are we to relate them to the broader contemporary context of which they are a part? Of course, in terms of their aesthetic make-up I have already attempted to describe and explore such a relation – claiming both their affinity to *and* their distinctiveness as expressions or forms of contemporary – which is to say, late or post-modern*ist* – culture (see, in particular, chapters 3 and 6). But what, more specifically, of spectatorship? How might the spectator experience involved in the reception or consumption of these forms relate to the general condition or circumstance of the current age: to so-called late or post-modern*ity* (where the latter is to be understood as designating broad transformations in economic, social and cultural domains, transformations that inevitably are viewed as calling forth corresponding shifts in forms of experience)?

I shall conclude by mentioning the consumption spaces of visual digital genres relative to some current ideas of contemporary life; and, more specifically, those conceptions that prioritise the linked elements of the media and consumerism as key to understanding contemporary forms of experience.

In a rather different way to the discrete culture of spectacle entertainments of the late nineteenth century, contemporary visual digital culture is part of a broader order that is definitively oriented around what can only be described as the voracious consumption of (material and immaterial) objects. Though the end of the nineteenth century might be viewed as the moment of change in which the onset of this consumer-oriented system first took shape, few could have predicted the extraordinary transformations its subsequent development would involve. It has evolved into a mass order that permeates and touches virtually all aspects of our everyday existence. Indeed, few today can escape the highly systematised imperative to consume and the generalised and thoroughly entrenched emphases on style, fashion and novelty that this entails (though many – and usually not through any choice of their own – are excluded from participating).

Of course, a central and inseparable dimension of the transformations involved in these developments has been the phenomenal growth and proliferation of systems of mass communication and representation. It is within this context that the formal and expressive character of visual digital production is, at least in part, shaped and instituted (chapters 3 and 6). Similarly, it is also the context within which the 'mixed economy' of public and private exhibition modes of the mass digital forms at issue here must be understood. They are part of a consolidated mass consumerist order that strives to capitalise on modes of novelty and excitement, not just through the constant reinvention of public exhibition sites, but also through the more recent cultivation of the home as primary site of cultural consumption.

'The society of the spectacle'

It is hardly surprising, given the above, that the cultural aspect of late twentieth-century Western society has variously been characterised as one that was thoroughly imbued with spectacular and sensational tendencies. Within this context, everyday forms of experience, including forms of spectating, have been cast or conceptualised in divergent ways. It was the Situationists who first applied the concept of 'spectacle' to contemporary Western societies, claiming that nothing remained untouched by it (for an introduction to the history of the Situationist movement, see Wollen 1993: 120–57). Guy Debord's *The Society of the Spectacle* wrested the concept of spectacle from its more usual and specific senses and turned it into a critical category that characterised everything that was problematic about late twentieth-century consumer society (Debord 1977). Debord claimed that, aided and abetted by the growth of a unilateral and (seemingly) unassailable mass media, modern capitalist society operated by substituting detached, mediated and illusory images for directly lived experiences and relations. In failing to recognise their alienation from genuine or real life conditions in the operation of the 'spectacle', the subordinated majority of society only perpetuate their enslavement through their passive consumption of its various illusions and diversions. Conceived in this totalising way, spectacle is, inescapably, an oppressive category – there is little point in attempting any kind of relative evaluation of particular modes, nor of engaging in any localised

185

comparative critique of their specific expressions. Clearly, under this approach the visual digital genres at issue here would receive short shrift, likewise their hapless spectators. The latter, surely, would be urged to see through the 'falsity' of such pursuits, to give them up and engage in other forms of more direct or participatory play or in recuperative acts of *detournement*.[8]

Yet, from the point of view of the present discussion, the notion of 'the spectacle' inaugurated by Debord's extraordinary critique continued to reverberate within late twentieth-century analyses of culture.[9] With hindsight *The Society of the Spectacle* can be located among an emerging current of criticism that in the 1960s began to produce prognostic understandings of a qualitatively new stage in social and cultural development (some key names here are Mumford 1970; Marcuse 1974; Lefebvre 1991). At the centre of many of these varied critical analyses lay the phenomenal rise in scale and intensity both of the media and of consumption. Amongst those attempting – albeit in quite diverse ways – to come to terms with these new developments in terms of the media and consumption were critics like Daniel Boorstin (1992), Marshall McLuhan (1968) and Roland Barthes (1973). Although, ultimately, none of the latter were as damning as the Situationists of the highly mediated and image-centred culture that had emerged in the second half of the twentieth century, all nevertheless recognised that it was something quite unprecedented. It was a crucial element shaping modern existence, something that was profoundly important to interrogate and understand – either as means to rectification and improvement (Boorstin, early Barthes) or as an element of destiny that we had to come to terms with (McLuhan). Indeed, from this point onwards (the 1960s) the critical and intellectual attention paid to mass mediation, in particular visual mediation, and questions of its place in the shaping of contemporary beliefs, relations and experiences intensified enormously. Moreover, whilst the radical utopian element of Debord's initial critique did not survive the critical turn of 1970s, other aspects did – most notably, his emphasis on the *uncoupled* and *substitutive* character of mass mediated images (for an informative overview, see Jay 1994: 416–34).

Consumers or recipients (spectators) of aesthetic cultural objects/commodities have been conceptualised as figuring in rather different ways in this new era where the image (both in direct and figural senses) is viewed as having assumed an axial position in all aspects of life. In ways that can be traced directly to the original critiques of *The Society of the Spectacle*, currently predominant *fin de siècle* accounts similarly operate with the notion of the media as an instrument of *surrogation, substitution, transposition*. Thus, Baudrillard – the contemporary commentator perhaps most indebted to the ideas of Debord – argues that the rise of the mass media has led to a fatal confusion between the real and its representation (see chapter 3). As the traditional ground of reference recedes and the 'circuits and networks' continue their expansion, Baudrillard posits the onset of an era where spectacle (which involved staging, theatricality, illusion) is being replaced by 'obscenity' (involving immediate transparency, 'pornography' or the 'all-too-visible'). Rather than individuals who are alienated by the 'spectacle' he sees people caught-up in *ecstatic fascination* and narcissistic acts of aleatory play (Baudrillard 1988: 11–27).

Zygmunt Bauman adopts the concept of *telecity* by way of describing the particular mode of substitution performed by the media (see Bauman 1993: 145–85). In an account that carries strong echoes of Baudrillard, Bauman conceives the modern-day spectator as retreatist. S/he is concerned – driven almost – to play and distraction by the novel modes of entertainment available, but increasingly only able or willing to do so in ways that involve the dual securities of symbolic and personal distance or safety. The typical cultural spectator of postmodernity is viewed as a largely home-centred and increasingly solitary player who, via various forms of 'telemediation' (stereos, game consoles, videos and televisions), revels in a domesticated (i.e. private and *tamed*) 'world-at-a-distance'. Behind the 'glass screens to which their lives are confined' the strangers and others who inhabit 'telecity' pose no threat; unlike those imagined others of the outside world they are safe if somewhat distant playmates – ultimately, superficial objects of voyeuristic enjoyment and amusement. This said, however, the 'screen worlds' this spectator seems to be so absolutely in command of are already someone else's: '*second-level*', designed and directed, 'carefully disguised as (managed) spontaneity' (1993: 177).[10]

Others have explored the idea of intensifying media substitution by focusing on what might be termed its inherent *vehicular* propensity. Thus Paul Virilio, pursuing his ruminations on speed and contemporary life, locates – in the development of the mobile film camera or the travelling shot – the birth of a 'static vehicle': a means of travelling without moving that may well herald the 'victory of sedentariness' (see Virilio 1986, 1989, 1991). According to Virilio, the developed audiovisual systems of late twentieth-century mass culture – radio, television and now digital simulation systems – are replacing earlier experiences of *extensive* time linked to an era of automotive modes of transport with experiences of *intensive* time linked to telecommunications and 'domestic inertia'. Physical or dynamic travelling (in automobile or passenger jet) and the static mode of travel instanced by audio-visual 'vehicles' begin to take on similar features, to merge experientially – yet there is no doubt where Virilio believes all this to be leading. In the event of the triumph of electronic simulation systems life will literally become film a 'spatial and temporal hallucination', the individual totally at the mercy of an electronic terminal. Indeed, Virilio invokes a nightmarish scenario of the 'cadaver-like inertia of the interactive dwelling' in which, ensconced in 'residential cells', individuals of the future occupy 'a canopy bed for the infirm voyeur, a divan for being dreamt of without dreaming, a bench for being circulated without circulating' (1989: 119).

Finally, someone who builds upon themes that in many respects echo both Virilio and Bauman is Anne Friedberg. She argues that the growth of cinema and television has cultivated a mode of mobilised and virtual visuality, the 'mobilised virtual gaze', which has now assumed a position of centrality within postmodern subjectivity (Friedberg 1994). Like Virilio, Friedberg locates the starting point of the novel mode of vicarious visual 'time travel' that she believes dominates the present in the late nineteenth century. New modes of physical transportation (railways, trams, later automobiles and aeroplanes) coincide with new modes of vicarious transportation (photography, later cinema and television). Like Bauman, the pleasures of *flânerie*, posited as symptomatic of the nascent metropolitan and consumerist society at the turn of the nineteenth century, have become ubiquitous today – though the strolling (and gazing) is now just as likely to involve imaginary rather than actual mobility. Perhaps the main contribution of this complex substitution – the 'instrumentalisation' of *flânerie* into 'commodity experiences' with the emergence of cinematic 'time machines' – has been an 'increasingly derealized sense of 'presence' and identity' (1994: 2). As spectatorship dissolves into everyday life, the contemporary individual's grasp of time and the real are altered. The phenomenal rise of modern systems of mediation is viewed as contributing to a fast disappearing sense of the past and the sensation of living a 'perpetual present'.

Local and *global*

Clearly, the conceptualisations sketched above (and admittedly, they are rather caricatured) are all striving to understand and explain what is generally held to be a new situation, one that involves a distinctive shift in our social and cultural condition. All, rightly, acknowledge that the rise of modern forms of mass audiovisual mediation has fundamentally shaped contemporary experiences. In these diagnoses aesthetics and culture are viewed as figuring far more centrally than previously in social life as a whole. Indeed, so thoroughly media saturated and dependent has contemporary society become that the act of cultural consumption itself is now proffered as the exemplary or paradigmatic form of post- or late modern subjective experience.

Conceptualising the experience of new times, it would seem, involves revisiting the idea of spectatorship: each of the critics mentioned attempts to definitively capture the typical mode of experience of postmodern spectators (and, thereby, postmodern subjective experience *per se*). Thus Baudrillard invokes the 'fractal subject' narcissistically wired to screens containing images that are increasingly transparent and lacking any symbolic depth. Bauman discovers a contemporary spectator desirous to play, yet fearful of the perils of inhospitable streets: driven to the safety and solitude of the managed playground or to the domestic sphere and its electronic pleasure machines where s/he enters into games of superficial, non-affective amusement. Virilio discerns an individual under construction who, in the displacement of travel by the media, is becoming increasingly sedentary. The impulse is towards a state of inertia and he invokes the image of the 'immobile simulator' – in which one runs or plays (golf, football and so forth) 'on the spot'. For Friedberg the contemporary subject is one who spends just as much time inhabiting, 'travelling' and gazing in vicarious mediated time and space as in actual time and space.

Clearly this impulse is not without foundation: with the rise of the modern mass media more people than ever before are involved in the activity of looking and otherwise engaging with forms of cultural production. Moreover, within the modern era the cultural/aesthetic mode of spectating has increasingly bled into and begun to fuse with the everyday. Indeed, such commonplace activities as driving and shopping are oft-cited examples of how this 'aestheticisation of everyday life' is occurring – the windows of shops and of private vehicles operating as part of a continuum of screens on the world.[11] Late modern consumer culture frames us as lookers/gazers in a manner that is qualitatively new.

Of course, the search for a culturally dominant mode of (spectator) experience under the new conditions of 'spectacular consumer society' is an intriguing and significant quest. It is both an inescapable impulse and a productive approach to understanding. Indeed, reviewing the analyses above one has the distinct sense, despite the divergence in overall aims, of the discovery of similar trends – of a certain convergence. This turns upon the generalised spread and intensification of spectator experiences that appear to revolve more and more around notions of *substitution, privatisation, transparency*.

However, such a search has, of necessity, to operate at an extremely high level of generality and abstraction (see – though by no means exclusively – Baudrillard). What we tend to lose sight of in such analysis is any sense of disparity, diversity, specificity and nuance. More often than not, the picture such accounts seem to paint is one of increasing unification and homogeneity: their 'global' ambition obliterates any sense that locality may still exist as an important consideration. Whilst the mass digital forms explored in this book share much with other contemporary forms (and with each other) – a commonality that it is important to acknowledge and define – understanding is not thereby exhausted by containment under one apparently unifying concept.

The consumption of digital visual genres is precisely a case in point. In large part this book has involved an attempt to begin to map a space of contemporary aesthetic consumption that is both particular to *and* subsumable under (within) a larger moment or situation. As we have begun to see, although the forms of visual digital culture all involve intensities of experience that devolve upon spectacle and sensation, this manifests itself in rather different ways – again, not only between forms but also often within them. Visual digital culture in the sense I am defining it is a discrete cultural space: it has its own peculiarities and aesthetic dominants and, as I have begun to indicate, we cannot assume any strict homogeneity between the sites in which it is consumed. Is it then the characteristic held in common – the underlying or overarching unifying idea that links it to contemporary culture in the broad sense – or the disparate ways in which this manifests itself that is to be privileged here? The level of correspondence between much of what I describe when exploring visual digital forms and expressions – both in previous chapters and in this one – and much of the

189

theorising upon the peculiarity of late modern experience, might lead one to prioritise the former, that is, blithely to subsume visual digital genres and their consumption under a comprehensive concept such as the 'society of the spectacle' or the 'order of simulation'. But I believe this would be wrong. It is important to hold on to both the general or shared *and* the specific or distinctive here – particularly when attempting to explore the aesthetic dimension.

For one thing, also attending to the local and specific – to the detail and differentials of form and reception – helps display the often subtly nuanced character of a general culture that increasingly (and for good reasons) is characterised in terms of uniformity and monotony. Just admitting that there are such distinctions also introduces the possibility that at the very least differing shades or degrees of spectator experience exist under the postmodern rubric. But, even more importantly, one is led to question whether the broadly shared aggregation of experiences and pleasures that typify the consumption of the expressions and genres at issue here actually *do* carry over to other kinds of mass visual culture. I do not believe they do – at least not in major part.

We must resist the tendency to essentialise: the aesthetic dimension of late modern culture is not homogeneous. On the contrary, it is highly sedimented with a multiplicity of image forms and corresponding kinds of spectator experience – even within the mass cultural sphere. Many of these experiences may turn out to be complementary (though this needs to be established) – and, of course, I am not against attempting to associate them by type. The suspicion remains however, that there may still exist highly differentiated and – if we are lucky – antagonistic modes of spectatorship. We must maintain that at one level at least, there is still a distinction to be drawn between consumption and consumerism as well as between the latter and reception and spectating. The tendency in many current diagnoses simply to reduce activities entailed in the reception/spectating couplet to those of consumerism can make us lose sight of the diversity of aesthetic spaces together with the distinctive forms of experience they engender.

CONCLUSION

Let me recover some of the main themes and questions raised as this text has unfolded. This book has isolated and begun to examine a dominant aesthetic current within certain recent forms or genres of mass visual culture closely tied to digital production technologies. I connect this aesthetic to a historical tradition of spectacle entertainments, the visual digital genres and expressions at issue being its most recent manifestation. At the same time I have sought to take account of the crucial shaping influences of the contemporary culture that surrounds this more circumscribed aesthetic and of which it is a vital part. This encompassing culture is oriented around mass production and consumerism. Based upon structural principles of ever intensifying repetition a dominant feature of its aesthetic make-up involves practices of 'recombination' and reinvention.

Continuity and difference

As we have seen the growth and *integration* of digital techniques within established media forms has happened in a relatively short space of time. Yet, although digital imaging techniques are new, the aesthetic uses they are put to and the forms they take are not – at least, not in the same radical way. Indeed, the latter are rather better described as 'different' or 'novel': they contain and display distinctive characteristics whilst at the same moment relying on prior and current cultural practices and forms for their shape and character. Thus one contention has been that cultural history is not always to be understood in terms of breaks or ruptures. Recognising continuities can also be illuminating. From this perspective I have pursued the persistence of a particular kind of aesthetic – though, once again, it is one that is firmly embedded in and moulded by the contemporary moment.

The aesthetic in question is that of spectacle in all its ephemeral and sensational guises. It is largely vision-centred and is about direct and immediate sensual pleasures. It has direct connections with illusion, magic and the special effect – with extravagant and extrovert and rhetorical image forms. Certain of the genres under consideration here appear to connect to this lineage in ways

191

that are quite direct – the new spectacle cinema and special venue attraction, for example – whilst in other cases the connection is perhaps more oblique. Thus the trend I have isolated within television advertising or the computer game, for instance, may not seem quite so obviously connected to such practices. Yet, the dazzling, diverting effects of advertisements are currently among the most sophisticated examples of visual trickery mobilised to produce astonishment and fascination. And the 'vicarious kinaesthesia' I have ascribed to the computer game – the impression of agency within an illusionistic space – carries vestiges both of illusion as spectacle (diorama, early cinema) and the 'real life' kinaesthesia of the amusement park. The continuities may be indirect and not as immediately apparent in this shallow and ephemeral genre of skill acquisition, competition, speed, action and illusory agency, but they are there nevertheless. From the aesthetic perspective most computer games, along with the sort of advertisements (and music videos) I have isolated, fall squarely within an aesthetic tradition of spectacle, surface and sensation. Their relation to established senses of drama, symbolism, depth of meaning and reflection is rather less straightforward. Indeed, games are perhaps the most intriguing of the genres I have explored within the conceit of 'visual digital culture'. Work on understanding their form and style, their modes and practices of production and the viewing activities they engender, has barely begun and clearly there is much more work to be done here.

I have supported conceptions of contemporary culture that understand its aesthetic as increasingly traversed by formal concerns: an aesthetic wherein the proliferation of recombinant and replicated images, styles and genres augur the displacement – the thinning down – of meaning and the symbolic (understood in its broadest sense). The 'culture of the depthless image', the 'era of simulation' and the 'age of the signifier' are all slogans that attempt to capture this new situation, to point within *mass* culture to a predominant tendency towards formal excitement within a realm of more or less uncoupled appearances. There is a clear harmony between such general conceptions of *fin de siècle* culture and the visual digital aesthetic I have isolated and begun to describe in this book. Indeed, given the prevalent tendency to visual display within culture generally it could be argued that it is hardly surprising that a reawakening of earlier modes of spectacle should be occurring, especially as the new digital technologies begin to provide the means to refresh the production of distinctive levels and kinds of visual excitation. The visual digital forms discussed here must be counted among the principal constituents of a new culture of surface play. But just how typical are they of the culture as a whole? I would resist any attempt to cast them as general models, if only because it is not at all clear to me that other prior or established non-digital genres succumb to or embody the culture of repetition and self-reference in the same ways. This is precisely one instance where difference becomes important. Too often the tendency is to characterise a whole complex cultural moment in sweeping and totalising terms. But what is gained in terms of scope and reach is often at the expense of detail and nuance.

A huge variety of visual cultural modes and their forms or genres make up contemporary culture. These have their own histories and one suspects they are variously both *more* and *less* affected by the propensity to repetition and recombination, surface and sensation that appears to be so prevalent in the genres that lie at the centre of this book. I would suggest that they manifest in rather different ways (*if indeed, they do so at all*) the preponderant aesthetic tendencies of the time, though clearly, further research is necessary to illuminate the character and extent of such distinctions.

Sensation

With regard to the genres and expressions at issue here I have sought to maintain their links both to a particular tradition and to the 'aesthetics of the sensual' that I believe this entails. To do with form, surface ('depthless images') and physicality, 'visual digital culture' manifests a highly specific aesthetic character – one indicating that something like a 'poetics' of surface play and sensation is required in order to begin to understand it in the first instance. Certainly, this aesthetic cannot simply be assimilated to Baudrillardian conceptions of simulation or ecstasy. For the cost of doing so entails the loss of particular textures and experiences. An approach that is sensitive to the complexly nuanced character of mass culture reveals that spectacle in the limited manner in which I have been exploring it is not the same as simulation. Similarly, sensation should not be reduced to Baudrillard's conception of ecstasy. Of course, I have not tried to deny the parallels and connections between visual digital culture and such suggestive (and ambitious) conceptions. Still, my focus has been more specific, having attempted to circumscribe an aesthetic space that displays its own peculiar aesthetic: a space that itself is not wholly consistent, yet one that variously manifests a preoccupation with form and surface and strives to engage spectators at such levels. Visual, stylistic and physical delights and sensations are the overriding *modus operandi* within this space.

All of the above is relevant to spectatorship, and though there is more to be done here I have begun to explore the particular character of spectator practice and experience within visual digital culture. Here it is important to assert that such experience is *aesthetic* and involves its own distinctive modes of exhibition and consumption. The tendency to explain contemporary aesthetic experience – in particular the modes and genres of mass culture – as *wholly* symptomatic (of broader social developments) has led many to collapse all consumption into aesthetic practice, but, once again, this obscures as much as it reveals. Of course, there are obvious and important similarities between the activities involved in buying and consuming objects such as refrigerators, automobiles, clothes and so forth and, for example, buying a console or a ticket and playing a computer game. The underlying dynamic of consumerism regulates all such activities. But there are also differences that must be held on to, for the practices and activities involved in the consumption of a computer game, special venue attraction or music video are not quite of the same order. The spaces of aesthetic consumption are more like playgrounds. Circumscribed and highly regulated (and appearing to lack all but the faintest trace of festival and carnival), still the games played therein have their own distinctive shapes, rules and pleasures – even those based on something as transient as spectacle. We have barely begun to analyse and understand the particular attributes and conventions that underpin such practices and the experiences they engender.

Interactivity

Even the computer game, in many respects perhaps the 'freshest' of the mass digital genres at issue in these pages, is both shaped and fed by other media and entertainment forms. True, it introduces the distinctive and potentially, perhaps, radical element of 'interactivity' – though what it does with this is far more continuous with forms such as the cinema, television and video than some would care to admit. Similarly, the 'game' genre is very much under the sway of the current more general 'culture of the copy'. Like the other digital forms at the centre of this discussion it lies close to the heart of the repetitive and super-ficial impulses that, it is argued, are coming to govern cultural production generally.

And yet there is something different occurring within the computer game genre and, clearly, this *has* much to do with its so-called 'interactive' aspect. In many respects interaction is not as new a concept as many would have us believe; it occurs in all aesthetic reception – be it perceptual, cognitive, psychical, interpretative. What is being signalled here, however, is a rather different mode of immediate engagement with technically reproduced art works. In computer games the spectator is positioned as a real-time participant within the diegetic space of the game world – given the ability to affect what happens and a certain agency and control over how the game unfolds. Although, clearly, the interactive player does not operate with anything approaching total freedom – rules and constraints are often all too apparent – nevertheless, it constitutes an intriguing and potentially impor-tant development.

I have argued that 'interactivity' in computer games is very much analogous to the moving image in early cinema. In a similar manner to the moving image in the early 'cinema of attractions', 'interactivity' itself is on display in the computer game. The vicarious kinaesthesia that comprises the major part of these (relatively) semantically shallow texts constitutes their primary attraction. They are, thereby, very much continuous with the aesthetic of surface play. My initial exploration of 'games' also suggested that, in keeping with the other expressions of visual digital culture at issue, a certain de-centring of narrative is normal within the genre. Relative to dominant modes of narrative form in established time-based genres – most typically classical cinema – games involve a distinctive mode of relatively open 'hands-on' direction which can only be recounted (as a kind of narrative) after each playing session. Clearly, more work is in order here, a more thorough understanding of the particular conventions of the computer games genre itself is needed. Part of this should include a more concerted attempt to grasp the particular character of interactivity. How, for example, might it differ from participation? How does it compare to notions of interactivity in other modes? More generally, if, as I suggest, there is a de-centring of narrative occurring within the genres of this recently emergent aesthetic space, then how significant is this? More precisely, what is happening to familiar forms of narrative and are other modes and genres involved?

The aesthetic dimension

The questions of form and surface and of continuity and difference that lie at the heart of this book sit rather uncomfortably with much of the work undertaken in the area of computers and culture to date. On balance, the scales here are tipped towards description as a means of persuading and understanding. I have paid little attention to interpretation as involving a search for hidden meaning, concentrating more on considerations pertaining to form and the manifest. There are several reasons for this. The first concerns the character of the material itself – the genres of visual digital culture. As I have endeavoured to demonstrate, these are characterised by an unusually high degree of formality at the aesthetic level. They foreground the phenomenal, outward dimension and its attendant qualities in a manner that many other genres do not. They encourage exploration at the level of the surface of the work because this, palpably, is what they are about.[1] At the same time, what seemed to me to be the apparent consonance between certain dominant conceptualisations of the direction and character of contemporary visual culture in general, and these digitally enabled forms in particular, suggested a more concerted exploration of the extent and detail of this relationship. More precisely, in what ways might these distinctive spectacular, decorative and visceral forms be associated with a culture in which traditional notions of representation are understood to be on the wane and in which groundless and 'depthless' image orders are in the ascendance?

This powerful sensation of the intensification of a formal disposition within contemporary visual culture must be set alongside two other reasons for electing to concentrate on the aesthetic dimension. The first is a desire to distance myself from much of the current commentary on (and many of the current approaches to) understanding the impact of digital technologies upon culture. The second is the contention that a more focused grasp of the aesthetic dimension is vital to any serious attempt to illuminate popular and mass cultural practices. Of course, these motives are not unconnected. Much of the highly speculative and future-oriented commentary that has accompanied the introduction of digital technologies in the cultural domain is naïve. It lacks any sense of the importance of history or of the numerous forces shaping technological development itself. In addition, much of the time at least, the mass cultural domain remains remote and ill-defined: prognoses are distant and disconnected from concrete practices.

The problem with the more warranted critical approaches – many of which are seeking to redress this problem – has been not so much their failure to take the aesthetic dimension seriously, as to reduce it precisely to a symptom or manifestation of other shaping forces. Once these have been explained and understood, then so has the aesthetic. All too often the aesthetic dimension disappears into broader considerations or it is deemed obvious and uninteresting and not in need of further exploration as such. It is as if the catch-all of 'postmodernity' obviates the need for more specific and local explanation. On the other hand, and almost as disconcerting, aesthetics is now dominated by hermeneutic approaches: controlled by various interpretative disciplines that, as David Bordwell says, talking primarily of the cinema, 'take the construction of implicit and symptomatic meanings to be central to understanding' (Bordwell 1991: 17). Once again, methods of understanding that stand outside of the purview of such approaches are viewed with suspicion and disregard. Of course, I do not deny that aesthetic forms and spectator experiences are shaped by the social and historical context in which they arise, or, that the 'deeper' symbolic or semantic dimension is crucial. I do contend, however – again following Bordwell – that there is more to (understanding) the aesthetic dimension than this. The material, sensuous aspect of mediation – the complexities of form and style – are crucial, as are immediate sites and spaces of exhibition and reception and the customs and practices they too might be seen to exemplify.

Indeed, this becomes especially apparent in genres that are primarily about spectacle and display: genres wherein surface appearances, formal and sensory qualities are so predominant and insistent. Spectacle is so elusive – it seems so obvious and yet is so little understood. In the senses I have discussed it in these pages spectacle is an aesthetic tradition that has flourished and blossomed at different historical moments. It has taken different forms at different times.[2] Understanding the spectacular and sensuous character of the mass forms that visual digital culture currently assumes entails taking spectacle seriously as an aesthetic. This book has been an attempt to do precisely this, though I would be the first to admit that it has only begun to scratch the surfaces that it is attempting to understand. More precise understandings of the history of spectacle as an aesthetic are in order – its moments of efflorescence, the differing institutional and generic characters it has assumed, formal and stylistic operations, production practices, exhibition modes and so forth. How has technology functioned within this aesthetic? What, for example, is the place and role of optical effects?

Meanwhile, alongside such work more rigorous analysis is required of the distinctive shapes and mechanisms that the still juvenile visual digital forms involve. Precisely how are they different from each other and their immediate predecessors in terms of form, style, modes of production, production practices and the experiences and effects they induce? This book has begun to sketch the terrain of a distinctive aesthetic space, but we must start to add more detail and accuracy, all the time checking these preliminary studies for the modifications that more sustained observation will bring.

NOTES

INTRODUCTION

1 I am concerned with *one* major dimension of contemporary visual digital culture: that relating to mass entertainment forms. Other dimensions, such as architecture, design, art practices and suchlike remain, for the most part, beyond the scope of this book.

2 I borrow this shorthand term from Peter Wollen (1993: 63) who uses it to point up the contrast between the cultural character of the present and the preceding era or age of 'mechanical reproducibility'.

3 Of course, mass culture theories (such as that of the Frankfurt School) cannot simply be dissociated from the 'high' versus 'low' culture tradition and its negative appraisal of popular forms. But then neither can more recent 'postmodernist' accounts: for example, Lyotard's espousal of neo-avant-gardist or experimentalist art practice, or Baudrillard's pessimistic prognoses, derived from a particular interpretation of the burgeoning growth of mass-mediated culture.

4 With spectacle it seems it has always been thus, even Aristotle viewed it as 'the least artistic of all the parts' of Tragedy (McKeon 1941: 1462).

5 I am not advocating here a counter-position that involves a reversion to some kind of simple populism. Rather, as *part* of the way to a more comprehensive understanding we should begin by taking the aesthetic space in question more seriously than we have in the past.

1 A BACK STORY: REALISM, SIMULATION, INTERACTION

1 General histories of the development of the modern computer include, for example, Shurkin (1984), Evans (1981) and Freiberger and Swaine (1984).

2 Other important contributors include James Whitney (John Whitney's brother), Stan Vanderbeek, Lillian Schwartz, Charles Csuri and John Stehura.

3 Whitney had already acquired a considerable reputation in the world of 'avant-garde' film-art when in 1966, IBM offered him a position as 'artist in residence'. The first and perhaps most famous film to emerge from this collaboration was *Permutations* (1968).

4 Knowlton's collaborations with computer artist Lillian Schwartz in the late 1960s and early 1970s are perhaps most indicative here.

5 I make further suggestions in chapters 2 and 3 as to other reasons that support and encourage this development.

6 In the late 1990s a new technique had been devised to aid the animator – especially one who is chasing naturalistic movement – it is called 'motion capture'.

7 Well over 80 since *Star Wars* at the time of writing.
8 Among this new canon of digital effects cinema are films such as, *Who Framed Roger Rabbit?* (1988), *The Abyss* (1989), *Terminator 2: Judgment Day* (1991), *Total Recall* (1990), *Robocop 2* (1990), *Jurassic Park* (1993), *True Lies* (1994), *Speed* (1994), *Casper* (1995), *Twister* (1996), *The Lost World* (1997) and *Armageddon* (1998).
9 I intend to use the term 'computer game' whether referring to arcade or home game platforms.
10 Indeed, for a time in the 1980s, there was even a period of game auteurism as the names of young hacker/hobbyists were associated with the games they had been responsible for programming for the home computer.
11 *Myst* is such a game: a time-travel-based exploration of a fantastic world rendered fully visible through sophisticated stylised graphics, sound effects and video sequences.
12 Thus in the mid-1990s giant electronics corporations such as Sony, Panasonic and Phillips had made incursions into the sphere of games machine production. The first two now produce dedicated home games consoles, whilst Philips has led the way in the development of PC CD-ROM machines.
13 A prime European example being Futuroscope, the 'Park of the Moving Image', situated at Poitiers in France.

2 GENEALOGY AND TRADITION: MECHANISED SPECTACLE AS POPULAR ENTERTAINMENT

1 The commercialisation of popular culture also clearly shaped performance as much as it shaped and altered prior forms. It introduced distinctive performance modes and new forms, just as it displaced and turned prior forms into outmoded ones.
2 The Boulevard du Temple was already established as a site of itinerant and quasi-itinerant popular entertainment before the entrepreneurs of the popular theatre set up business there, thus accounting for their choice of location.
3 In the latter part of the nineteenth century diluted forms of the Phantasmagoria migrated to the travelling fairground in the form of the 'ghost show'. Many of its techniques were refined and adapted to become frequently used devices in the acts of stage magicians (illusionists and conjurers) (Heard 1996: iii).
4 On the connection of these pre-cinema forms with developing techniques of optics and lighting, see Neale (1985) and Schivelbusch (1995).
5 Such late nineteenth-century amusements as the public displays of the dead at the Paris Morgue and the recreated scenes of the Musée Grévin waxworks also evince a taste for realism. Here realism is also spectacle – though its morbid and voyeuristic character demonstrates that not all of the popular entertainments of the time were light and frivolous. See Schwartz (1995).
6 See the critics Simmel, Benjamin, Kracauer who attempted to theorise the sensational and stimulus-oriented character of early twentieth-century culture in terms of a shift under way in the human sensorium as a result of the momentous social transformations introduced by the processes of modernisation. For an explication of these ideas which ties them explicitly to popular commercial culture, see Singer (1995).
7 Emerging as a commercial form almost a decade after the first film screenings, Hale's Tours attempted to take the realistic illusion of actuality films a stage further by simulating the experience of train and trolley travel (see Fielding 1970).
8 This does not mean that the high art forms of the middle classes played no part at all in the aesthetic make-up of the early cinema (see, for example, Burch 1978/9). However, for the most part, the first decade of the cinema has a particularly close association with popular entertainments.

9 I do not mean to imply that early cinema – indeed, popular spectacle forms in general – were wholly devoid of the voyeuristic element which is so central to classical narrative cinema. In fact, within early cinema itself there quickly emerged a corpus of 'keyhole' films involving striptease and erotic subjects. I do suggest, however, that the dominant mode of spectacle involved in these popular entertainments was of a rather different order: a shallower, more immediate and ephemeral experience, from which complex (deep) modes of signification were largely absent – at least at the aesthetic or poetic level.

10 In relation to the idea of 'the look' or 'looking' in classical narrative cinema I am thinking here of the related though somewhat different analyses of Metz (1976) and Mulvey (1975).

11 Indeed, by the end of the 1920s Hollywood also had synchronised sound which it could use to compete with radio for audiences. However, the two modes of entertainment were so different (and dominant) that they hardly had to compete – they maintained, rather, a wary coexistence.

12 I am generalising here, of course, and what I am describing was probably more applicable to early American television. The latter did not operate with the same kind of public (national) broadcasting remit as, say, that of Britain.

13 Of course, this is a vastly expanded and much changed sphere, one that I discuss in more detail in the next chapter.

3 SHAPING TRADITION: THE CONTEMPORARY CONTEXT

1 In what follows I shall assume a certain familiarity with other aspects of Baudrillard's theoretical writing. For those requiring more background, I would suggest the following: Baudrillard (1981, 1983b) and Poster (1990).

2 Baudrillard's notion of 'implosion' also owes much to McLuhan. However, whilst agreeing with McLuhan that the social world is now imploding, Baudrillard significantly reverses the implications which the former draws from this (see McLuhan 1968; Baudrillard 1983a).

3 'Tactile' is a notion that was first introduced by Benjamin as a description of what he viewed as the radical and novel spectating experience introduced by film mediation.

4 In this instance, it is theories of depth or latency – theories which urge that understanding can only be gained by looking beyond the appearance of things, for hidden, or not immediately apparent causes, structures, meanings or some such – that Baudrillard takes issue with (Marxism, psychoanalysis and structuralism are seen as the principle representatives of such 'rationalist' theories, and are thus the ultimate object of his criticism). In their place, Baudrillard now proposes a strategy centred on a conceptualisation of what he calls 'seduction'. In a way which extends his previous category of symbolic exchange, Baudrillard conceives of 'seduction' as the radical challenge to the reality principle, i.e. to production (in all domains, not just the material) – which forms the basis of the Western world.

5 This is because, as Baudrillard understands it, the 'pure form' of *trompe l'oeil* (the features of which he rigorously specifies), are not confined to one period, having appeared at various times to exercise their metaphysical power.

6 'Hyperreality' is a term that Baudrillard introduces in his later theorising to describe the condition of the collapse or effacement of the real and its representation.

7 Given Baudrillard's notion of seduction and his attack on the idea of 'latency', 'depth' and any theory which would attempt to attribute an underlying, hidden dimension, beyond, or in some way masked by appearances, something suspiciously like a contradiction begins to appear in his theory here. For at first sight, the notion of a code (variously described as 'genetic', 'cybernetic' and 'digital') governing every

level and aspect of our contemporary world smacks of a kind of neo-structuralism: a deep and hidden regulation of the hyperreal. Baudrillard's way of escaping this contradiction is through an extraordinary collapsing of appearances and code, so that together they come to constitute the (irreal) world. Representation is no longer distinguishable from that which it represents, a new modality emerges; the hyperreal, which is itself pre-coded, programmed.

8 At the time the paper was written (mid-1980s) this theory was at the centre of a flourishing debate in Italy, conducted 'under the standard of "a new aesthetics of seriality"' (Eco 1985: 180).

9 Later in the same essay, Baudrillard claims that, 'cinema plagiarises and copies itself, remakes its classics, retroactivates its original myths, remakes silent films more perfect than the originals, etc.' (1987: 31).

10 See Jameson (1989: 32) where he explicitly acknowledges that his analysis of postmodernism 'owes a great debt to Baudrillard'.

11 For Jameson, of course, ultimately this is a manifestation of capitalist (social and economic) development.

12 Thus, although such theorists as Jameson and Eco follow Baudrillard by supporting his radical re-emphasis on formal factors, like him believing them to be key to understanding contemporary culture, they are not prepared to follow him in extending this formalism to make it, somehow, constitutive of the world itself.

4 SIMULATION AND HYPERREALISM: COMPUTER ANIMATION AND TV ADVERTISEMENTS

1 This was produced – in part – by introducing unprecedented levels of spatial and temporal verisimilitude into the fictional world via the continuity system, the use of psychologically rounded characters to ground and motivate the narrative thrust, and an enhanced literality in the drawn imagery itself (inspired by the 'impression of reality' of live-action photography).

2 The fact that one of the characters from the film *Toy Story* (Buzz Lightyear) became – once the publicity and merchandising machine had cranked up – the most sought-after character toy for young boys in 1995 and 1996, does little to alter this claim.

3 *Shots* – an industry oriented publication – has since the beginning of the 1990s released a bi-monthly compilation tape (VHS format) showcasing ads and music video. For more information, contact *Shots*, 8 Tottenham Mews, London, W1P 9PJ, UK.

4 They are, an advertisement for the insurance company Eagle Star screened in the early 1990s and a series of related ads produced for Smirnoff vodka and screened in the mid- to late 1990s. Whereas the Eagle Star example is national-context-specific, the Smirnoff examples have had – or so I conjecture – international exposure.

5 Of course, neither is the imagery in dominant feature films. Nevertheless, there is still a difference at the formal level between neo-Hollywood blockbusters and such advertisements.

6 In a similar way, there is a pattern to the linkages between the separate scenes of the ad. This has to do with graphic configurations, framing bias and the direction of movement within the closing and opening shots of contiguous scenes.

7 See, for example, Magritte's paintings *La Condition humaine* (1933), *La Cascade* (1961) and *La Bataille de l'Argonne* (1959).

8 In particular, its non-narrative associational character ties it both to metaphor and metonymy. For example, the carry over of circular and parallel linear forms throughout the diverse scenes of the text, the detailed use of the colour gold with its

connotations of wealth and security, or the fact that each scenario stands as a specific instance of a larger (and insurable) realm.

9 It is virtually impossible for the untrained eye to detect the quite phenomenal amount of fabrication involved in these scenes, even when they are viewed on a frame by frame basis, so seamless is the work of combining and retouching involved.

10 The most stunning, perhaps, involves the moment when a woman fires a gun at her accomplice/lover, and the whole image – with the exception of the bullet itself – freezes. The camera tracks with the bullet, travelling in slow motion, to its moment of impact with a bottle of Smirnoff. At which point, normal speed is resumed and the bottle – viewed in close-up – smashes spectacularly.

11 I am think here of a dazzling black and white advertisement for the Saab 9000, appearing on screens in Europe at the time of writing. Such impossible zooms have become a standard trope, particularly within advertising and music video (see, for example, Abbey National's ad 'Changes' and the Michael Jackson video *Black or White*). See also Gitlin 1986: 136–61.

5 THE WANING OF NARRATIVE: NEW SPECTACLE IN CINEMA AND MUSIC VIDEO

1 I do not want to argue that spectacle fails to signify in such films, only that its special or excessive quality as imagery is what takes precedence. It is the dual focus on sensation and artifice that defines spectacle. The experiential character of spectacle tends to displace, demote (or, perhaps, delay), concern with meaning-making in its traditional senses, substituting instead the immediacy of wonderment at what is shown and, frequently, at how it was possible. For a critical approach to spectacle that *is* primarily concerned with content or meanings see, Tasker (1993).

2 Indeed, Steve Neale (1990) has argued as much. Drawing on the work of Metz, Neale operates with the psychoanalytic concept of 'disavowal', thereby producing an argument which, in significant respects, is closely related to that of Mulvey.

3 'Narrative image', in the sense defined by Ellis (1982), is still the fulcrum of those multiple modes of subsidiary circulation which revolve around the cinema's highly developed marketing strategies. Only now, particularly with the technological blockbusters, 'the promise' purveyed is just as likely to rest upon an indication or reassurance of the centrality of certain visual pyrotechnics and the portrayal of stunning actions as it is traditional story enigmas.

4 The thing that unifies the texts of these blockbuster films is that they are avowedly effects driven. This in itself, however, hardly seems to be enough to qualify them as constituting a genre. This is further reinforced by their tendency to cut across previous genres and the frequency with which they consist of a mélange of references, pastiche and allusions to a host of prior film kinds.

5 I should also point out that I am tending to emphasise one dimension of the spectacular character of such films here. The other dimension is that of action: these films all involve periods of sustained and fast-paced action sequences (some – *Speed*, for example – are relentless in this respect).

6 An intriguing forerunner of such simulacra is the film *Zelig* (1983).

7 Thompson refers specifically to the following essays: Heath (1975) and Barthes (1977).

8 An excellent if somewhat obvious example of this is the well known sequence in the film *True Lies* (1994) involving shots of a Harrier Jump Jet above a city street and depicting events and actions of ludicrous impossibility.

9 So too do most of the other expressions of visual digital culture at the centre of this book. It is just that this is, perhaps, more immediately apparent in the case of music video.

10 Other examples include Mike Oldfield – *Tubular Bells 11*; Orchestral Manoeuvres in the Dark – *Dream of Me*; Enigma – *Age of Loneliness*; Jamiroquai – *Space Cowboy* and *Virtual Insanity*; Madonna – *Bedtime Story*; and Tori Amos – *Caught a Lite Sneeze*.

11 Of the many TV advertisements which operate with a similar aesthetic, among the most striking on UK screens in the late 1990s was the Halifax Building Society's ad 'Kaleidoscope'.

12 One of the films in the impressive Betty Boop series made by Fleischers in the 1930s.

13 Indeed, many of the Fleischers' films of the time, including this one, have been cited as early forerunners of the music video form itself, involving as they did musical performance and the occasional appearance of popular musical figures such as Rudy Vallee, Ethel Merman and Louis Armstrong.

6 THE DIGITAL IMAGE IN 'THE AGE OF THE SIGNIFIER'

1 This does not mean that before technological reproduction, repetition was an insignificant factor or element in cultural formations. See, for example, Eco (1985) and Latour (1985).

2 At the same time, however, he warned that – in the wrong hands – they might well turn into something altogether different. Indeed, were Benjamin alive today, he would no doubt consider – with some consternation – that it has been the more cautionary aspects of his prognostications that have been vindicated.

3 A clear example of such 'difference within repetition' is manifest in the range of classical animated cartoon series of the middle period of this century (see Warner Brothers' cartoon series, *Road Runner*).

4 See Calabrese (1992: 27–46) for a searching application of the notion of rhythm to a poetics of the series and the serial in general.

5 Such techniques, when they were first introduced in the visual arts, initially in Cubist painting, later in works of the various avant-gardes of the 1920s; Dadaism, Futurism, Constructivism, Surrealism and so forth, constituted radical challenges, and provoked shock in the recipients of the time.

6 That it is photographic imagery that is being simulated, definitively problematises any attempt to make a privileged link between photographic representation and the real.

7 Useful overviews of the idea of authorship in relation to the cinema appear in Caughie (1981), Lapsley and Westlake (1988) and Cook (1985).

8 George Lucas, Steven Spielberg, James Cameron and Paul Verhoeven are, perhaps the best known.

9 Respectively, they are John Lasseter and Douglas Trumbull.

10 Significantly, when more extended discussion of music video production and authorship occurs, then this is frequently found within writing from or associated with the domain of experimental video, where video artists are seen as engaging in crossover work.

11 Indeed, if, as is perhaps most often the case, the promo is viewed on TV (think of MTV) then production credits do not get seen at all.

12 Perhaps the clearest paradigm for authorship's attenuation in the contemporary context is television.

13 For significant insight into the romantic origins of modern concepts of authorship see Abrams (1953).

14 This is Wollen's striking characterisation of 'the new systems of imagery' emerging from this integration of the established media and new media (see Wollen 1993: 66).

7 GAMES AND RIDES: SURFING THE IMAGE

1 One notable exception has been the somewhat anomalous work of David Myers who has pursued questions relating to game experience and game structure using approaches that range from empirical analysis to structuralism (see, for example, Myers 1990, 1991, 1992).

2 I have borrowed this phrase from Robins (1996).

3 Many games designed for home consumption, particularly those produced for dedicated game consoles, introduce the 'back story' in a glossy, special effects-laden video sequence at the beginning of the game disc. Back stories are a standard feature of most computer games.

4 There is, perhaps, more of an affinity with the distracted, repetitious and inconclusive spectatorship of the TV viewer – though, even here, there are considerable differences.

5 The work of Paul Ricoeur on problems with the configuration and refiguration of time by narrative, in particular his discussion of the distinction between historical narrative and fictional (literary) narrative, may offer ways of developing our understanding of narrative in new 'interactive' genres such as games (see Ricoeur 1984, 1985, 1988).

6 Stallabrass (1993: 98–9) compares this aspect of computer games to Benjamin's notion of allegory.

7 The character definition in games tends to be of the lowest order. Given this token status, it is hardly surprising – when characters do begin to take on individuating traits – that stereotyping of an extremely basic type is palpable, more conspicuous because more directly and simplistically framed: for example, Lara Croft, 'star' of the popular 3-D platform game *Tomb Raider*.

8 Indeed, even a slower-paced game such as *Myst* in which *something* of the life and traits of three characters and the relations between them is slowly revealed as the game progresses, is not, ultimately, so much *about* them or their stories. The more central pleasures are those of puzzle solving and the visual exploration of 'childishly romantic' and aseptically rendered fantasy environments.

9 See Ricoeur (1984, 1985, 1988), especially volume 2, *The Configuration of Time in Fictional Narrative*.

10 See Myers (1992) who discusses the 'subjective experience of time during play'.

11 There are exceptions to this, i.e. in the pre-constructed film sequences that punctuate the game itself and at certain moments when lift buttons, location maps, data and image analyser screens are viewed and controlled from a subjective point of view.

12 Indeed, it has been argued that the most striking thing about the film itself was its *mise-en-scène*: the futuristic city and its denizens as star. See, for example, Chevrier (1984).

13 It is largely for such reasons that the so-called 'strategy guide' has become such an important component of computer game playing. Whether in book form or as a feature in one of the many games periodicals the misnamed 'strategy guide', provides the reader with step-by-step ways through the puzzles, tics and idiosyncrasies of a particular game. These game solutions appear almost simultaneously with the publication of the game itself.

14 'This is the fun, challenge and skill derived and learned from controlling the options presented on the TV screen' (Hayes and Dinsey with Parker 1995: 6).

15 On the other hand, see Myers (1990: 382–3), whose study suggests that 'replayability' is 'an important component of its success'.

16 I have borrowed the expression 'sense of presence' from a paper published in the field of computer science research. See Slater and Usoh (1993).

17 For ways in which games may function beyond the primary level of formal/aesthetic operations (poetics) to reinforce deep ideological meanings (rhetoric) see, for example, Kinder (1991) and Stallabrass (1993).

18 This is perhaps even more apparent in so-called 'sim' games. Here it is the act of competing in a Formula One motor race or of flying a plane involved in air combat that is the object of such participative representation.

19 I support the frequently drawn parallels between such mechanical 'thrill' rides and the other forms under discussion here. This aesthetic relationship has been made most frequently in discussion and criticism of contemporary action or spectacle cinema. See, for example, Hartley (1996).

20 In this respect it is clear that the increasingly sensational character of conventional thrill rides (the Big Dipper and so forth) in today's burgeoning leisure and theme parks is also part of this cultural space.

21 It is claimed that 'game addicted youngsters ... often have extraordinary semiotic skills' (see, for example, Wark 1994). This may be so, still, it would seem important to ask what is the nature of these increased semiotic capabilities? Are we talking of mythology of the kind that Barthes was involved in (i.e. sophisticated ideology critique), higher levels of intertextual recognition (see Kinder 1991), an increased capacity for spatial cognition or the ability to become quickly familiar with the 'rules of the game'?

22 The so-called 'tie-in' phenomenon is important here, i.e. the emergence of films, games and rides that are connected by the same title. For an interpretation that links this aspect of computer games to notions of subject construction and gender, see Kinder (1991).

8 SURFACE PLAY AND SPACES OF CONSUMPTION

1 Bordwell's arguments for a rejuvenated poetic criticism are concerned primarily with the cinema. Echoing earlier concerns by the likes of Erich Auerbach (1953), Susan Sontag (1967) and Jonathan Culler (1975) that hermeneutics is suppressing the sensuous perceptible aspect of art he advocates a return to modes of understanding that take far more account of form and style.

2 For a suggestive and lucid account of how this – or something very much like it – may occur in certain narrative films, see Bordwell (1985: 274–310).

3 Caillois claims that *paidia* and *ludus* are not categories of play itself but relate rather to ways of playing. He describes their invariable opposition thus: 'the preference for cacophony over a symphony, scribbling over the wise application of the laws of perspective' (1962: 53).

4 I am not, however, trying to insinuate that the genres of what I term visual digital culture do not contain expressions of violence, suffering and death – clearly they do.

5 The expression 'frenzy of the visible' is from Comolli (1980: 122).

6 Some would argue that the contemporary theme parks, electronic leisure centres and so forth have substituted a far more ordered and managed (rationalised) kind of space: a space in which the term 'exoticism' takes on rather sanitised and clinical connotations. See, for example, Nelson (1986).

7 Of more direct relevance perhaps, are mass forms and genres such as 'white-knuckle' rides, performance based modes such as sport and popular music (see Sky Sport and MTV), rejuvenated forms of the circus such as *Cirque du Soleil* and *Archaos*, new illusion and magic spectacles by the likes of David Copperfield, and forms of contest such as *Gladiators*.

8 The concept of *detournement* is a Situationist strategy or technique that appears to bear some resemblance both to avant-garde art techniques such as montage and

collage and to certain postmodernist practices involving recombination (though one would have to say that it is far removed from simple pastiche), the intention being to turn or in some way to redirect the spectacle against itself using its own genres, images and icons in the process.

9 In the way it augments traditional Marxist accounts; in its concern with the notion of 'everyday life'; in its direct and productive engagement with the critical cultural project of the artistic avant-gardes – fractured and strained though this was – and, in its espousal of participatory play and festival as a direct countervailing force to the spectacle itself. See Wollen (1993).

10 In each of these accounts the *play element* figures prominently. However, it does *not* operate as a subversive category as with the Situationists, being conceived somewhat differently (see Baudrillard 1988a: 25; Bauman 1993: 169).

11 Indeed, each of the authors discussed here invokes the image of the automobile and modern means of transportation in their discussions of changing forms of experience.

CONCLUSION

1 Once again, let me state what I am *not* claiming. I do not suggest that this is all that these forms are about or that the broadly poetic approach I have adopted here is the only way in which they are to be understood. I maintain only that it is one frequently underestimated dimension of understanding their function and significance.

2 For obvious reasons I have fixed upon recent modern manifestations of the spectacle aesthetic. However, it is clear that it has a far longer history than this. Of particular interest perhaps, are its full-fledged manifestations within the cultures of the Baroque and Imperial Rome.

BIBLIOGRAPHY

Abrams, J. (1995) 'Escape from Gravity', *Sight and Sound* 5, 5: 14–19.

Abrams, M.H. (1953) *The Mirror and the Lamp: Romantic Theory and the Critical Tradition*, London: Oxford University Press.

Altman, R. (1989) *The American Film Musical*, London: BFI Publishing.

Auerbach, E. (1953) *Mimesis: The Representation of Reality in Western Literature*, trans. W.R. Trask, Princeton, NJ: Princeton University Press.

Aufderheide, P. (1986) 'The Look of the Sound', in T. Gitlin (ed.) *Watching Television: A Pantheon Guide to Popular Culture*, New York: Pantheon Books.

Baker, R. (1993) 'Computer Technology and Special Effects in Contemporary Cinema', in P. Hayward and T. Wollen (eds), *Future Visions: New Technologies of the Screen*, London: BFI Publishing.

Balio, T. (ed.) (1976) *The American Film Industry*, Madison and London: University of Wisconsin Press.

—— (ed.) (1990) *Hollywood in the Age of Television*, Boston: Unwin Hyman.

Barnouw, E. (1981) *The Magician and the Cinema*, New York, Oxford: Oxford University Press.

Barthes, R. (1973) *Mythologies*, London: Paladin.

—— (1975) *The Pleasure of the Text*, New York: Hill and Wang.

—— (1977) *Image-Music-Text*, London: Fontana.

—— (1984) *Camera Lucida: Reflections on Photography*, trans. R. Howard, London: Flamingo.

—— (1990) *S/Z*, Oxford: Blackwell.

Battock, G. (ed.) (1975) *Super Realism: A Critical Anthology*, New York: Dutton.

Baudrillard, J. (1981) *For a Critique of the Political Economy of the Sign*, St Louis: Telos Press.

—— (1983a) *In the Shadow of Silent Majorities*, New York: Semiotext(e).

—— (1983b) *Simulations*, New York: Semiotext(e).

—— (1984) 'Game with Vestiges', *On the Beach* 5: 19–25.

—— (1987) *The Evil Demon of Images*, Sydney: Power Institute Publications.

—— (1988a) *The Ecstasy of Communication*, New York: Semiotext(e).

—— (1988b) 'The Trompe-l'Oeil', in N. Bryson (ed.) *Calligrams; Essays in New Art History from France*, Cambridge: Cambridge University Press.

—— (1990) *Revenge of the Crystal: Selected Writings on the Modern Object and its Destiny, 1968–1983*, London and Concord, MA: Pluto Press.

—— (1996) *The System of Objects*, London and New York: Verso.

Bauman, Z. (1993) *Postmodern Ethics*, Oxford, UK and Cambridge, MA: Blackwell.

Bazin, A. (1967) *What is Cinema?*, trans. H. Gray, Berkeley and Los Angeles: University of California Press.

—— (1971) *What is Cinema? Volume II*, trans. H. Gray, Berkeley and Los Angeles: University of California Press.

Belton, J. (1992) *Widescreen Cinema*, Cambridge, MA: Harvard University Press.

—— (1990) 'Glorious Technicolor, Breathtaking Cinemascope, and Stereophonic Sound', in T. Balio (ed.), *Hollywood in the Age of Television*, Boston: Unwin Hyman.

Bender, G. and Druckery, T. (eds) (1994) *Culture on the Brink: Ideologies of Technology*, Seattle: Bay Press.

Benjamin, W. (1973) *Illuminations*, London: Collins/Fontana Books.

Boorstin, D.J. (1992) *The Image: A Guide to Pseudo-Events in America*, New York: Vintage Books.

Bordwell, D. (1985) *Narration in the Fiction Film*, Madison: University of Wisconsin Press.

✳ —— (1991) *Making Meaning: Inference and Rhetoric in the Interpretation of Cinema*, Cambridge, MA and London: Harvard University Press.

Bordwell, D., Staiger, J. and Thompson, K. (1985) *The Classical Hollywood Cinema: Film Style and Mode of Production to 1960*, London: Routledge.

Brand, S. (1972) 'Space War: Fanatic Life and Symbolic Death Among the Computer Bums', *Rolling Stone* (December): 50 –6.

Bryson, N. (ed.) (1988) *Calligrams: Essays in New Art History from France*, Cambridge: Cambridge University Press.

Buck-Morss, S. (1989) *The Dialectics of Seeing: Walter Benjamin and the Arcades Project*, Cambridge, MA and London: MIT Press.

Burch, N. (1978/9) 'Porter or Ambivalence', *Screen* 19, 4: 91–105.

—— (1990) *Life to Those Shadows*, London: BFI Publishing.

Caillois, R. (1962) *Man, Play, and Games*, London: Thames and Hudson.

Calabrese, O. (1992) *Neo-Baroque: A Sign of the Times*, Princeton, NJ: Princeton University Press.

Cameron, A. (1995) 'Dissimulations: The Illusion of Interactivity', *Millennium Film Journal* 28: 32–47.

Carlson, M. (1974) 'The Golden Age of the Boulevard', *The Drama Review: Popular Entertainments* 18, 1: 25–33.

Caughie, J. (ed.) (1981) *Theories of Authorship: A Reader*, London, Boston and Henley: Routledge and Kegan Paul.

Charney, L. and Schwartz, V.R. (eds) (1995) *Cinema and the Invention of Modern Life*, Berkeley, Los Angeles and London: University of California Press.

Chevrier, Y. (1984) '*Blade Runner*, or, The Sociology of Anticipation', *Science-Fiction Studies* 2, 1: 50–9.

Clarke, S.W. (1983) *The Annals of Conjuring*, New York: Magico.

Collins, J., Radner, H. and Preacher-Collins, A. (eds) (1993) *Film Theory goes to the Movies*, New York and London: Routledge.

Comolli, J.-L. (1980) 'Machines of the Visible', in T. de Lauretis and S. Heath (eds), *The Cinematic Apparatus*, London: Macmillan.

Comrie, B. (1976) *Aspect*, Cambridge: Cambridge University Press.

Cook, P. (ed.) (1985) *The Cinema Book*, London: BFI Publishing.

Coyle, R. (1993) 'The Genesis of Virtual Reality', in P. Hayward and T. Wollen (eds) *Future Visions: New Technologies of the Screen*, London: BFI Publishing.

Crafton, D. (1982) *Before Mickey: The Animated Film 1898–1928*, Cambridge, MA: MIT Press.

Culler, J. (1975) *Structuralist Poetics: Structuralism, Linguistics and the Study of Litera- ture*, London: Routledge and Kegan Paul.

Darley, A. (1990) 'From Abstraction to Simulation: Notes on the History of Computer Imaging', in P. Hayward (ed.) *Culture, Technology and Creativity in the Late Twen- tieth Century*, London: John Libbey/Arts Council of Great Britain.

—— (1995) 'The Computer and Contemporary Visual Culture: Realism, Post-Realism and Postmodernist Aesthetics', unpublished DPhil. thesis, University of Sussex.

Davis, D. (1973) *Art and the Future: A History/Prophecy of the Collaboration Between Science, Technology and Art*, New York: Praeger.

de Lauretis, T. and Heath, S. (eds) (1985) *The Cinematic Apparatus*, New York: St Martins Press.

Debord, G. (1977) *The Society of the Spectacle*, London: Practical Paradise Publications.

Dixon, W.W. (1995–6) 'The Digital Domain: Some Preliminary Notes on Image Mesh and Manipulation in Hyperreal Cinema/Video', *Film Criticism* 20, 1–2: 55–66.

Eco, U. (1986) *Faith in Fakes: Essays*, trans. W. Weaver, London: Secker and Warburg.

—— (1985) 'Innovation and Repetition: Between Modern and Post-Modern Aesthetics', *Daedelus* 114: 161–82.

Ellis, J. (1982) *Visible Fictions: Cinema: Television: Video*, London: Routledge and Kegan Paul.

Elsaesser, T. with Barker, A. (eds) (1990) *Early Cinema: Space, Frame Narrative*, London: BFI Publishing.

Evans, C. (1981) *The Making of the Micro: A History of the Computer*, London: Gollancz.

Ewen, S. (1976) *Captains of Consciousness*, New York: McGraw-Hill.

—— (1988) *All Consuming Images: The Politics of Style in Contemporary Culture*, New York: Basic Books.

Featherstone, M. (1991) *Consumer Culture and Postmodernism*, London: Sage.

Fell, J.L. (1983) *Film before Griffith*, Berkeley: University of California Press.

Fielding, R. (1970) 'Hale's Tours: Ultrarealism in the Pre-1910 Motion Picture, *Cinema Journal* 10, 1: 34–47.

Fiske, J. (1994) *Television Culture*, London and New York: Routledge.

Foster, H. (ed.) (1988) *Vision and Visuality*, Seattle: Bay Press.

Foucault, M. (1983) *This Is not a Pipe*, Berkeley, Los Angeles and London: University of California Press.

Franke, H.W. (1971) *Computer Graphics/Computer Art*, London: Phaidon.

Freiberger, P. and Swaine, M. (1984) *Fire in the Valley: The Making of the Personal Computer*, Berkeley: Osborne/McGraw-Hill.

Friedberg, A. (1994) *Window Shopping: Cinema and the Postmodern*, Berkeley, Los Angeles and London: University of California Press.

Fyfe, G. and Law, J. (eds) (1985) *Picturing Power*, London: Routledge and Kegan Paul

Gane, M. (ed.) (1993) *Baudrillard Live: Selected Interviews*, London and New York: Routledge.

Gernsheim, H. and Gernsheim, A. (1968) *L.J.M. Daguerre: The History of the Diorama and the Daguerreotype*, New York: Dover Publications, Inc.

Gitlin, T. (ed.) (1986) *Watching Television: A Pantheon Guide to Popular Culture*, New York: Pantheon Books.

—— (1987b) 'Music Video in the (Post) Modern World', *Screen* 28, 3: 36–55.

Gombrich, E.H. (1984) *The Sense of Order: A Study in the Psychology of Decorative Art*, London: Phaidon Press.

—— (1996) *Art and Illusion: A Study in the Psychology of Pictorial Representation*, London: Phaidon Press.

Goodwin, A. (1987a) 'From Anarchy to Chromakey: Music, Video, Media', *One TwoThreeFour: A Rock and Roll Quarterly*, Special Issue 5: 16–32.

Gunning, T. (1989) 'An Aesthetic of Astonishment: Early Film and the (In)credulous Spectator', *Art and Text* 34: 31–45.

Haber, R.N. (1987) 'Flight Simulation', *Scientific American*, 257: 90–7.

Haddon, L. (1988) 'Electronic and Computer Games: The History of an Interactive Medium', *Screen* 29, 2: 55–7.

—— (1993) 'Interactive Games', in P. Hayward and T. Wollen (eds) *Future Visions: New Technologies of the Screen*, London: BFI Publishing.

Hansen, M. (1990), 'Early Cinema – Whose Public Sphere?', in T. Elsaesser (ed.), *Early Cinema: Space, Frame, Narrative*, London: BFI Publishing.

Hammond, P. (1974) *Marvellous Méliès*, London: Gordon Fraser.

Hartley, R. (1996) 'That's Interaction! Audience Participation in Entertainment Monopolies', *Convergence* 2, 1: 103 –23.

Hayes, M. and Dinsey, S. with Parker, N. (1995) *Games War: Video Games – A Business Review*, London: Bowerdean Publishing Company Ltd.

Hayward, P. (ed.) (1991a) *Culture, Technology and Creativity in the Late Twentieth Century*, London, Paris and Rome: John Libbey Press.

—— (1991b) 'Industrial Light and Magic: Style, Technology and Special Effects in the Music Video and Music Television', in P. Hayward (ed.), *Culture, Technology and Creativity in the Late Twentieth Century*, London, Paris and Rome: John Libbey Press.

Hayward, P. and Wollen, T. (eds) (1993) *Future Visions: New Technologies of the Screen*, London: BFI Publishing.

Heard, M. (1996) 'Pepper's Ghost – An Introduction', in J.H. Pepper, *The True Story of Pepper's Ghost* (reprint of the 1890 edition of *A True History of the Ghost and All About Metempsychosis*), London: The Projection Box.

Heath, S. (1975) 'Film and System: Terms of Analysis', *Screen* 16, 1: 7–77.

Hecht, H. (1993) *Pre-Cinema History: An Encyclopaedia and Annotated Bibliography of the Moving Image before 1896*, London: Bowker Saur (Reed Reference Publishing).

Hopkins, A.A. (1977) *Magic, Stage Illusions and Scientific Diversions*, New York: Arno Press.

Huettig, M.D. (1976) 'The Motion Picture Industry Today', in T. Balio (ed.), *The American Film Industry*, Madison: University of Wisconsin Press.

Huhatamo, E. (1996) 'Encapsulated Bodies in Motion: Simulators and the Quest for Total Immersion', in S. Penny (ed.), *Critical Issues in Electronic Media*, New York: State University of New York Press.

—— (1995) 'Armchair Traveller on the Ford of Jordan: The Home, the Stereoscope and Virtual Voyaging', *Mediamatic* 8: 13–23.

Huizinga, J. (1955) *Homo Ludens: A Study of the Play Element in Culture*, Boston: Beacon Press.

Huyssen, A. (1980) 'The Hidden Dialectic: The Avant Garde – Technology – Mass Culture', in K. Woodward (ed.), *The Myths of Information: Technology and Post-Industrial Culture*, Madison, WI: Coda Press.

—— (1984) 'Mapping the Postmodern', *New German Critique* 33, 5–52.

—— (1988) *After the Great Divide: Modernism, Mass Culture and Postmodernism*, London: Macmillan.

In Camera (1994) 'Doug Trumbull's Vision of the Future in Sharp Focus', *In Camera* autumn: 10.

Jameson, F. (1984) 'Postmodernism, or The Cultural Logic of Late Capitalism', *New Left Review* 146: 53–92.

——(1989) 'Marxism and Postmodernism', *New Left Review* 176: 31–45.

—— (1991) *Postmodernism, or The Cultural Logic of Late Capitalism*, London: Verso.

—— (1992) *Signatures of the Visible*, London and New York: Routledge.

Jay, M. (1994) *Downcast Eyes: The Denigration of Vision in Twentieth-Century French Thought*, Berkeley, Los Angeles and London: University of California Press.

—— (1988) 'Scopic Regimes of Modernity', in H. Foster (ed.), *Vision and Visuality*, Seattle: Bay Press.

Jhally, S. (1990) *The Codes of Advertising: Fetishism and the Political Economy of Meaning in Consumer Society*, New York and London: Routledge.

Kaplan, E.A. (1987) *Rocking Around the Clock: Music Television, Postmodernism and Consumer Culture*, New York and London: Routledge.

Kasson, J.F. (1978) *Amusing the Million: Coney Island at the Turn of the Century*, New York: Hill and Wang.

Kinder, M. (1991) *Playing with Power in Movies, Television, and Video Games: From Muppet Babies to Teenage Mutant Ninja Turtles*, Berkeley, Los Angeles and Oxford: University of California Press.

Kuhn, A. (ed.) (1990) *Alien Zone: Cultural Theory and Contemporary Science Fiction Cinema*, London and New York: Verso.

Lapsley, R. and Westlake, M. (1988) *Film Theory: An Introduction*, Manchester: Manchester University Press.

Latour, B. (1985) 'Visualisation and Social Reproduction: Opening One Eye whilst Closing the Other ... A Note on Some Religious Paintings', in G. Fyfe and J. Law (eds), *Picturing Power*, London: Routledge and Kegan Paul.

Laurel, B. (1991) *Computers as Theatre*, Reading, MA: Addison-Wesley.

Lefebvre, H. (1991) *Critique of Everyday Life*, London: Verso.

Le Grice, M. (1974) 'Computer Film as Art', in J. Halas (ed.), *Computer Animation*, London and New York: Focal Press.

Leiss, W., Kline, S. and Jhally, S. (1990) *Social Communication in Advertising: Persons, Products and Images of Well-Being*, New York and London: Routledge.

Levy, S. (1984) *Hackers: Heroes of the Computer Revolution*, New York: Anchor Press/Doubleday.

Lord, A.B. (1960) *The Singer of Tales*, Cambridge, MA: Harvard University Press.

Lyotard, J.-F. (1986) *The Postmodern Condition: Report on Knowledge*, Manchester: Manchester University Press.

McKeon, R. (ed.) (1941) *The Basic Works of Aristotle*, New York: Random House.

McLuhan, M. (1968) *Understanding Media: The Extensions of Man*, London: Routledge and Kegan Paul.

McNamara, B. (1974) 'Introduction' and 'The Scenography of Popular Entertainment', *The Drama Review: Popular Entertainments* 18, 1: 3–4 and 16–24.

Magid, R. (1996) 'Digitising the Third Dimension', *American Cinematographer* August: 45–6, 48, 50.

Marcuse, H. (1974) *One-Dimensional Man*, London: Abacus.

Mellencamp, P. (1977) 'Spectacle and Spectator: Looking through the American Musical Comedy', *Cine-tracts* 1: 28 –35.

Merritt, R. (1976) 'Nickelodeon Theatres 1905–1914: Building an Audience for the Movies', in T. Balio (ed.), *The American Film Industry*, Madison: University of Wisconsin Press.

Metz, C. (1974) *Film Language: A Semiotics of the Cinema*, trans. M. Taylor, New York: Oxford University Press.

—— (1976) 'History/Discourse: Note on Two Voyeurisms', *Edinburgh 76 Magazine* 1: 21–5.

—— (1977) '*Trucage* and the Film', *Critical Enquiry* 2, 4: 657–75.

Morley, D. (1993) *Television, Audiences and Cultural Studies*, London: Routledge.

Mulvey, L. (1975) 'Visual Pleasure and Narrative Cinema', *Screen* 16, 3: 6–18.

Mumford, L. (1970) *The Myth of the Machine: The Pentagon of Power*, New York: Harcourt, Brace, Jovanovich.

Murray, J.H. (1997) *Hamlet on the Holodeck: The Future of Narrative in Cyberspace*, New York: The Free Press.

Myers, D. (1990) 'A Q-Study of Game Player Aesthetics', *Simulation and Gaming* 21: 375–96.

—— (1991) 'Computer Games Semiotics', *Play and Culture* 4: 334–45.

—— (1992) 'Time, Symbol Transformations, and Computer Games', *Play and Culture* 5, 4: 441–57.

Neale, S. (1980a) *Genre*, London: BFI Publishing.

—— (1980b) 'Hollywood Strikes Back – Special Effects in Recent American Cinema', *Screen* 21, 3: 101–5.

—— (1985) *Cinema and Technology: Image, Sound, Colour*, London: BFI Publishing/Macmillan.

—— (1990) ' "You've Got to be Fucking Kidding!" Knowledge, Belief and Judgement in Science Fiction', in A. Kuhn (ed.), *Alien Zone: Cultural Theory and Contemporary Science Fiction*, London and New York: Verso.

Nelson, S. (1986) 'Walt Disney's Epcot and the World's Fair Performance Tradition', *Drama Review* 30: 106–46.

Noll, M. (1967) 'The Digital Computer as a Creative Medium', *IEEE Spectrum* October: 89–94.

Nye, R. (1970) *The Unembarrassed Muse: The Popular Arts in America*, New York: The Dial Press.

Onosko, T. (1984) 'Mathemagicians: Computer Moviemakers of the 1980s and Beyond', in D. Peary (ed.), *Omni's Screen Flights/Screen Fantasies: The Future According to Science Fiction Cinema*, New York: Doubleday and Co.

Parslow, R.D. and Green, R.E. (1970) 'Introduction', *Advanced Computer Graphics – Economics, Techniques and Applications*, Proceedings of the International Computer Graphics Symposium, Brunel University.

Peary, D. (ed.) (1984) *Omni's Screen Flights/Screen Fantasies: The Future According to Science Fiction Cinema*, New York: Doubleday and Co.

Peirce, C.S. (1931) *Collected Papers* vols I–VIII, C. Hartshorne and P. Weiss (eds), Cambridge, MA: Harvard University Press.

Penny, S. (ed.) (1995) *Critical Issues in Electronic Media*, New York: SUNY Press.

Pepper, J.H. (1996) *The True Story of Pepper's Ghost* (reprint of the 1890 edition of *A True History of the Ghost and All About Metempsychosis*), London: The Projection Box.

Poster, M. (ed.) (1988) *Jean Baudrillard: Selected Writings*, Cambridge: Polity Press.

Pourroy, J. (1991) 'Through the Proscenium Arch', *Cinefex* 46: 30–45.

Provenzo, E.F. (1991) *Video Kids: Making Sense of Nintendo*, Cambridge, MA and London: Harvard University Press.

Qualtier, T. (1991) *Advertising and Democracy in the Mass Age*, New York: St Martin's Press.

Reichardt, J. (1968) 'Introduction', *Cybernetic Serendipity; Studio International*, Special Issue, 5.

—— (1971) (ed.) *Cybernetics, Art and Ideas*, London: Studio Vista.

Ricoeur, P. (1984, 1985, 1988) *Time and Narrative*, vols 1–3, Chicago and London: University of Chicago Press.

Robins, K. (1996) *Into the Image: Culture and Politics in the Field of Vision*, London and New York: Routledge.

Robley, L.P. (1984) 'Digital Simulation for *The Last Starfighter*', *American Cinematographer* November: 84–91.

Schatz, T. (1981) *Hollywood Genre: Formulas, Filmmaking and the Studio System*, New York: Random House.

—— (1993) 'The New Hollywood', in J. Collins, H. Radner and A. Preacher-Collins (eds), *Film Theory Goes to the Movies*, New York and London: Routledge.

Schivelbusch, W. (1995) *Disenchanted Night: The Industrialisation of Light in the Nineteenth Century*, Berkeley, Los Angeles and London: University of California Press.

Schwartz, V.R. (1995) 'Cinematic Spectatorship before the Apparatus: The Public Taste for Reality in *Fin-de-Siècle* Paris', in L. Charney and V.R. Schwartz (eds), *Cinema and the Invention of Modern Life*, Berkeley, Los Angeles and London: University of California Press.

Shurkin, J. (1984) *Engines of the Mind: A History of the Computer*, New York, London: W.W. Norton and Co.

Singer, B. (1995) 'Modernity, Hyperstimulus, and the Rise of Popular Sensationalism', in L. Charney and V.R. Schwartz (eds), *Cinema and the Invention of Modern Life*, Berkeley, Los Angeles and London: University of California Press.

Skirrow, G. (1986) 'Hellivision: An Analysis of Video Games', in C. MacCabe (ed.), *High Culture/Low Theory: Analysing Popular Television and Film*, Manchester: Manchester University Press.

Slater, M. and Usoh, M. (1993) 'Representations Systems, Perceptual Position, and Presence in Immersive Virtual Environments', *Presence* 2, 3: 221–33.

Sontag, S. (1967) *Against Interpretation and Other Essays*, London: Eyre and Spottiswoode.

Sørenson, P. (1984a) '*The Last Starfighter*: Imagery Wrought in the Total Forge', *Cinefex* 17: 54–71.

—— (1984b) 'Simulating Reality with Computer Graphics', *BYTE* March: 106–34.

Speaight, G. (1980) *History of the Circus*, London: The Tantivy Press.

Stallabrass, J. (1993) 'Just Gaming: Allegory and Economy in Computer Games', *New Left Review*, 198: 83–106.

—— (1996) *Gargantua: Manufactured Mass Culture*, London and New York: Verso.

Sutherland, D. (1976) 'Electronic Clones are Coming: Will the Real Peter Fonda Please Stand Up?', *Popular Photography* December: 106–7, 144–8.

Tasker, Y. (1993) *Spectacular Bodies: Gender, Genre and the Action Cinema*, London and New York: Routledge.

Thompson, K. (1981) *Eisenstein's Ivan the Terrible: A Neoformalist Analysis*, Princeton, NJ: Princeton University Press.

Toles, T. (1985) 'Video Games and American Military Ideology', *Critical Communication Studies* 3: 207–23.

Turkle, S. (1984) *The Second Self: Computers and the Human Spirit*, London: Granada.

—— (1996) *Life on the Screen: Identity in the Age of the Internet*, London: Weidenfeld and Nicolson.

Vanderbeek, S. (1970) 'New Talent – The Computer', *Art in America* January: 86–91.

Virilio, P. (1986) *Speed and Politics*, New York: Semiotext(e).

—— (1989) 'The Last Vehicle', in D. Kamper and C. Wulf (eds), *Looking Back on the End of the World*, New York: Semiotext(e).

—— (1991) *The Aesthetics of Disappearance*, New York: Semiotext(e).

Wark, M. (1994) 'The Video Game as an Emergent Media Form', *Media Information Australia* 71: 21–9.

Weinstein, R.M. (1992) 'Disneyland and Coney Island: Reflections on the Evolution of the Modern Amusement Park', *Journal of Popular Culture* 26: 131–64.

Weizenbaum, J. (1984) *Computer Power and Human Reason: From Judgement to Calculation*, London: Penguin.

Whitman, S. and Kluver, B. (1967) 'Theatre and Engineering: An Experiment', *Artforum* 5: 26–33.

Whitney, J. (1971) 'Animation Mechanisms', *American Cinematographer* January: 26.

—— (1981) 'Motion Control: An Overview', *American Cinematographer* December: 1220–3, 1236–7, 1242–3, 1261–3.

Wolff, J. (1981) *The Social Production of Art*, London: Macmillan.

Wollen, P. (1969) *Signs and Meanings in the Cinema*, London: Thames and Hudson.

—— (1982) *Readings and Writings: Semiotic Counter-Strategies*, London: Verso.

——(1988) 'Ways of Thinking about Music Video (and Post-Modernism)', in C. MacCabe (ed.), *Futures for English*, Manchester: Manchester University Press.

—— (1993) *Raiding the Icebox: Reflections on Twentieth-Century Culture*, London and New York: Verso.

Wollen, T. (1993) 'The Bigger the Better: From Cinemascope to Imax', in P. Hayward and T. Wollen (eds), *Future Visions: New Technologies of the Screen*, London: BFI Publishing.

Woodward, K. (ed.) (1980) *The Myths of Information: Technology and Post-Industrial Culture*, Madison, WI: Coda Press.

—— (1994) 'From Virtual Cyborgs to Biological Time Bombs: Technocriticism and the Material Body', in G. Bender and T. Druckery (eds), *Culture on the Brink: Ideologies of Technology*, Seattle: Bay Press.

Youngblood, G. (1970) *Expanded Cinema*, London: Studio Vista.

—— (1989) 'The New Renaissance: Art, Science and the Universal Machine', in R.L. Loveless (ed.), *The Computer Revolution in the Arts*, Tampa: University of South Florida Press.

AUTHOR INDEX

SUBJECT INDEX